D0443276

BY SARAH SENTILLES

Stranger Care

Draw Your Weapons

Breaking Up with God

A Church of Her Own

Taught by America

Stranger
Care

Stranger Care

A MEMOIR OF
LOVING WHAT
ISN'T OURS

Sarah Sentilles

RANDOM HOUSE
NEW YORK

Published in the United States by Random House, an imprint
and division of Penguin Random House LLC, New York.

RANDOM HOUSE and the HOUSE colophon are registered
trademarks of Penguin Random House LLC.

Library of Congress Cataloging-in-Publication Data

Names: Sentilles, Sarah, author.
Title: Stranger care: a memoir of loving what isn't ours / Sarah Sentilles.
Description: First edition. | New York: Random House, [2021]
Identifiers: LCCN 2020032793 (print) | LCCN 2020032794 (ebook) |
ISBN 9780593230039 (hardcover) | ISBN 9780593230053 (ebook)
Subjects: LCSH: Adoptive parents—United States. |
Adopted children—United States
Classification: LCC HV875.55 .S47 2021 (print) | LCC HV875.55 (ebook) |
DDC 362.734092273—dc23
LC record available at lccn.loc.gov/2020032793
LC ebook record available at lccn.loc.gov/2020032794

Printed in Canada on acid-free paper

randomhousebooks.com

9 8 7 6 5 4 3 2 1

First Edition

Book design by Jo Anne Metsch

For C., forever and ever and always.

*And for the half a million children
in foster care in the United States
and the people who care for them.*

Author's Note

The names and identifying characteristics of some people mentioned in this book (including social workers, court advocates, and associates of the woman I call "Evelyn") have been changed to protect their privacy.

Preface

Faded pink construction paper letters taped to the wall of the Department of Human Services classroom spelled W E L C O M E T O D H S. Eric and I sat in the back, near the door, on blue cushioned chairs with wheels. On every long table, a scattered handful of hard candy—peppermints, butterscotch, Tootsie Pops.

We'd eaten dinner at 4:45 so we'd arrive on time. Though the department's office was less than ten miles from our house, class started at six, and in Portland's traffic, the drive could take an hour, which it did. The classroom was cold. I took off my jacket, but not my scarf, thankful Eric had brought us insulated mugs of herbal tea.

The facilitator stood at the front of the room. "Our goal at DHS is to keep biological families together," she said. "The first plan is always a return-home plan, but in the meantime, kids need a safe place to go."

A man in an orange sweater at the table next to us crunched one Tootsie Pop after another, scrolling through his phone's Facebook feed while the facilitator talked.

"Kids in foster care are our most vulnerable citizens," she said. "And the state doesn't make a very good parent." She handed us posters outlining foster children's rights: access to free soap and shampoo, to clean drinking water, to a working phone.

"Hang it somewhere visible in your home where your foster kids can see it," she said.

She wheeled an ancient television into the middle of the room, inserted a VHS tape into the VCR, and pressed Play so we could watch a video about being "mandatory reporters," which meant when we were certified as foster parents, we would be required to report any suspected violence. As the video played, she sat with her back to the television, doing paperwork. When the tape froze and wavy lines filled the screen, she didn't notice, until we told her. "Nothing important happens at the end," she said and turned off the TV.

I walked out of the classroom during a break and into a larger room with glass-walled offices on one side and a waiting area on the other. Couches, chairs, toys, games, multicolored rugs—a place for parents to visit their children, who have been taken away.

"Remember," the facilitator said when we returned, "forming a healthy attachment to a child is very different from making a claim on that child. Foster families have to parent knowing the child will leave." She looked around the room. "How many of you are relatives of a child in care?" she asked, and everyone, except Eric and me, raised their hands. Our classmates were there to be certified as foster parents so they could care for nephews and nieces and grandchildren whose biological parents couldn't care for them.

"You're doing a good thing," she told them. "There are about four hundred foster homes in this county. Sixty percent of those homes are like you—*relative care providers*—but they take care of less than half of the kids in the system. The rest of the kids are living with people who aren't blood relatives." She gestured to Eric and me.

"We call it *stranger care*," she said.

I still think about that meeting in Portland six years ago, about that version of myself, with my hope and my fear pointed in the wrong direction, afraid I wouldn't be able to love someone else's child, unaware of the joy to come, and the heartbreak, the helplessness.

"Given what you know now, would you do it again?" people

ask, and I know what they are trying to say is that they wish they could lift this grief from me.

But it isn't the right question. Because this is how we find you.

Some say children come from stars, look down from that hot bright fire to this cool green blue and choose their families. Others say children arrive by stork, winged through sky, cradled by beak and blanket and brought to doorstep. But you will come by phone. For this reason, we have a landline, a word I like to say out loud because of the earth it names and roots me to, plumb line, divining rod, beacon to find your way home. There will be ringing and a voice saying "Are you ready?" Then we will ask questions, and the voice will answer, and you will wait, patient, already knowing our *yes* because you decided it. You will teach us that family is everywhere, well beyond the cul-de-sacs of our narrow minds, taking the edges of the ideas we have about who can be loved and who belongs to whom and stretching them wide.

There will be a social worker who will tell us there will always be holes in your story, missing pieces we can't provide. "You won't be able to tell them what it felt like when they kicked your ribs," she will say, and I will want to tell her I knew you before I had ribs. I knew you before bone, before marrow. I knew you when we were dust gathered and mixed with water and animated by wind. Seed, egg, division, explosion—countless are the ways you've been born.

You have so many mothers. The one who birthed you. The one who brought you home. The earth. The mountains visible outside your bedroom window. The three spruce trees in our yard. Ocean. Rocks. Rivers. Moon. Stars.

I remember a children's book about a baby bird looking for his mother. "Are you my mother?" he asked a cat. A dump truck. A wrecked car.

"Are you my mother?" he asked a cow.

"How can I be your mother?" said the cow. "I am a cow."

"Are you my mother?" he asked a dog.

"I am not your mother. I am a dog," said the dog.

But in your story, the one I tell you now, everyone answers, *Yes*.

Contents

I

SHOW YOURSELF
TO BE A MOTHER

trailing spouse

I always imagined myself a mother. I kept a list of possible names for my future children, pictured myself pregnant and listening to fast fetal heartbeats, looking in wonder at the image on the screen. But I had reservations. I'd absorbed the messages in the cultural ether that framed motherhood as both holy work and trap. My ambivalence grew.

When Eric and I married in 2004 we agreed we'd eventually have a child, but we were busy doing other things—writing dissertations, writing books, chasing academic jobs around the country—and by the time we started talking in earnest about becoming parents, I was in my midthirties, and Eric was close to forty.

We moved to Southern California in 2007 and lived in a townhouse subsidized by the university where we both taught. Eric had been hired for his first tenure-track faculty position in a graduate school of education, preparing teachers for public school classrooms. I was the "trailing spouse," language that reminded me of the signs along some California highways that show an adult holding the hand of a small child who appears to float in the wind, feet not touching the ground.

Eric liked our life as it was. He liked our freedom, the ease of escaping to the Sierras to backpack and to the Alabama Hills to climb, the unfettered time for activism, for work that might make a difference. We could turn our attention and our resources toward all children, he reasoned, not just our own.

"You're enough for me," he said. "I'm okay if it's just the two of us."

My friends had desperately wanted to be pregnant, and many had been willing to do anything to make pregnancy possible—take hormones, give themselves shots, find egg donors, buy sperm, endure IVF procedure after IVF procedure, go into debt, hire surrogates. Their certainty threw my uncertainty into relief.

"I don't know what I want," I said.

"Figure out what you want," he said, "and we'll do whatever you decide."

I'd struggled for most of my life to name my desire, separate it from other people's expectations. To know my answers to even the smallest questions—pizza or burrito, hike or bike ride, comedy or documentary—I had to meditate, write in my journal. And when I did manage to figure out what I wanted, it was hard for me to say it. I didn't trust my knowing. Especially when someone else wanted something different.

Eric does not suffer from indecision. He knows what he wants, and he isn't afraid to say it. For him, this isn't about control. It's about integrity and honesty. It's about not making other people read your mind. He says what he needs, and he trusts I will do the same.

But I didn't do the same. When it was time for us to figure out if we wanted to have a baby, I hadn't been saying what I wanted for years. And Eric was always so sure. If I didn't know what I wanted for dinner, then why not eat what he wanted to eat? Why not watch what he wanted to watch? Why not hike where he wanted to hike?

These little deferrals accumulate.

I imagine it feels good to be married to someone who accommodates, especially if you don't know that's what's happening. It makes it easier to say "We'll do whatever you decide" because past experience indicates we always agree.

Until we didn't.

Until I wanted a baby, and he did not.

the biggest gift

I wanted a baby, but I'd also swallowed whole the story that being a mother would ruin my writing, ruin my life. *If I have to play with trains for one more second,* a friend texted me, *I'm going to shoot myself.* Everyone I knew who had kids complained about it. There wasn't enough money. There wasn't enough sleep or sex or play. There wasn't enough time to paint or write or read. There wasn't enough time alone or time off or time, period.

"Work, kids, marriage, health," Eric said on repeat after he read some article in some magazine about parenthood and its demands. "Choose three."

I didn't believe that scarcity narrative, but I couldn't point to anyone's life where it wasn't true.

Sometimes when we shopped at Target, we'd see tired parents wheeling carts filled with plastic through the aisles, kids running behind them. "Why do you want to be a mother?" Eric would ask me while a toddler screamed and threw himself on the floor next to shelves and shelves of detergent.

"Because I want to" was all I could muster.

Eric didn't want to have a baby because of the stress parenthood would bring, but there was a deeper resistance, too. Eric loves the earth and hates what people do to it. He follows me around the house turning down heat, turning off lights. "When did you two become vampires?" a friend asked when she came over for cocktails and walked into our dark kitchen. The environmental argument against making another human was a logical one for him to make, an ethical extension of his worldview. "We're a cancer," he said and emailed me article after article about overpopulation and melting ice and the great Pacific garbage patch and how much an American child consumes compared to a child born somewhere else. "The biggest gift I can e to a planet under stress is not creating another human," he said.

Knowing that Eric thought having a baby would cause the earth harm made it harder for me to admit my longing for one. How do you pit personal desire against planetary destruction?

the wisdom of mother trees

In the forest, underground, there is another world. In a single footstep, hundreds of miles of fungal networks are buried in the soil. The ecologist Suzanne Simard studies how trees use those networks to talk to each other, to communicate their needs and help their neighbors. These pathways connect trees, allowing the forest to behave as if it were a single organism. Through the fungal threads, trees share carbon. They send warnings and distress signals to one another. And they look for kin.

Scientists have mapped those underground grids, which look like our brain's neural networks. The trees are the nodes and the fungal highways are the links. The busiest nodes are called hub trees or mother trees. A mother tree might be connected to hundreds of other trees. She nurtures her young, the new growth of the understory.

Simard wanted to know if mother trees could tell the difference between their seedlings and seedlings from other trees. And if they could, did they favor their offspring? She did an experiment. She grew mother trees alongside both kin and stranger seedlings. And it turned out mother trees knew their offspring. They colonized their kin with bigger mycorrhizal networks than they did the stranger seedlings. They sent them more carbon. They even reduced their own root competition to make room for their young. And when the mother trees were injured or dying, they sent carbon and defense signals to their seedlings, messages of wisdom that increased the resistance of their young to future stresses.

But trees also help strangers. They cooperate and share. As the climate changes, as the earth heats up, ponderosa pine, a lower elevation species, will replace Douglas fir. In a greenhouse, Simard and her team grew Douglas fir and ponderosa pine seedlings. They then injured the Doug fir that was acting as the mother tree. When the mother fir was injured, she gifted her carbon to the ponderosas. She also sent them a warning, information that gave the ponderosas an advantage as they took on a more dominant role in the ecosystem. She shared what she knew about the warming world with the trees that would take her place.

brave enough to have your heart broken

Eric and I met in divinity school in 1999. I was studying to become an Episcopal priest; he was studying to confirm that if people think they know God it is not God they know. RADICAL AGNOSTIC read the bumper sticker on his car. I DON'T KNOW AND YOU DON'T EITHER. In school, instead of *Does God exist?* we were taught to ask *What do our ideas about God do? Whom do they harm? Whom do they help?* We learned to engage not whether someone's belief about God is *true*—because how could you prove it?—but rather the ways faith affects people's lives. That can be measured, observed, evaluated, changed.

Humans play a crucial role in creating the world in which we find ourselves, its beauty and its terror—about this, Eric and I agree. We understand that the world is made and believe it can be unmade and remade to be more just and life-giving for the most vulnerable among us.

But Eric thinks humans, as a species, will never choose to do that.

And I think we might.

This difference was at the root of our disagreement about whether to have a baby. Running alongside Eric's love for the earth was a fear he rarely spoke about: Picturing our child in the world made him feel vulnerable, afraid, helpless. All those people who don't take care of one another. All those systems that exploit and pummel and hoard. "I don't want to give my kid to this world," he said. "To be a parent, you have to be brave enough to have your heart broken, and I can't imagine a worse heartbreak than watching our child get hurt."

I didn't see things that way. When I imagined our child in the world, I felt joy, a sense of possibility, a hope that what is broken might be repaired.

We were at an impasse; we decided to see a therapist. At the end of our first session she said, "Eric, you don't need to come back. Sarah, I'll see you next week," and I thought, *Did I win?*

show yourself to be a mother

The oldest known image of Jesus's mother is a third-century fresco painted in red on red rock in a Roman catacomb that shows baby Jesus feeding at Mary's exposed breast. All through the Middle Ages, Mary was called "the wet nurse of salvation." It was believed she offered balm to communities suffering from disease or enduring the violence of war. People reported lactation miracles. They built milk shrines. Saint Bernard of Clairvaux, the story goes, knelt in front of a statue of Mary and Jesus. "Show yourself to be a mother," he said, and Mary pressed her breast to his mouth and nourished him with milk.

Through the Renaissance, breast milk was believed to be processed blood. People thought there was a vein that turned menstrual blood into milk, which meant Mary fed Jesus with her blood, just as Jesus later fed believers with his blood. In some paintings of the crucified Jesus from these years, the wounds on his side leak milk. In one image by the Renaissance painter Quirizio da Murano, Jesus sits on a throne. He opens his garment and exposes his breast, sending milk into the open mouth of a kneeling monk.

With the invention of the printing press came mass-marketed pornography and the reproduction of anatomical drawings used as medical texts. No longer was the female body viewed as divine. It was a sexualized object, demystified, scientific. The breast became inappropriate to see in church. Instead of Mary's body, the Bible became the holy thing. Text above experience; mind above body. By 1750, the image of a mother nursing her child as the primary symbol for God's love for humanity was replaced by the image of a father sacrificing his child. Not the breast, but the cross.

when you least expect it

I went to see our therapist, who was now just my therapist, week after week, and in between visits, the question *Do I want to have a baby?* ran through my mind, until one day the question shifted: *Do I want to be a parent?*

Adoption began to feel like a viable option, and I wondered why I'd never considered it before. Why make a new child when there are already so many children who need homes? A different version of motherhood, of parenthood, became visible to me. It was not dependent on pregnancy or genes. It suggested we all might belong to one another, might be responsible for one another.

But I was still afraid.

What if I couldn't love a child I didn't give birth to?

What if the child arrived traumatized beyond repair?

My friend Maylen came to visit and led me through a writing exercise. She told me to write for ten minutes without stopping, without lifting the pen from the page. She lit a candle and set a timer. I wrote and wrote and in those words I heard a voice. The voice was mine and also not mine. The words came from me yet surprised me. It was the voice of myself as an old woman, wise and strong and clear. *A child will come when you least expect it, and you will recognize them,* she said. The hair on my arms stood. *Open your heart,* she said. *We are waiting for you.*

stronger than everything

The video shows a four-story building in Syria that has been bombed into rubble, and from somewhere inside that pile of rocks comes the sound of a baby crying. A group of rescuers called the White Helmets can't get her out. They're worried she'll die. For more than two hours, they dig, careful, slow. When her rescuer, Abu-Kifah, finally pulls her from the wreckage—one month old, wearing a yellow onesie, face covered in dust—he holds her. He can't stop crying. "When I first laid eyes on her," he says, "I felt as if she were my own daughter."

In another video about a three-story house in Syria hit by barrel bombs, a mother tells the White Helmets that her infant is in the rubble. A boy. Two weeks old. They can hear him crying. He's in a place nearly impossible to reach. If anything more were to fall on him, he would not survive.

Rescuers dig for twelve hours.

"This is a life," Khaled Farah, a White Helmet, says. "One has to be delicate dealing with life."

They carve a hole in a large rectangular rock, scrape the dust away with their hands. You can still hear the baby crying. Then you see his head, the stone a birth canal the child is pulled through. A cheer goes up from the crowd. Farah lies down, holds the baby on his chest, cradles him like a new mother. Other hands reach for the child, and Farah pushes them away, tears on his cheeks.

"This baby was stronger than barrel bombs, stronger than collapsed ceilings, stronger than everything," Farah says, days later.

waiting room

I shared with Eric what I'd heard during the writing exercise, the words my old-woman-self had said to me. "Let's adopt," I said.

We could become parents without creating another human, I offered. We could choose to take care of a child already in the world.

At our kitchen table, we each agreed to write four letters—one to the biological child we wouldn't have, one to the earth, one to ourselves honoring the decision we'd made, and one to the child we would someday welcome home.

"If we're not having a biological child," Eric said, "I should get a vasectomy."

We scheduled the surgery. We bought a special electric razor and followed the directions on the handout the nurse gave Eric during the class he was required to take before the procedure. "No hair at all," she'd said, brandishing a razor and waving it around her groin. "Or I will have to shave you."

The night before the surgery, Eric's sister called. "I'm pregnant," she said.

I ran upstairs to find the other phone. I ran upstairs to be alone. I ran upstairs because I wanted to be the one calling to tell people I was pregnant.

"Why are you crying?" Eric asked when we got off the phone.

"I'm happy for your sister," I said, which was not the whole truth.

The next morning, I went on an early run and my stomach hurt so much I had to turn around and race home. I threw up.

Maybe I'm pregnant, I thought.

I hope I'm pregnant, I thought.

I didn't share my doubt, didn't speak my longing. Instead, I drove Eric to his appointment. We sat in the waiting room, and the nurse called his name immediately. He stood. "I'll be right here," I said.

I'd hoped to make my way through my pile of unread *New Yorkers*, but I'd been waiting for less than half an hour when Eric walked in, slowly, carefully.

"Did it hurt?" I asked.

"We'll talk about it in the car," he said.

We picked up codeine at the hospital pharmacy. We read the instructions that told us what recovering from a vasectomy looks like: No exercise for one week, no baths or showers for three days, pain killers every four to six hours, no sex for two weeks.

In the car, Eric told me that while he'd waited for the doctor, he'd been visited by the biological child we didn't have. He'd watched her walk away.

The doctor had tried to talk Eric out of the procedure. "I'm going to do my best to convince you not to go through with this," he'd said. "What if you later change your mind?"

"I won't," Eric said.

"How old is your wife?" the doctor asked.

He made the first cut.

"You can still back out," the doctor said and held up the knife. "What if you marry someone else?"

mate for life

Most hornbills build their nests in existing tree hollows that have been created by other animals. The hollow might be made like this: A woodpecker pecks the tree in search of insects. Then the woodpecker's hole is enlarged by fungus. Later a bee colony moves inside, and when a bear scrapes the tree to find the honey in the bees' nest, she makes the hole even bigger.

Hornbills mate for life. When it's time to lay eggs, a couple choose a hollow for their nest, and the female seals herself inside. The male brings her material—lumps of soil moistened with saliva, chewed wood and bark, whatever he can find that makes a good wall. He swallows mud and regurgitates it to the female. She then builds the wall from the inside.

In that dark hollow, with a narrow opening just wide enough for feedings, the female waits. Just before laying her eggs, she molts and casts out her tail feathers. At that point, if she decides the male is not dependable or the nest is not safe enough, she can still fly away. But once she lays eggs—fertilizing them with sperm she has stored from her mate—she molts her wing feathers too, rendering herself flightless, unusual behavior for birds and not yet fully understood by scientists. She incubates the eggs until they hatch. When there are chicks, the male makes as many as seventy feeding trips a day. He brings geckos and seeds, insects and frogs, slugs and berries, figs and spiders, sometimes even a snake. The mother and her young remain inside the nest for months. They are dependent on the male for their survival until the mother regrows her flight feathers, which she does just before leaving the nest.

say it out loud

I told a friend I was having breastfeeding dreams, and she sent me an article about adoptive mothers who lactate. While they wait for the babies they will adopt, these women stimulate their breasts by hand and with a breast pump. Sometimes it takes months. Sometimes weeks. Sometimes all it takes is their infant's sucking to stimulate the milk supply.

Another friend sent me a link to a video of a cat nursing a baby squirrel alongside her kittens. In the video, the squirrel purrs.

"I keep having baby dreams," I told my new therapist, Juliana.

"What are you doing with the babies in your dreams?" she asked.

"Holding them," I said.

"Is that all?" Juliana asked.

"Yes," I said.

"Really?" she asked.

"Yes," I said.

"Really?" Juliana asked again.

"No," I said. "I'm breastfeeding them."

"Why do you make this so hard?" she asked. "Why can't you admit you want to have a baby?"

"Fuck," I said. "Fuck fuck fuck fuck fuck."

"Say it," she said. "Say, 'I want to have a baby.' Say, 'I want to have a baby with Eric.'"

"I want to have a baby," I said. "I want to have a baby with Eric."

Driving home I thought, *I'll tell him, and he'll have his vasectomy reversed, and I'll get pregnant, and we'll have a baby.* I laughed until I cried. My body relaxed. I'd been holding back, steeling myself, trying to find a way through, but deep down I'd known what I wanted—a baby. I hadn't let myself fight for it it because I knew Eric didn't want a baby, and I had my own doubts about what mothering might do to my life, so I'd tried to bury my yearning. But it had been there all along, a seed, growing, reaching for the light. Admitting it, I felt free, giddy.

Eric was watching the U.S. Open when I got home, the tennis ball flying back and forth across the net.

"I want to have a baby," I said.

He turned off the TV.

"I want to have a baby with you," I said.

"I had *surgery,*" he said. "How can you ask me to undo something I've already done to my body?"

I remembered the signs advertising vasectomy reversals I used to see along the highways when I was an elementary school teacher in California. "It's not that hard to reverse," I said.

"We decided," he said.

"But what if I've changed my mind?" I asked.

"Some child out there needs a home," he said, "and we can provide one."

He'd said it was up to me, that we'd do whatever I decided, and I had decided to adopt. But I made that choice, in part, because I knew it was the only way Eric would agree to become a parent—an existing child, not a new one. It was a compromise. We understood the stakes. We both knew we'd have to choose between our longings and our marriage. Adoption was our middle ground, but we didn't yet live in that shared landscape.

That day with the U.S. Open on TV, when I finally said what I wanted, confessed the deepest truth of it, I was too late.

II

FAMILY PICTURE

three births

We moved from California to Oregon for Eric's new job in 2011. He was a professor at a graduate school of education in Portland. I worked part-time as an adjunct professor at an art school downtown, and I wrote. I was working on a book about photography and war, about what difference art might make in the face of violence that feels as if it can't be stopped. I still wanted to have a baby and Eric still didn't, but we'd found our way to a tenuous agreement: We would adopt a child through the foster care system.

Because it was, at first, a compromise, there was no urgency for either of us. We were in the doldrums. And we didn't talk about it with anyone, both of us feeling that we were doing something wrong. Our secret shame turned us defensive.

Not being a mother when so many people around me were parents was its own kind of storm. Parents make assumptions about what the lives of people without children look like, about the kind of love their hearts can feel.

"Do you have kids?" strangers asked almost every day.

"No," I said, not wanting to explain, because, really, it's an unimaginative question, full of their beliefs about what family means, about who counts as kin, and it's a hard question for anyone with a complicated relationship to family making, for those of us who've experienced miscarriage or failed adoptions or the death of a child, for those of us estranged or embattled or in grief. It's a question I now refuse to ask. "Tell me about your family," I say instead, because I know belonging comes in all shapes and sizes, visible and invisible, hidden and made and chosen and found.

A couple of years after we moved to Portland, in 2013, I joined a feminist earth-based spirituality group. I didn't want to. My friend Amy made me. After graduate school, I'd left the ordination process and Christianity. Too much sexism. Not enough activism. I'd earned a doctorate in theology and still considered myself a theologian, still liked thinking and writing about the language people use to talk about God, but I wanted nothing to do with organized religion of any kind.

"You need community," Amy said when she invited me to join the spirituality group. She knew I was struggling to become a mother, knew I felt alone in that labor.

"Fuck community," I said.

"You need community."

"Fuck community."

This went on for some time.

"Trust me," she said.

I signed up. I met with the local circle in Portland. I liked it, liked that I didn't have to leave parts of myself behind to participate. My politics, my feminism, my body—everything welcome. A year later, I traveled to the group's national gathering. At the end of the weekend retreat, there was a healing circle. Each person was invited to lie on the ground with people singing all around you. I lay down, not sure what to expect. Someone cradled my head. Someone bent my legs at the knees, put the soles of my feet on the ground. A birthing position.

And in a dream in the center of all that singing, I gave birth three times: To myself. To the biological child we would not have. To the child we would adopt.

In graduate school, I took a course called "Mysticism and Literature," and most of my classmates spent seminar after seminar arguing about whether people actually had the religious experiences they claimed to have. Did Julian of Norwich really see a little thing the size of a hazelnut in the palm of her hand? Did Margery Kempe really see a purple-robed Jesus sitting on her bed? Did she really hear him tell her to stop eating meat and to stop having sex with her abusive husband? Did the enslaved man named Morte really hear God calling him to preach the good news to White people that the chained and oppressed were God's chosen people? But the veracity of these religious experiences didn't interest me; what mattered was what those claimed experiences allowed people to do. They'd been shut up and shut out—but now, doors opened.

On the ground in that healing circle, my body tingled, vibrated. I didn't speak. I didn't tell anyone about giving birth. Someone bathed me in water, washed my face, my head, my chest. Someone anointed me with cedar oil, rubbed it under my nose. "In some traditions," a woman whispered in my ear, "cedar oil is the first thing infants smell when they enter the world."

I went home and told Eric what had happened, what I'd experienced on the ground, in that song. I didn't need him to change his body again. My longing to be pregnant was satisfied. I'd had the birthing experience I'd been dreaming of. I was now ready to adopt.

"I wish I'd been there," he said. "I wish I'd witnessed the birth of our child."

pick a picture

Though we'd decided to adopt, we'd been dallying for years. An intro meeting here, an informational phone call there, a training here, another phone call there. After my birthing experience in the healing circle, I called the Department of Human Services and enrolled us in the official process of becoming certified as foster parents.

"But if you wanted to adopt, then why did you foster?" people ask me now, and I don't know what to tell them. There are nearly half a million children in the foster care system in the United States on any given day. Eric and I wanted to share our home with a child who needed one. Though we had done some research, we didn't yet understand the ins and outs of the foster care system, how it works or what it would require of us or how likely it would be that we could adopt. We knew we might have a foster child in our home temporarily before we found our forever child, but we underestimated what our attachment to that foster child would feel like, how immediate, how deep.

DHS sent an enormous stack of paperwork to complete that asked about our medical records and our finances, our families and our employment records, our philosophies about child-rearing and punishment, our drinking habits and our sexual histories. We were assigned a social worker named Kay, who was tasked with determining whether a foster child would be safe in our home.

Before her first visit, in the fall of 2015, we cleaned the house. Swept. Mopped. Folded the blanket on the couch just so. Checked the kitchen counters, which were speckled and looked clean until you put your eye at counter level and saw crumbs and dust and hair because our two cats walked on the counters no matter what we did to try to make them stop.

Eric brewed coffee. I heated water for tea and set out a plate of cookies I'd baked. We'd been told Kay would be looking for fire extinguishers, for carbon monoxide detectors on every floor.

We talked to our cats before Kay arrived. "Please be good," we said. I turned on my desk lamp so they would sleep there in that heat, stay put and not come into the kitchen. One of our cats takes antianxiety medication. She has to be fed in a bathroom by herself, undisturbed, so she doesn't vomit. I used to call the bathroom Hedgebrook, after the writing residency I love, as if it were her sanctuary, but since she started pooping on the rug if we let her out of the bathroom too early, we call it her panic room.

Will Kay think this makes us good parents?

We adopted our two cats. I'd adopted my first cat, too. I'd only had dogs as a child. One of our dogs was epileptic. My siblings and I were supposed to give him a pill every day, wrapped in American cheese, but sometimes we forgot, and he would convulse on the ground.

If the social worker knew this, I thought, she would not give us a child.

The doorbell rang. Kay stood on the front stoop with another woman, a social worker in training named Renee. I poured tea. We sat at the kitchen table, Kay took a cookie, and within minutes, one of the cats jumped onto the table. "Get down," I said and pushed him off.

"Good parenting," Kay said, and I knew she was watching everything I did. "How did you two decide to become foster parents?"

"We want to grow our family through adoption," I said. "And working with DHS feels like a good way to do that."

"Do you have infertility issues?" she asked.

"No," I said.

"Not that we know about," Eric said.

"We were teachers," I said. "I taught elementary school and Eric taught middle and high school."

"We both had students who were foster kids in our classrooms," Eric said.

At that time in Oregon, there were more than eight thousand children who'd been taken into care and were living with people other than their biological parents. Nearly two thousand of those kids would be reunited with their biological parents or another family member, but almost eight hundred children would be legally adopted, a number that, year after year, continued to rise.

In the United States about half of the children who exit foster care return to their parents or a previous caregiver in a given year, but more than fifty thousand children who cannot return to their biological parents are adopted, most often by a relative or by the foster parent they had been living with. I'd read about the trauma caused when children in foster care are moved from foster home to foster home to foster home, from school to school to school. A child in care is moved an average of four to six times. Sometimes they are moved as many as fifteen times. Being foster parents who wanted to adopt—foster parents who could give the child in our care a permanent home if needed—felt like a useful thing to be.

Kay explained that once she certified us, once she declared us safe, our house safe, then we would be given a link to a website and a password. The website would show photographs of children available for adoption, children whose parents' rights have been terminated, who will never return home.

"You'll scroll through the pictures of available kids," Kay said. "And if you see a child you think is right for your family, you'll need to make a photo album. You'll say, 'We think David or Abigail or whoever is right for our family,' and you'll send in your album, and other possible adoptive parents will send in their albums, too, and social workers like us will sit around a table and look through your album and your file to decide if you're the right family for the child, if you're a good match."

Kay explained what the album should include. "Photograph yourselves doing things you like to do," she said, and I imagined a picture of me sitting at my desk typing. A picture of me lying on the couch reading.

"Photograph your kitchen table," she said. *This is where you will eat.*

"Photograph the child's bedroom." *This is where you will sleep.*

"Photograph the local park." *This is where you will play.*

The handout she left recommended buying special scissors, glitter, glue, making it fun.

these are our babies

In the photograph, the man rests his head on the rhino's head, rests his hand between the rhino's eyes. This northern white rhino, named Sudan, is the last male of his subspecies, and in the photograph, he is dying. Joseph Wachira is comforting him.

National Geographic's Ami Vitale captured the moment. She'd first met Sudan when he'd been moved to Ol Pejeta Conservancy in Kenya from a zoo in the Czech Republic nine years before. Poachers kill rhinos for their horns, and Sudan was one of just eight remaining northern white rhinos. The room to roam and the Kenyan climate were supposed to "entice them to breed." They were watched around the clock, guarded, protected. But now Sudan was one of three remaining, the only male, and he was dying. Vitale came back to say goodbye.

"It was really hard on all of his keepers," Vitale said. "They've fallen in love with him. They say they wake up in the morning and see [the rhinos] often before they see their own children. They say, 'These are our babies.'"

want to see

We drove to a required DHS introductory meeting in a downpour. We parked and took the back staircase to the second floor of a beige building with long hallways and low ceilings. We signed in at the table at the front of the room. Next to my name were two boxes—one to check if I was interested in foster care, one to check if I was interested in adoption. I checked both. The facilitator handed me a red folder and a booklet.

A handout inside the folder explained that this meeting was designed to help us decide whether fostering and/or adopting children in the care of DHS was the right thing for our family. A bulleted list gave examples of why we might decide it wasn't a good fit. Maybe you're not ready to parent a child with special needs. Maybe you have young children who are too vulnerable or are going through challenges of their own. Maybe you have a criminal or child abuse history. Maybe you don't have enough money.

Most of the meeting was spent listening to the facilitator tell us we wouldn't be allowed to foster or adopt until our homes were certified as safe by the department. "You must have a working telephone," she explained. An operable heating system. Safe drinking water. Carbon monoxide detectors. Fire extinguishers. Escape routes and locking windows and fire ladders. No bedrooms with doors that lock from the outside, because you aren't allowed to punish your foster children by trapping them inside. She told us what to do if we had a pool or a pond or a water feature. "You'll need to have a fence," she said. "You'll need to make sure your child can't get into that water."

"Can't you just put a camera back there?" one of the potential foster parents asked.

"No," the facilitator said.

"Not just one camera," the woman said, and to clarify, she

described the elaborate surveillance system she planned to use to watch her foster kids, cameras everywhere to make sure they didn't do anything bad.

"No," the facilitator said again. "Cameras are explicitly against the rules. You can't use cameras to monitor your foster kids. The only camera allowed would be a video monitor if you happen to be fostering a baby."

When my out-of-town friends who have babies or toddlers visit me, they bring video monitors so they can watch their kids sleep, see when they wake from a nap or in the night. A friend who lives in San Francisco told me that once, after putting her child to bed, she plugged in her video monitor and set it on the kitchen counter to watch while she cooked, but on the miniature screen, instead of her own two-year-old, someone else's child appeared. There are so many monitors in that city that signals get crossed.

When I was growing up, we didn't have video monitors. You had to listen for a baby's cry. There was a time when kids weren't being watched, when we were out of view. No constant stream of shared pictures uploaded by parents. Kids in Halloween costumes, in high chairs with food smeared on their faces, on the first day of school, in the bathtub, blowing out birthday candles, missing teeth, napping on couches, sitting on the toilet. Every second recorded and made public.

The imagined lives of others show us our own longings. I saw a photograph on Facebook one afternoon posted by a friend from graduate school. She'd shared a series of photographs of her two boys holding two adorable puppies. I wanted *that* life. I wanted the kids, the dogs. I called her. "You seem happy," I said. "Your life looks so happy."

"It's all a lie," she said. "I posted those pictures to make myself feel better. I had a really shitty day." Her back door had been kicked in. Her house robbed. Everything gone.

On my Facebook page, I posted about drones and war and books and art and the fucked-up things our government is doing. One friend, a doctor with kids, told me she imagines that Eric and I talk about politics over long, quiet dinners, have amazing sex, and then lie around and read poetry to each other before falling into blissful and uninterrupted sleep.

"Eric hates when people read out loud to him," I said.

"For some reason that makes me feel better," she said.

The potential foster parent still didn't understand why she couldn't use cameras to watch her future foster children, but the facilitator had moved on to outline more rules about photographs. "You're not allowed to post any images of foster kids on social media, but that doesn't mean you shouldn't take pictures when the child is living with you," she said. "You need to take pictures of significant life events. Birthdays. Halloween. Soccer games. Graduation. School plays. The children's biological parents will miss those events, and they'll want to see them."

"Sixty-seven percent of foster kids will be returned to their biological family," she added.

I kept shutting that information out.

bring her family home

The biologist Louis Agassiz—a careful observer of the natural world and a racist—tried to use photography to substantiate his claim that not all human beings belonged to the same species. He wanted empirical evidence to justify the enslavement of Black bodies by White bodies. In 1850, Agassiz traveled to the Taylor plantation in Columbia, South Carolina. He set up a photography studio and hired J. T. Zealy to take daguerreotypes. He then chose the enslaved people he wanted photographed: five men of African birth and two African American women, daughters of two of the men.

Imagine that room with the camera set on its tripod, Ariella Azoulay proposes in *The Civil Contract of Photography*. Imagine enslaved men subjected to the gazes of the camera and of the White men gathered there. Then imagine fathers forced to watch their daughters as they were photographed, daughters who were ordered to strip, to peel down their flowered dresses, to expose their breasts, a reenactment of the auction block, where naked women were groped by sellers and potential buyers, their bellies and their breasts grabbed, so enslavers could determine how many children the women could bear and nurse, how many more enslaved people they could produce.

Yet even as they stood within that violence, Azoulay writes, the subjects of Agassiz's images could see there was a small opening: The camera would capture not their inferiority but their equality, their humanity. "Photography subverted Agassiz's presumption," Azoulay writes. Rather than documenting the subhumanity of the enslaved, the images document the inhumanity of the owners.

I wrote about Azoulay's ideas for *The New Yorker*, and alongside the article, the magazine published one of Agassiz's images. *Renty, a man taken from the Congo, in Columbia, South Carolina, in*

1850, the caption said. Shirtless, the man in the photograph looks right at the camera. His hair is gray, his skin illuminated, his abdomen scarred.

Two months after the essay was published, an email arrived in my inbox with this subject line: *Renty in the Slave Daguerreotypes is my Grandfather.* The email was from Tamara Lanier, the great-great-great-granddaughter of the man in the photograph. "I grew up hear[ing] my Mom tell stories about Papa Renty," Lanier wrote to me.

The first time Lanier saw the image of Renty, "It was almost like we made eye contact," she said. "It was an immediate feeling of kinship." And she had the same feeling when she saw images of his daughter Delia, Lanier's great-great-grandmother.

Agassiz had been a professor at Harvard, and the university now stores the images in a museum on campus. Lanier has accused Harvard of profiting from these photographs of her relatives taken without their consent, and she is suing the university. "Slavery was abolished 156 years ago, but Renty and Delia remain enslaved in Cambridge, Massachusetts," the 2019 complaint states. "Their images, like their bodies before, remain subject to control and appropriation by the powerful, and their familial identities are denied to them." Lanier is demanding that Harvard allow her to bring her family home.

handle with care

In a series that she titled *Holding,* the artist Michal Heiman collected newspaper photographs taken by photojournalists, images of rescue—one figure holding another. A man wearing a headlamp holds a woman whose eyes are closed. A man in an emergency worker's vest holds a woman whose arm covers her face. A man holds a barefoot boy whose arm is around the man's neck. A child holds a baby.

I thought of these images years later when I saw a photograph of an aid worker carrying three-year-old Alan Kurdi, whose body washed up on the beach of an island in Greece. A photographer took pictures of the dead boy, and they were on the front page of every newspaper, the boy at the edge of the surf, facedown in the sand.

"You don't leave home unless home is the mouth of a shark," I read in a poem by the poet Warsan Shire.

In "Shoulders," the poet Naomi Shihab Nye writes about a man crossing the street in the rain, his son asleep on his shoulder. The father carries "the world's most sensitive cargo," she writes, but it's unmarked. "Nowhere does his jacket say FRAGILE, HANDLE WITH CARE." In the father's ear, the sound of his son's breathing. He feels the boy's dream thrumming deep inside. He must keep the boy dry, must keep him safe, protect him from harm. "We're not going to be able to live in this world if we're not willing to do what he's doing with one another," she writes. "The road will only be wide. The rain will never stop falling."

the only way

The second time Kay and Renee came to our house, Kay had with her the stack of paperwork we'd completed weeks before. She wanted to review it. She divided us: She'd stay with me upstairs, Renee would go downstairs with Eric to the basement. I hadn't thought to clean the basement. I hadn't vacuumed the carpet. It hadn't occurred to me that anyone would sit on the small blue couch where we watched TV.

When we were alone, Kay opened a manila folder and took out my questionnaire. I could see she'd highlighted some of my answers in yellow.

"You're one of four kids, right?" Kay said.

"Yes," I said.

"I was such a tired mom," Kay said. "I sometimes wanted to hit my kids. Did your parents hit you?"

"No," I said.

"I wanted to hit my kids," she said. "I yelled at them. Did your parents yell at you?"

"No," I said.

"Then why have you been in therapy for so long?" she asked.

"I think everyone should be in therapy," I said, and Kay wrote something on a piece of paper.

"What diagnosis has your therapist given you?"

"Diagnosis?"

"Is there depression in your family?" she asked. "Smart people are always depressed."

"I'm not depressed," I said.

"From what I see here, it sounds like you're a perfectionist," she said. "It sounds like everyone in your family is a perfectionist, so accomplished, all those fancy jobs, all those degrees. What are you going to do when you adopt a kid who can only make C's in school?"

I didn't know how to answer her question. I didn't know the right thing to say. Should I say I don't care about grades—or would that make it sound like I wouldn't help my child in school? Should I say I'd want the child to do their best—or would that make it sound like I'd apply too much pressure?

"I'd want to help them thrive," I said. "Whatever that looks like for them."

"What about church?" Kay asked. "Will you take your kid to church?"

"No," I said. I'd already told her I was almost ordained as an Episcopal priest. She knew I'd written a book called *Breaking Up with God*.

"I grew up Catholic like you did," she said. "I hated it. But I took my kids to church. I wanted them to have that."

Have what? I thought. Then I said, "Maybe I'll take them to the Unitarian church downtown." I knew I wouldn't, but I said it anyway.

"Not there," she said. "I went to that place once. It doesn't feel like a church. It feels like a basement. It feels like you could be anywhere. You need to take them somewhere, though. How else will you give them a sense of community? Really, that's the only way."

After an hour of questions about my family, about eating disorders, about shame and perfectionism, my face was hot. I was sweating. "Are you not going to let us have a kid because of all this?" I asked. "Will we not be allowed to be parents?"

"Oh, no," she said. "These problems are minor, minor, minor."

I heard Renee and Eric climbing the stairs, laughing. Renee and Kay adored Eric, laughed at all his jokes, were impressed by his expertise in adolescent development and public education. Their expectations for him, the future father, were gentler than their expectations for me. He treated their visits like a game; he understood the rules and played well. But it was not a game to me. I thought I needed Kay and Renee to like me if I wanted to be a mother, and my desperation for their approval triggered all my pleaser-good-girl energy and made me act weird.

I heard Eric telling Renee about the family photographs lining the staircase wall—images of my great-grandparents and me smelling roses, of Eric's extended family gathered at a cottage on a lake, of my grandfather as a young boy driving a cart pulled by a goat, of our nephews, of trees and pets and mountains and rivers. We'd left empty spaces on that wall, too, with the hope that one day our child's picture would hang there, and our child's biological parents' pictures, too, and maybe their parents' pictures and their parents' and theirs. We will not hide any of the bodies that made our child.

"What the fuck did you two talk about?" I asked Eric after the social workers left. Renee hadn't asked Eric anything about his parents hitting him. Nothing about church. Nothing about therapy. She hadn't asked him questions like that at all.

"I want to work with Renee next time," I said.

"These questions are just a proxy," Eric said. "They don't really care what you say. They just want to see if you get upset.

"And look," he added. "You're getting upset."

III

ONE OF OUR OWN

one

The third time Kay and Renee visited our house, we sat at the kitchen table to review some paperwork. "We're getting closer to getting you those two kids you want," Kay said.

"Two?" I asked.

"Two," she said.

"We only want one," I said.

"I have *two* written down right here," she said.

"One," Eric said.

"But I wrote down two," she said.

On their first visit, we'd given them a tour of our house. It was an A-frame with a reverse floor plan—the kitchen on the upper level, the bedrooms down below. On one of the triangular walls in the kitchen, above the stairs, was a high shelf with nothing on it because it was impossible to reach. Everyone who visited our house commented on that shelf the first time they saw it. "What's up with the shelf?" people asked. I imagined it a prank played by the builder, who later went bankrupt and couldn't be found.

"What's up with the shelf?" Kay asked.

"That's where we thought the kid would sleep," Eric joked, and I loved him for it. I'd been so worried during that first visit, so stiff, but Eric was charming, funny.

"You're right," Kay said, "I could see three or four kids sleeping up there," and everyone laughed.

We showed them our bedroom and my writing room, and then we took them to the lowest level of the house, which opened into the woods. We showed them a small room Eric used as an office, and then we showed them the guest bedroom, which would soon become the kid's room.

Eric had tried to persuade me to use the guest room as my office because it was the most beautiful room in the house—big and light, large windows opening to green, to ferns, to Doug firs, a place to watch coyotes, to look for elk—but I wanted to leave it open for our child. A room in waiting seemed like an intention, like a welcome.

We stood at the bedroom's doorway and looked inside. "You could fit a lot of kids in there," Kay said, and we thought she was joking, because we'd just joked about the shelf. "A couple sets of bunk beds," she said, and Eric and I laughed again and said, "Yes, bunk beds."

And that must have been when she wrote *two* on her form. *They want two.*

other people's children

A gynecologist, a specialist to whom I'd been referred by my primary care physician because of irregular and heavy bleeding, tried to talk me into getting pregnant. She looked at my chart. "You're getting older," she said. "No time to waste."

When I told her we were planning to adopt, she made the sound people make when they see a puppy or a baby duck. Then she asked, "But don't you want babies of your own?"

I didn't answer her then because it's hard to talk during a vaginal ultrasound, but I wish I'd told her what I'd come to realize. That any child we bring into our lives will be *ours,* and that all children—whether we give birth to them or find them some other way—are also *not ours.* They are strangers, mysterious beings whose becoming we get to witness and support.

People who learned Eric and I wanted to adopt a child often told us stories of adoptions gone wrong. The adopted child incapable of attachment. Who became a drug addict, a runaway, who drained bank accounts, ruined marriages. "I have a friend who adopted," these stories began. "It was a nightmare." How often this happened surprised me. Over drinks, over dinner, at the park, in lobbies and living rooms, on planes and buses and trains, people told us to fear other people's children.

And their stories did make me afraid, convinced me I was the vulnerable one whose life was at risk. Listening, I'd forget the abandoned, the neglected, the children curled on the floor of some empty-cabinet kitchen or crying in some school bathroom stall or shaking in some crib. I'd forget that these children belong to all of us. If they wield knives in the dark or hit heads against walls or refuse to speak, they signal our failure, not theirs.

stranger danger

When I was five years old, I walked to kindergarten by myself. Stayed on sidewalks, as my mother had instructed me to do. Looked both ways to cross streets. Steered clear of a cluster of bushes where a mean girl sometimes hid to jump out and scare me. My mother warned me about a man who'd been spotted driving a van and showing kids his underwear. "Stay away from men in vans," she said. "Even if they offer you candy."

In the neighborhood where I grew up, signs stapled to telephone poles said WARNING: NEIGHBORHOOD WATCH and showed an image of a figure wearing a cloak and a hat that partially hid his face. As a child, I'd assumed the man on the sign represented the neighborhood watchman. Only recently did I understand my mistake. He wasn't the watcher; he was the *watched*. He was the stranger.

Oppression is tied to sight. *Stranger danger* hangs on the belief that our eyes will tell us who belongs and who doesn't, who's foreign and who's native, who's an intruder and who's a neighbor.

Now the Department of Homeland Security tells us what to do: See something, say something. Report suspicious activity. If you notice anyone you know shouldn't be there, tell someone. Only you know what's supposed to be in your everyday, their website says.

In *Strange Encounters*, Sara Ahmed argues that when we call someone a "stranger," it doesn't mean we don't recognize them. Rather, it means we recognize them as *stranger*, and in doing so, we assert our own belonging to the exclusion of someone else's. What is viewed as "uncommon" lets the "common" take shape, she writes. The stranger is "a mechanism *for allowing us to face that which we have already designated as the beyond.*" Boundaries become most visible when you imagine someone trying to cross them.

appear to be innate

Jackdaws, birds in the crow family, live in colonies. They have lifelong companions with whom they conduct most of their daily activities. When a jackdaw is raised in isolation, without a colony, he adopts companions. If a fledgling jackdaw is taken from her mother for even just a few days, the fledgling will imprint so deeply on a new mother—a person, a dog, a squirrel, a robin—that the connection will appear to be innate.

At the Amsterdam Zoo, a male heron fell in love with the director of the zoo. That heron was supposed to mate with the female heron, but the director's presence hindered copulation, so the director stayed away, and the herons mated. When there were eggs in the nest, the director thought it would be safe to visit again, but as soon as the male heron saw the director, he chased the female off the nest and bowed to the director repeatedly, his way of telling the director to take his rightful place in the nest.

i was a stranger

The kingdom of heaven will be like this: When the Son of Man comes, when he sits with his angels on the throne of glory, when all nations are gathered around him, he will separate them into two groups, place one on his left and the other on his right. To those on his right, he will say, "For I was hungry and you gave me food, I was thirsty and you gave me something to drink, I was sick and you took care of me, I was a prisoner and you visited me, I was a stranger and you welcomed me." To those on his left, he will say, "You did not give me food or drink or welcome or clothing. You did not visit me. You did not welcome me home." And they will say, "We didn't know it was you." And he will say, "Just as you did not do it to the least of these, you did not do it to me." And he will send them away.

you never know

After I learned my friend Emily's son, Ronan, had been diagnosed with a fatal disease, I visited her in New Mexico. I held Ronan for hours, his two-year-old body against my chest. Warm. Heavy. Emily cooked prunes, whirled them in a food processor, then spooned them into Ronan's mouth. She placed him in a carrier with pillows and stuffed animals arranged to support his head, which he could no longer hold up. We walked with him for miles through the desert.

Emily has a prosthetic leg. I remember walking with friends through city streets late at night after drinking together at a bar during graduate school, and Emily was walking slightly behind.

"Hurry up, Emily," one of us said. "Why are you walking so slowly?"

"Because I only have one leg," she said.

We'd been friends for months, and none of us had known.

She'd always refused to get a disability permit for her car. Didn't need it, she'd said. Didn't want it. But when Ronan was diagnosed, when she had to carry his heavy body everywhere, she got the placard to hang on her rearview mirror. The first time she parked in a reserved spot and was loading her dying toddler into his carrier, a man drove by and shouted out his car window, "Move your car! You don't look handicapped." This happened more than once.

In restaurants or libraries or doctor's offices, strangers peered inside the carrier to look at Ronan, his head propped up by a lion, a giraffe, a seal, his eyes open but unseeing because he'd gone blind.

"What's wrong with your baby?" one man asked.

"He doesn't like you," Emily said.

A few months after Ronan died, Emily visited me. I scheduled pedicures for us. "Remember to get half off for me because, you know, I only have one leg," she said.

Days later, we sat in the salon, talking, Emily soaking her leg in a tub scented with lavender healing salts, and the owner of the salon walked by.

"Why do you only have one leg in the water?" she asked.

"Because I only have one leg," Emily said, and knocked on her prosthetic one.

"That's hilarious," the owner said, and Emily laughed.

The owner was mortified by what she'd said, but Emily thought it was the best response she'd ever gotten.

That's hilarious. We texted those words back and forth for months.

Before Ronan died, on one of our walks, Emily and I took turns pushing his stroller uphill, and we talked about adoption. Emily was considering adoption, too, if she ever decided to have another child. I told her what people say when I tell them I might adopt: *But you never know what you're going to get.* As if biology is any kind of guarantee.

"Fuck them," Emily said.

But you never know what you're going to get. People said this to me, yes, but they also said it to Emily, who'd given birth to a child with a fatal disease passed on genetically, an extremely rare disease that needs both parents to be carriers, a baby she was watching die.

Belief in biology runs deep. Fear of the unknown, of the unrelated, runs deeper.

not on the list

To be certified as foster parents by the state, Eric and I were required to take a series of classes. You can take the classes at
night once a week for several weeks, or you can take all the
classes in a single weekend. We signed up for the weekend version, but a few weeks later, a woman called and left a message.
"This is Megan from DHS, and I'm trying to reach Lorenzo and
Madigan," she said. "You signed up for the class this coming
weekend, but our records indicate you are not a relative caregiver, so you can't attend."

I called her back. Her recorded message said, "Today is October twenty-first, and I'm not in the office all week." It was
December.

I called again in a few days and told her she'd called Sarah
and Eric, though she'd left a message for Lorenzo and Madigan.
"The website says the classes this weekend are open to everyone, relatives and nonrelatives."

"I don't know anything about the website," she said. "I have
to take you off the class list."

The next time Kay came to our house, we told her we
weren't allowed to take the classes we'd signed up for, and she
took her cellphone out of her pocket and dialed the number for
another organization that offered the required classes and registered us for the weekend series.

"If it doesn't work for your schedules," she said, "call this
number to cancel."

That week I found out I'd been accepted to attend a writing
workshop on the Oregon coast during that same weekend.

"What should I do?" I asked Eric.

"What do you think you should do?" he said.

I thought this was my chance to prove the child mattered to
me more than anything else, to demonstrate the sacrifices I was

prepared to make to be a mother. "Don't take the writing workshop?" I said.

"But we can take the adoption classes anytime," he said. "This writing workshop won't be offered again."

I signed up for the writing workshop, paid the deposit, and called the organization offering the classes to ask them to take our names off the list.

"You aren't signed up for this class series," the woman who answered the phone said. "You aren't on the list."

"But I heard our social worker sign us up," I said.

"I don't know what you heard," she said, "but you're not on the list."

"She was sitting at our kitchen table when she did it," I said.

"I'm not sure what to tell you," she said. "I'll sign you up for the next class, which will be offered in May." It was January.

why are you crying

Mary Magdalene weeps in the garden, outside the tomb, which is empty, Jesus's body gone. "Why are you crying?" two angels ask her, one sitting where Jesus's head should have been, the other at his feet.

"They have taken my lord," she says. "I don't know where they put him."

She turns from the angels and sees a man in the garden. "Did you take my lord?" she asks. She thinks he's the gardener.

"Mary," the gardener says, and hearing him speak her name, she knows he's Jesus. She reaches for him. "Don't hold on to me," he says.

One winter night, when Eric and I were on vacation in Idaho visiting my family for the holidays, I soaked in a heated community pool under the stars and watched a group of teenagers. They laughed. Splashed each other. Whispered. Dived into snowbanks and back into the warm water. Then their talk turned to Jesus. "Our generation is really lucky," one of the girls said. "Jesus is definitely coming back in our lifetime."

"Yeah," said another kid. "The proof is right there in the Bible. Pastor showed me."

If Jesus ever planned to return to the world that killed him, he must have come already, a second time, a third, a fourth and fifth, but again and again, we didn't recognize him. While we watched for the blond blue-eyed Jesus of stained-glass windows, he was a woman thrown over the bow of an enslaver's ship, a refugee turned away at the border, an ancient oak cut down to make room for more condominiums, a honeybee.

a neighbor is there

"They're keeping kids with their biological parents as long as possible," Kay said, reaching for a cookie. "Keeping the family intact, giving parents more time to get their lives together." She gave us an example. "Let's say the mother is doing meth. Let's say the mother is doing meth and having people over to the house to do meth. We can make the mother not do meth in the house, we can make the mother not invite people over to do meth, by asking, for instance, a neighbor to move in. That way the kid is with her biological parents, but a neighbor is there to watch."

"What?" I asked. "You ask a neighbor to move in?" I thought of our next-door neighbor, who walked her dog several times a day, who left coupons for the local grocery store in our mailbox at Christmastime, who yelled at the coyotes howling in the woods at night ("Out of there!" she shouted, aiming a strobe light into the trees. "Out of there!"). I imagined Kay calling to ask her to move in with us to make sure we didn't do meth.

"It usually doesn't work," Kay said. "And all it means is that children are kept in traumatizing situations for more time than they should be, sometimes for as long as two years. So now the kids we're seeing have been traumatized for longer. They're in even worse shape."

What kind of pain and suffering did Kay witness on a daily basis? We must have annoyed her, with our insistence on one child even though we lived in a house big enough for many more, with our desire to adopt, with our slowness and resistance and questions and high-maintenance cats. The need for foster homes is urgent, the violence real. Children need safe places to live. And there aren't enough safe places. We live in a country where we don't take care of one another, where we don't take care of children, and we make ourselves feel better about our refusal to care for those who need us by talking about kids in foster care as if they are scary or dangerous or defective. As if they are the ones to blame.

Day in and day out, Kay saw firsthand the worst we do to the most vulnerable among us. And she tried to work within the overtaxed system that is supposed to respond to that suffering, alleviate it, repair it, be some kind of salve for it. To do her job, she must have had to shut parts of herself down, to turn off her heart, her emotions. Otherwise it would be impossible to function.

Kay rearranged some of the manila folders stacked on our table, reached for another cookie, took a bite. "They say they keep kids at home in bad situations because it's good to keep them with their biological family as long as possible," she said. "But it's really because there's nowhere else for them to go."

Kay asked us to draw our house. Floor by floor. Eric drew each room on the graph paper Kay provided. We thought we were making the drawing for Kay to include in her files, but when Eric handed it to her, she wouldn't take it. "It's not for me," she said. "Tape it to your wall."

"I would have drawn it more carefully if I'd known we'd be hanging it up," Eric said.

"It's an escape plan," she said. "Your child needs to know where to go if there's a fire. You need to decide where you'll meet if something goes wrong and everyone has to leave the house."

Eric and I studied the drawing.

"By the mailbox, for example," she said. "You can say you will meet by the mailbox."

Meet by the mailbox, Eric wrote in pencil at the bottom of the page.

the list

The next time the social workers came to our house, they asked if they'd given us "the list." They often had trouble remembering what they'd given us and what they hadn't.

"The list?" I asked.

"That form that asks you what kind of kid you're willing to take."

"Yes," I said. "You gave it to us, but we haven't filled it out yet."

"You don't actually have to fill out the form," Kay said. It was never clear to me what was required and what was optional. "We can just go through it now, together," she said. "You need to tell us what qualities you will accept or not accept in a child in your home. Just say yes or no. It's important to be honest about your limits."

Schizophrenia?

Cruelty to animals?

Learning differences?

Developmental delays?

Public masturbation?

Wiping excrement on the walls?

Defiance?

Conceived by rape?

Addiction?

Fetal Alcohol Syndrome?

When we finished going through the fifteen-page document, I worried we'd said *no* too much or *yes* too much. I worried there were right answers but I didn't know them.

"I really just want a resilient child," I said. "A child we're the right parents for. A child who will thrive in our home."

"Maybe you're shopping at the wrong store," Kay said.

"Oh! One more thing!" Renee said. She clapped her hands. "We forgot this one because it's not on the form. What about kids who have been sex trafficked?"

"Sex trafficked?" I asked. Around Kay and Renee I felt like Jesus's dumb disciples who never understood anything Jesus said and just repeated his words back to him. "A mustard seed?" they asked. "Lost sheep? Fig tree with no fruit? Cast our nets *where?*"

"Yes," she said. "Some of the older kids in our care have been trafficked."

"I don't know," I said. "I hadn't thought about that." I knew Oregon had a huge sex trafficking problem along the I-5 corridor, but I hadn't connected that with foster care. Later, I learned the FBI estimates that more than a hundred thousand children in the United States are victims of sex trafficking, and 60 percent of all child sex trafficking victims have histories in the child welfare system. Knowing that children in foster care are vulnerable, that they often don't feel loved or cared for, traffickers target them, send already trafficked girls into group foster homes to try to lure other girls to leave.

"You'd really need to think about where you put the computer in your house," Kay said. "I wouldn't let them have a computer in the bedroom."

"Right," I said. "As if that would be the only thing to worry about. Good thing we have a desk in the kitchen." I pointed to the built-in desk on the other side of the room.

"Computers are how these predators try to contact them," Kay said.

"Are you open to taking a teenager who has a baby?" Renee asked.

"We just want one," Eric said.

Kay took a stack of manila folders out of her briefcase. "I

want to make sure you have a sense of what you're getting into," she said. "Let's see. Yes, okay, this little guy might be just perfect for you: Marcus. He's five. He loves to read."

I pictured him in my head. Marcus. Our son.

"Oh, never mind," she said. "He has a sibling who has already been adopted by another family in town, and we'll want to keep them together."

She opened another folder. "Nick," she said. "He's one of many siblings, they're all a little feral. Their father sometimes punished them by making them live outside."

I pictured him in my head. Nick. Our son.

She opened another folder. "Okay, Mikah," she said. "She's a little older, about thirteen. She's defiant. Punched her foster mother in the face. Pretty angry."

I pictured her in my head. Mikah. Our daughter.

"Take it with a grain of salt," Kay said. "You can't really trust what the foster parents report. Sometimes they make up stories about what their foster children do so they can get paid more by the state. The amount of money you receive each month is determined by how difficult the child is."

She read folder after folder after folder, described kid after kid after kid, and I wasn't sure what the point was, how I was supposed to listen to the information, whether it was appropriate that Kay was sharing their stories with us, whether we had a right to hear them. My heart hurt, my head hurt. It was hard for me to listen for even a few minutes to what these children had experienced, but Kay lived that violence, watched it, day after day, went into the homes where it happened and took children out, and then she searched for places where they might be safe, for a day or a month or a year or forever.

"Are all these children available for adoption?" I asked. "Are you asking us if we'd like to have them in our home?"

"Not necessarily," she said.

where is your coat

A woman in Germany was waiting for her morning train when she noticed the man standing next to her on the platform. It was below freezing, the woman said, and he wasn't wearing a proper coat.

"Where is your coat?" she asked the man. He didn't have one, he explained. He'd just arrived from Syria, a refugee. He'd left everything behind.

"Come with me," the woman said, and she brought him home and gave him a coat and a place to live.

"We're family now," she said.

respite care

"Can I sign you up for respite care?" Kay asked. She didn't think we'd had enough experience with kids. My two years teaching elementary school and Eric's six years teaching middle and high school didn't count. "Teaching and parenting are not the same," she said.

If we signed up for respite care, we'd give other foster parents a break. Their foster kids would live at our house for a weekend, for a few days, for a night or two. In Oregon, you can only leave foster children with people who've been approved by the system. Grandparents, aunts and uncles, parents of children's friends, anyone who lives in your house, anyone your foster kid spends more than one night with—they're all required to get background checks, required to be fingerprinted.

"You should do it," she said. "When you're trying to adopt your kid, you'll need to be able to say you have experience with children when you go in front of the judge."

I didn't want to do it. Respite care felt like a setup. If Kay already had doubts about the kind of parents we'd be, what would she think if the weekend went wrong? Would it become evidence to be used against us? And how could it not go wrong? If we agreed to offer respite care, we'd be signing up to take care of someone else's kids, who were someone else's someone else's.

"Sure," Eric said. "Sign us up for respite care."

"No," I said. "Don't sign us up."

"What?" Kay asked. "Why?"

"I never really liked babysitting other people's kids," I said.

"Adoption will feel like babysitting," Kay said. "For quite some time."

IV

MATERNAL IMPRESSION

lots of ways to have a baby

In 2014, I became an aunt for the fourth time, but I did not become a mother. A few weeks after my sister gave birth, I went to visit her. I cooked vats of chili and butternut squash soup, stayed up late with my new nephew, let him sleep on me for hours while my sister and her husband slept in a quiet room on the other side of the house.

My brother-in-law took a picture of me with their baby on my chest, and later that year, at Christmastime, my sister gave me the photograph. I took the photograph home and cried in a room by myself. I wanted that to be me. Me with my baby on my chest. But I was forty-one. But my husband had had a vasectomy.

I put the photograph on my altar.

My therapist, Juliana, talked to me about freezing my eggs. About sperm banks. "There are lots of ways to have a baby," she said.

I brought it up with Eric. "But why would you make a new baby when there are already all these children who need homes?" he wanted to know. "You want to spend thousands of dollars making another human when there are already too many of us?"

Eric and I also disagreed about the age of the child we wanted to adopt. I wanted a baby; Eric wanted a teenager. Eric is an expert in adolescent development. He has written books about middle school and high school students and how to support them better in the classroom. Eighth graders—aghast at history's injustices, outraged at unfairness, trying to understand why things are the way they are and how they might be changed—are his favorite. He knew that the foster care system struggled to place older children in foster homes, especially older boys of color. The average age of children in foster care is eight; the average age of children adopted from foster care is six. I wanted to be a parent for a child's entire life, beginning as close to birth as possible, but my desire for a baby seemed selfish in the face of such need.

"What age child would you like to adopt?" Kay asked.

"I'd prefer a baby," I said.

"There are very few babies available for adoption through the foster care system," Kay said. "Really, getting a baby would be nearly impossible."

"I'd prefer an older child," Eric said.

"So, maybe, three or four or five years old?" I said, and Kay wrote something in her notebook.

unrelated pain

Sixty—that's how many years one woman carried a baby inside her, and when she finally gave birth at age ninety-two, it was to a stone. *Lithopedion,* from Greek words meaning *stone* and *baby.* An ectopic or abdominal pregnancy fails and the fetus, too large to be absorbed by the body, calcifies to protect the mother from its dead tissue. Of four hundred or so recorded cases of lithopedion, most tell the story of a pregnant woman whose water breaks, who labors and labors, but no baby appears. She's sent home empty-handed. It's not until many years later that a doctor, examining the woman for what everyone thinks is unrelated pain, finds the stone. In France, one woman complained her whole life of pain in her abdomen, which was hard to the touch and swollen, but no one listened to her. When she died, an autopsy was performed, and doctors found a calcified fetus, which she'd been carrying for twenty-eight years.

lots and lots of babies

One of my aunts adopted her daughter from foster care, and when that aunt was in town, we had breakfast together. "How's the adoption process going?" she asked.

"The social workers are coming back tomorrow," I said. "They're going to ask us about sex and drugs." I told my aunt how at the end of her last visit, Kay had said, "Next time: sex, drugs, and rock and roll," and Eric and I had wondered if she'd be expecting lines of cocaine on the kitchen table instead of tea and cookies.

"It sounds like it's exactly the same process as it was thirty years ago," my aunt said.

Like Kay, my aunt's social worker had separated her from her husband. "How many times a week do you have sex?" the social worker had asked.

"Get your stories straight in advance," she warned.

What is the right number of times to tell a social worker you're having sex with your spouse per week? Which number will make them think you'll be a good parent? Which number will make them think you'll be a bad parent?

Twice a week, Eric and I decided we'd say. I made my aunt laugh. *What do you mean by "sex"?* I told her I'd ask Kay. *Should I show her my vibrator?* I joked.

When Kay and Renee arrived for the sex, drugs, and rock and roll conversation, they separated us again. Renee and Eric stayed in the kitchen. Kay took me to the basement. I didn't make any jokes about vibrators. I didn't make any jokes at all. Though we'd prepared for the sex questions, they didn't ask a single one.

"How many drinks do you have per week?" Kay asked me.

"One or two beers," I said. "Though sometimes I like a shot of tequila when I'm cooking."

"Oh, no," she said. "Don't say tequila. I'm not going to write that down. My boss has a thing about tequila."

What else did she not write down?

"Do you ever drink before work?" Kay asked.

I laughed. "No," I said.

Did I drink in high school? Do we have pornography in the house? Have I used drugs? Do I use drugs? Now that marijuana is legal in Oregon do I smoke pot? We made it through her list of questions quickly, and when we finished, we could hear Renee and Eric talking upstairs.

"Let's give them some more time," Kay said. "Have you considered getting a baby?"

"What do you mean?" I asked.

"Would you want to adopt a baby?"

"I told you I wanted to adopt a baby," I said. "But you said there were very few babies available for adoption through the foster care system."

"There are tons of babies," she said.

"You told me there weren't any," I said.

"There are lots and lots of babies," she said.

"But you said it would be impossible."

"No, I didn't," she said. Kay told me she used to work with women who'd been drinking and doing drugs during their pregnancies. Addicts. Meth mostly. Lots of alcohol. Whatever the substance they'd been abusing while pregnant, Kay would work to get the mothers into rehab immediately after the birth of the baby, and she'd try to get the women into programs that would allow them to bring their babies with them. "Because that's the best-case scenario," she said. "They bring their babies and get clean. If you take the babies away, the mothers feel so much shame that rehab doesn't do any good and they don't get better. Plus, in rehab they have all those other adults around who can help them learn how to be a good parent.

"It doesn't always work," she added. "Really, it usually doesn't work. That's why there are all these babies available for adoption. We should get you one."

maternal impression

On a September day in 1726, Mary Toft, a peasant who worked in hop fields in rural England, called out for her neighbor, who was a midwife. When the midwife arrived, she found Mary in labor and writhing in pain. She positioned Mary for birth and delivered what looked like a jumble of animal parts.

The midwife took the pieces to a local surgeon, who inspected the remains and wrote that they resembled *three legs of a cat of tabby color, and one leg of a rabbet . . . in them were three pieces of the backbone of an eel.*

The surgeon was skeptical. He didn't trust Mary, and he didn't like her, either. [*Mary is*] *of very stupid and sullen Temper,* he wrote. But then, in a few days, before his eyes, Mary gave birth again. This time to a dead baby bunny.

When news about a woman giving birth to rabbits reached the king, he sent two doctors to investigate. Mary explained that she'd recently miscarried. During her pregnancy, she said, she'd intensely craved rabbit meat. She couldn't get enough rabbit. She chased rabbits, hunted them, dreamed she held rabbits in her lap. The doctors watched her, day in and day out, yet even with the king's two doctors present, Mary continued to give birth to dead rabbits.

As news of Mary's births spread, nearly all of Britain stopped eating rabbit.

Maternal impression: the belief that a mother's emotions and imagination can cause birth defects and disorders. The belief that a pregnant woman can pollute her fetus with her thoughts. If a pregnant woman is sad, she can imprint depressive tendencies. If she hears a loud sound, her baby might be deaf. If she looks at a blind person, the possibility of sightlessness. The Elephant Man's mother, it is said, was spooked by an elephant when she was pregnant with him.

Two months after she first gave birth to the animal parts, Mary was taken against her will to London to be studied. She was locked in a bathhouse. She broke into a fever. She fell in and out of consciousness. And she stopped giving birth to rabbits.

While dukes took turns watching her, one of the king's doctors dissected some of the specimens Mary had given birth to. The rabbits appeared to have been cleaved with a knife. One contained droppings of corn and hay.

Within a week of Mary's arrival in London, a porter was caught sneaking a baby rabbit into the bathhouse. He said Mary had bribed him. A separate investigation found that Mary's husband had bought a suspicious number of rabbits from the town's butchers.

The doctors threatened Mary. They told her if she didn't admit what she'd done, they'd perform a painful pelvic surgery, said they'd send in a *chimneysweep's boy* to do it.

Mary confessed.

She'd been pregnant earlier in the year, she said, but she'd miscarried. While her cervix was still open, the body of a cat and the head of a rabbit were put inside her womb. To keep up the charade, she'd sewn special pockets inside her skirts, which she filled with bits of rabbit. When doctors weren't looking, she put the rabbit parts inside herself and feigned labor. Mary thought this would be her ticket out of poverty.

Toft was sentenced to prison. When she was finally released, the Duke of Richmond presented her at dinner parties to his curious guests. It is said she gave birth to a healthy, human child less than a year later.

more baby dreams

After Kay told me there were lots and lots of babies, my baby dreams returned. A baby on my back. A baby rocking in a bassinet. A baby strapped to my chest. In the dreams, I was always in Idaho, standing on the top of a hillside at the midpoint of one of my favorite hikes. My family had been visiting Idaho's Wood River Valley for decades. I'd spent summers there. Eric and I had lived in Ketchum for two years while writing our dissertations. I love that land. But we hadn't been able to figure out how to make money in a ski town as two academics.

I'd been an adjunct professor at an art school in Portland for five years, and I'd finally been hired as a full-time professor, chair of a master's program, exactly the job I would have designed for myself. But the master's program had been founded by people the school was scared to fire, so instead of firing them, they hired me to try to force them out. I didn't want to be part of that. I'd been offered a visiting professorship at another university an hour away. I told the art school I'd redesign the master's program and recruit students for it while teaching at the other university, and then I'd come back when they'd worked things out.

The university where I was a visiting professor paid for me to take a writing workshop, and while I was at the workshop, my agent called to tell me she'd sold the manuscript for the book I'd been writing for a decade, and when she shared this good news, I thought, *I could quit my job.* Then I tried to put that thought out of my mind.

But it wouldn't leave.

At home, I told Eric about wanting to quit my job at the art school. I told him that when I pictured my life, I saw myself as an artist, a writer, not as the chair of a graduate program. I told him about my Idaho baby dreams. Eric never remembers his dreams. If he did, I imagine he'd say he dreams of mountains. Backpacking. Hiking. Paragliding. Snowboarding. Mountain biking. He'd always wanted to live in a mountain town, and we planned to move to one when he retired. He wasn't a professor anymore. He now worked remotely for an educational non-profit headquartered in Boston. Really, we could live anywhere.

Eric relaxed in the mountains. He was joyful, fun, at ease. "Your husband is like a happy little kid when he's snowboarding," my brother would report when they'd come back from a day on the hill. I knew Eric would be a better parent in the mountains than in a city. A small town would make everything easier—a grocery store just down the street, friends a bike ride away, no traffic, clean air, wide open vistas, more time, more space, more play.

My parents live in Idaho for part of the year, and I wanted our child to know them, to spend time with them. Kay was always telling us that we were too busy, that we didn't have enough family support in Portland, that we'd need to shift our lives around when we welcomed a child.

"I could quit my job, and we could move to Idaho," I said.

Though I often struggled with small decisions, most big decisions—except for motherhood—have never been hard for me. When the stakes are high, I can be decisive, as sharp as a blade. For such a well-trained good girl, I have a surprisingly bold streak. Intrepid. It often catches other people by surprise.

Eric was packing his suitcase. He was about to drive to the airport to fly to a meeting for work. "Don't quit your job while I'm out of town," he said.

"I won't," I said.

But I did.

V

FAMILY TREE

draw the branches

We sold our house in Portland and bought a house in Idaho. Before we moved, I called the organization that ran the foster parent certification classes in Portland and told the woman who answered the phone that we wouldn't be attending the class in May. I knew there was a waiting list. I wanted someone else to have our spot.

The week after we had been supposed to attend the classes, Kay called. "Just checking to see how the classes went," she said on our answering machine. "Your home study is almost done."

I called her back. I told her we were moving to Idaho and apologized for wasting her time. I thanked her. "You always wanted us to have more family around, and you thought we were too busy," I said. "I quit my job. We're moving closer to a network of support."

Our last night in Portland, which was the night of the 2016 presidential election, we sat on two orange folding chairs, a pizza between us, to watch the returns come in. We'd packed everything except our television and those two chairs. "There's going to be a female president," Eric said. "And I'm going to get laid."

Neither of those things happened.

The next morning, men loaded our belongings into a moving truck. Then we drove nine hours to Hailey, Idaho, a small mountain town in the Wood River Valley just south of Ketchum and Sun Valley.

Two weeks after we arrived, I called the Idaho Department of Health and Welfare and learned we'd need to start the certification process all over again. Nothing we'd done in Oregon—not the home study, not all the meetings with Kay and Renee, not the introductory classes—counted.

I was relieved. I wanted a do-over.

I also wanted a baby. I'd always wanted a baby. I didn't need to be pregnant, I didn't need to give birth, I didn't need any kind of genetic relationship to our child, but I did need to be a mother to an infant. I had let Eric's preference for an adolescent and the social workers' initial insistence that there weren't any babies and the dire need for homes for older foster kids push my knowing down. Bury it. Their resistance let me tiptoe around my deepest desire, pretend it wasn't there. But it was there. And feigning that it wasn't had become a slow-drip acid eating away at our marriage.

In the weeks before we moved to Idaho, I gave Eric an ultimatum: baby and me, or no baby and no me. We each took time alone to think about what I'd said, slept in different parts of the house, scheduled our hours in the kitchen. I spent the weekend meditating, journaling, reading; Eric went to an RV show.

The word "ultimatum" comes from the Latin noun *ultimatum,* meaning "a final statement," and from the Latin verb *ultimare,* meaning "to come to an end." The plural *ultimata* was used by the Romans as a noun to mean "what is farthest or most remote; the last, the end." In the 1820s, "ultimatum" was slang for "buttocks."

And that slang use of the word seems about right, because people assume those who give ultimatums are assholes. If you share with anyone that you gave your partner an ultimatum, they look at you like you put a gun to someone's head. An ultimatum is seen as violent, a sign of weakness, a way to force someone to do what you know they don't want to do. An ultimatum is a threat: Do what I want, or I'll end our relationship.

But resentment ends relationships too. When you know what you want but you pretend otherwise, it's a poison everyone is drinking. It took this years-long fight for a baby to teach me to say what I want, to teach me that when you don't, you aren't doing anyone any favors, you aren't being the better person, the more generous one. You're being dishonest.

Why did I believe my desires couldn't be trusted? I'd had dreams and visions. I could see our baby. I'd always been able to.

At the end of our time apart, Eric and I met in the living room to talk.

"Okay," he said.

"You're saying yes to a baby?"

"I'm saying I don't want to live without you," he said. "I'm choosing to trust your vision of the world. I'm choosing to believe you know what's best for our family."

The afternoon sunlight yellowed the green woods outside the window. The leaves glowed.

"But I need a map," he added. He'd been trying for months to talk with me about what our daily lives would look like when we were parents—who'd be with the child when, who'd work and who'd cook and who'd stay up all night—and I'd been refusing to have those conversations, my denial of his requests my own little rebellion. "You've been minimizing the kind of planning that makes me feel safe," he said. "I need us to talk about schedule."

"Okay," I said.

Eric reminded me that I'd been right about the biggest decisions we'd made in our lives together so far—where to move, when to move, which jobs to keep, which jobs to quit, which houses to buy. I'd taken the lead on the decisions we'd made that other people told us were colossal mistakes, decisions they said would bring ruin to our finances, to our careers. But our choices didn't bring ruin. They brought joy, made our lives better, our bodies healthier.

Eric trusted me. Now it was my turn to trust myself.

I registered online as a family interested in fostering and adoption. The department sent us a stack of paperwork, much of it identical to what we'd completed in Oregon. We filled it out and mailed it back. A few weeks later a social worker named Eliza called to explain how the process worked.

I told Eliza we wanted to adopt a baby. She told me that her daughter wanted to adopt, too, but that she was pursuing adoption through an agency instead of trying to adopt through the foster care system. "I told her there are plenty of children available for adoption in foster care," Eliza said. "You'll have no trouble adopting a baby here. I wish my daughter would do what you're doing."

The curriculum for the classes we were required to take was called PRIDE (Parents' Resource Information Development Education), and Eliza told us she was trying to organize classes in Hailey, but then she called and said she couldn't find enough families in our town who wanted to adopt or to become foster parents, so we'd have to attend the classes in Jerome, an hour and a half south.

Eric and I drove to the first class on a Friday night, passed fields of volcanic rock and snow-covered sagebrush, signs inviting us to tour ice caves, cows standing in mud, stacks of hay covered in plastic. The car's GPS directed us to an access road lined with abandoned buildings and warehouses, every window dark or broken. We stopped at a gas station convenience store to ask for help, and a nice man dressed in full-body camouflage told me the place we were looking for was probably on the other side of the highway, though he'd never heard of it.

We typed in the address again, and this time our GPS took us to a car dealership. "This can't be right," I said. We were late, so I ran into the lit-up showroom, and a salesman approached me, eager, as if I were there to buy a car just before closing on a Friday night.

"Is there a meeting room here?" I asked. "A foster parent training class?"

"Upstairs," he said.

The dealership's lot was full, so we parked in front of the payday loan shop next door. We entered the dealership, climbed the stairs to the second floor, and at the first landing, halfway up, I stopped. I wanted to mark the moment, add some ceremony to what we were doing, acknowledge it as the beginning of a new life. "Let's find our baby," I said to Eric and kissed him.

We were the last people to arrive. The facilitator, a woman named Dawn, handed us a white binder and two pieces of paper and told us to fold the paper into table tents and write our names on them. The room was windowless, the gray tables arranged in a U, and in the corner by the door was a large cardboard box that held plastic toys and a few American flags.

"Welcome to PRIDE," Dawn said. "Let's start by getting to know each other a little bit. Just say your name, why you're here, and something you like to do."

The introductions started on the other side of the U. "I like to hunt," said the first person. And the second and the third, fourth, fifth.

I couldn't think of a thing to say. My mind went blank.

"I like to read," I said when it was my turn.

"Jesus," I heard Eric say under his breath.

"I like to car camp," Eric said when it was his turn.

After everyone had introduced themselves, Dawn showed us a stack of gridded paper, our names listed in a column on the left-hand side of each long page. "We'll take notes about the things you say here," she said. "They will become part of your home study."

The feeling of being watched and not knowing what, exactly, the watchers were looking for returned to me.

"Let me be clear," she said. "We're not an adoption agency. Our goal is always reunification. We support children and their biological families to come back together. We help children return home. Of the three hundred children in care at any one time in our area, only ten percent are available for adoption."

I did the easy math—thirty kids available for adoption at any given time. That number was small, but it wasn't zero. The other facilitators helping Dawn had all adopted from foster care, more than once. One woman told us she had ten children at home, eight of whom she'd fostered and then adopted.

Dawn explained that within a week of a child's being placed in a foster home, there would be an "icebreaker" meeting with the child, the bio parents, the foster parents, and the social workers, so the child could see you interacting with their family and the child's family could see you interacting with their child. "The message you need to communicate is 'I'm here to *take care of* your child, not to *take* your child,'" Dawn said.

I raised my hand. "We want to adopt," I said. "That's what brought us here. Are we in the wrong place?"

"We don't find kids for homes; we find homes for kids," Dawn said.

"Okay," I said.

"How would you feel if the people you trusted to help you get your children back really wanted to keep them away from you?" she asked.

"Should we leave?" I asked.

"I hope you'll stay," she said. "I hope you'll come back tomorrow."

I didn't hear much more after that, my mind spinning. I'd been clear with Eliza on the phone that we wanted to adopt a baby, and she'd assured me adoption wouldn't be a problem, that there were plenty of babies who needed permanent homes, but now it seemed it was a problem.

I'd worked hard to get to that room at the car dealership. I'd fought with Eric to become a parent. I'd fought for a baby. I'd moved us to Idaho. How could I leave now? Plus, there was a desperate need for foster parents. We might have to foster for a while, but I was sure we'd eventually find our child. Kids in cages at the border. Child refugees drowning in the sea. Hundreds of thousands of children in foster care. I wanted to be a person who could meet a small part of this need.

At the end of class, Dawn assigned homework, which included several worksheets and directions for making a family tree. We'd been required to make a family tree when we lived in Portland, too. At our kitchen table, Kay had pulled out a small piece of paper that looked like a scrap, one edge jagged where it had been ripped. "First things first," she'd said. "I need to draw your family tree." On that scrap, she'd penciled names in tiny handwriting as we said them. Grandparents, parents, aunts, uncles, siblings, nephews. The dates they were born. She wanted to know if they had children, if they were married, divorced. She wanted to know who was alive and who was dead and how they'd died.

A tree is a strange symbol for kinship. It's not how trees reproduce, and it isn't even how they grow—from crown to roots. But mapping family onto a plant makes the constructed system feel natural, as if family is inevitable, a process of passing genetic material from one generation to the next to the next.

At the end of class, I used the bathroom before our long drive home, and when I came out, there was a couple waiting for Eric and me in the dark hallway at the top of the stairs. They were there to adopt, too, they whispered. These classes are just a technicality, they explained. "Once you're certified, you can do whatever you want. You can even work with a different adoption agency, even a private agency," the woman said. "There are plenty of available children who need good homes."

I cried most of the way home.

"Why didn't Eliza tell me the truth when we talked on the phone?" I said. "I was clear from the beginning that we wanted to adopt."

"Think of what these social workers have seen," he said. "Think of what they see every day. They're worried about kids who need a home to go to right now, abused kids, traumatized kids. That's their job. They don't care about some woman in some class who wants to adopt a baby, and they shouldn't. It isn't about you."

It was nearly eleven o'clock when we got home, and we had to wake up at five to drive back to Jerome for the second class, which started early the next morning. We fed our cats, who were famished because it was late, hours past their dinnertime, so they ate too fast, and one crawled under our platform bed and vomited in a spot unreachable unless we moved the bed, which was impossible to budge without first taking the mattress off the platform, so we took it off, then pushed the platform with our legs, our backs against the wall, pushed as hard as we could to get the bed to move, inch by inch, the weight crushing, insurmountable.

tree friends

Look up into the forest canopy, Peter Wohlleben writes in *The Hidden Life of Trees*. The average tree will grow her limbs until they encounter the branch tips of a neighboring tree of the same height. Each tree reinforces its extended branches, but once they touch, the tree doesn't grow wider because air and light in that space are already taken. It might look like a shoving match up there, but "a pair of true friends is careful right from the outset." They don't grow thick branches in each other's direction because they don't want to take anything away from their friend. Most humans, when they look into a forest, misunderstand what they see. They don't see friends. They don't see family.

When trees grow close together, they share. Nutrients and water are "optimally divided among them all so that each tree can grow into the best tree it can be." Thinking that trees need space to grow, humans thin the forest, believing we're helping individual trees by removing their competition. But we're wrong. "The remaining trees are bereft," Wohlleben writes. "They send messages out to their neighbors in vain, because nothing remains but stumps."

Tree friends are sometimes so tightly connected at the roots that they die at the same time. If they don't die together, if one friend dies before the other, the still living tree will tend the stump, whatever is left of her friend, trying to keep her alive.

eco-map

The next morning, we parked in front of the payday loan place again, and the pine tree at the edge of the lot was filled with tiny singing birds. "You came back," Dawn said when she saw us.

"But why did you go back?" friends ask me now, and I don't know what to tell them.

I probably went back because it felt like my only option. Just being in those classes felt like a victory. Private adoption was not on the table for us at that time. We'd talked to people who'd gone through the private adoption process, and they'd told us about a price list, about White babies costing more than Black or Brown babies, and we didn't want anything to do with that. I now understand we got incomplete information, even misinformation. I know it's hard to believe we didn't do our own research about adoption agencies, but we didn't. We barely researched foster care in Idaho. We didn't know Idaho is a "reunification state." We didn't know reunifying foster children with their biological parents is considered a victory here, even when it's not, ultimately, the safest situation for the children. We didn't know Idaho's reunification statistics are higher than almost anywhere else in the country; the national average is 50 percent, but in Idaho, reunification takes place 72 percent of the time.

A friend asked, "But what if you foster a baby for a few weeks and then you have to give the baby back to the biological family?" Her months-old baby was sitting on her lap.

"Then we'll have given that baby a good home for those few weeks," I said.

My answer was naïve. Ignorant. Defensive.

I'd been told ostriches bury their heads in the sand because they think if they can't see you, you can't see them. My denial was ostrich-like. People kept pointing out the savanna's dangers, reminding me I couldn't fly, and I'd shrug my small wings, as if they were the ones who didn't understand the situation, as if they couldn't see what I was capable of.

I was wrong about so much. I was even wrong about ostriches: They don't put their heads in the sand because they're afraid. They dig holes in the dirt to use as nests for their eggs. They put their heads in those holes to turn the eggs. Ostriches aren't hiding; they're tending their young.

Eric and I sat in the same seats we'd sat in the night before, next to a man wearing an NRA shirt with a picture of an eagle on the back, each wing feather made of a different kind of gun. He and his wife were our age, and they'd had their first child while still in high school. Their kids were now grown and out of the house. They wanted to be foster parents so they could offer a safe place to children for as long as needed. We became friends.

"There are three components to parenting," Dawn said and wrote them on the board: 1. Giving Birth; 2. Protecting and Nurturing; and 3. Legal Responsibility. "Number 1 belongs to the bio parent, and number 3 belongs to the department," she explained. "Number 2 is where the foster parents come in."

To protect and nurture the children in their care, foster parents need to help them maintain the existing relationships in their lives, as long as those relationships don't cause harm, Dawn explained. She gave us each a handout with a large circle in the center of the page and smaller circles all around, an eco-map, she called it. Dawn read us the profile of a foster child named Will and told us to listen for the meaningful connections in his life and fill in the eco-map accordingly. "Will is inside that large circle," she said. "The smaller circles represent all the other people and activities in his life." She told us to draw lines connecting the smaller circles to the large circle. A solid line indicated a strong relationship, a dotted line meant the relationship was weak, and a line with hash marks showed the relationship was stressful.

Will lived in Chicago, Dawn read. He was eight years old. His mother struggled with addiction. His father wasn't around. But he'd been seeing the same pediatrician since he'd been born, and he liked to go to her office, often stopped by after school to visit with the receptionist. He took the bus to school every morning and talked about baseball with the driver. He played soccer and loved his coach, who was the father of his good friend and who usually invited him over for dinner after practice. On Saturdays, Will liked to walk around his neighborhood, and he spent hours sitting on the stoop of a local market down the street from his apartment, the shopkeeper talking with him about school and books and sports, slipping Will a free piece of candy or two every time he saw him. Will spent several nights a week with his upstairs neighbor, an older woman who was like a grandmother to him, gentle and kind, and who cooked his favorite food (spaghetti) whenever his mother had to work late or didn't come home because she was drunk or high or in jail.

"Will was put in foster care in the suburbs, miles away from where he'd been raised," Dawn said. "What relationships would you include in his eco-map?" The upstairs neighbor, we said. The coach. The bus driver. The shopkeeper. The pediatrician and her receptionist. His friends from school.

"Helping children develop and maintain lifelong relationships," Dawn said. "This is our role."

I raised my hand. "As a foster parent, how will I find out the child in my care had a meaningful relationship with a shopkeeper?" I asked.

"When a child is placed in your home, we'll make an eco-map for them within sixty days of placement," Dawn said. "Hopefully, someone will be able to tell you."

But how would that someone know?

Sometimes we don't even know which relationships are the most meaningful in our own lives until they are lost. My father grew up in New Orleans, and after Hurricane Katrina, he talked with a friend who still lived there. He told my father it felt like his entire life had been washed away. It was the relationships he'd thought about the least whose loss affected him the most, like the woman who worked at the dry cleaner in his neighborhood. "I saw her all the time," he said. "Almost every week. We talked. Enjoyed each other." But he knew only her first name, and after the flood, the dry cleaner never reopened. A sign on the front door said they'd gone to live with family in a different state. He tried to find her, but it was impossible.

screen filled with images

After the couple told us about the organization that has a website with photographs of children available for adoption, I typed in the URL and my screen filled with images of kids. Six children sitting on an orange couch, ages fifteen, fourteen, twelve, eleven, eleven, and nine—a *sibling set,* in the language of the foster care system. A smiling girl standing in front of her elementary school, wearing a backpack and a shirt with the name of a sports team on it. A boy leaning against a beige wall, blue hooded sweatshirt zipped tight. Five siblings gathered in an arcade, arms around one another, the oldest making bunny ears over the head of the youngest. A five-year-old girl in a Spider-Man T-shirt standing in front of a Christmas tree, candy-cane-colored ribbons tied to every branch.

I turned off my computer.

expected and unexpected loss

The theme of the next PRIDE class was "Loss and Grief," and a man named Ben joined Dawn as a co-facilitator. He was a middle school assistant principal and a foster parent. He and his wife, Kate, had seven kids—two biological kids, one adopted kid, one foster kid who'd been with them for six months, and three new foster kids, siblings who had just arrived two days ago, including a baby who'd been born addicted to meth and was still in the neonatal intensive care unit. Ben, like all the people who were involved with DHW, rarely said the words *children* or *kids* or even *babies*. He said *kiddos*. He said *littles*.

The department had called Kate to see if they might be willing to house that sibling set of three, and Kate had texted Ben at work to see if he was okay with it, and when he didn't respond to the text within five minutes, she said yes. Their family grew from four kids to seven kids in one afternoon. "She hates when I don't respond to her texts," Ben said.

"We need to work out a different system," Eric whispered to me. "If I don't text back right away, that doesn't indicate a *yes*."

"We're going to do an activity called sculpting," Dawn said, and she told Ben to sit in the chair in the center of the room. "Each of you will represent a relationship in Ben's life," Dawn said. "And how close you stand to him will show how close the relationship is." It was like a live version of the eco-map we'd made the day before.

"Who wants to be his wife?" Dawn asked.

"I will," I said.

"*Ooooohhhhhh,*" the class said in unison, like we were in seventh grade, and everyone laughed.

"Do you have a close relationship with your wife?" Dawn asked.

"Yes," Ben said.

"Stand close to him," Dawn told me.

Wife—close. Kids—close. God—close. Church—close. Parents, siblings, friends, colleagues. Basketball. Coaching. Teaching. Other people in our class stood near to Ben or far from him, depending on the strength of the relationship.

"I apologize, but now we're going to pretend things go wrong in your life, Ben," Dawn said. "Let's say your wife and kids are driving home from an event at church, and they get in a car accident, and one of your kids dies."

The person representing the child who died left Ben's side, sat back down.

"The grief is terrible. You start drinking," Dawn said. "You get drunk all the time. You get fired."

His colleagues returned to their seats. His students sat down, his basketball team.

Soon his wife and God were the only ones left standing next to him.

"You hit your wife," Dawn said.

I sat down. Then it was just Ben and God.

"There are expected losses and unexpected losses," Dawn said. "Expected losses are shared by all human beings. These losses come with cultural support. They're considered normal. You might experience regret, but you won't experience shame. You're generally prepared by life to anticipate losses like this. But when we experience unexpected losses, we're unprepared to cope. These kinds of losses are not shared equally by all human beings. There is often little understanding or support. You might feel shame or blame. Your loss won't be seen as normal. It will be seen as different. This complicates the grieving process."

Ben drew a big T on the board. He labeled one side "Expected" and the other "Unexpected," and then Dawn called out life events, and we had to place them in the correct category.

The death of a child?

Unexpected.

The death of a parent?

Expected.

Moving? Aging? Illness? Job loss?

Ben recorded each loss in the appropriate column.

"What kind of loss do children experience who are coming into care?" Dawn asked.

"Unexpected," someone said.

"Yes," she said. "Everything is unexpected. Siblings. Parents. Home. School. They lose their whole life."

"How can you help kids manage loss like this?" Ben asked us.

The room was quiet.

"You can say things to the child in your care like, 'I know you don't want to be here, I know you miss your mom, but you're here, and we're in this together,'" Dawn said.

I raised my hand. "You can tell them you'll keep them safe," I said.

"You should never tell them that," Dawn said. "It's a promise you can't keep."

upbringing

Mother trees raise their children, and the upbringing they offer is strict: light deprivation. With their enormous crowns, mature trees form a thick canopy that admits only 3 percent of available light for new trees. "With that amount of sunlight, a tree can photosynthesize just enough to keep its own body from dying," Wohlleben writes. "There's nothing left to fuel a decent drive upward or even a thicker trunk." Rebellion in the shade is impossible, he insists, because the young tree doesn't have enough energy to sustain resistance.

With this light deprivation, tree mothers teach their tree children, raise them strong. Living to old age requires unhurried growth, so mother trees know to slow their children's development, because when a tree grows slowly, the inner wood cells of the young ones' trunks are tiny and contain almost no air, which renders the trees flexible, harder to break in storms and resistant to fungi, which have a hard time invading their tough exterior.

Human time is nothing compared to tree time. We forget what old age would be for a tree in an untouched ancient forest. Many hundreds of years, even thousands. Modern forestry practices impose a human life span onto trees, planting trees that are allowed to grow for only 80 to 120 years before they're cut down and turned into cash.

In the forest Wohlleben tends, young beech trees wait under their two-hundred-year-old mother trees, patient. They've waited for decades and will wait for decades more before it's their turn to rise through the canopy. To make the wait time bearable, the young trees' mothers pass along sugar and other nutrients through their root systems. "You might even say they are nursing their babies," Wohlleben writes.

spare the rod

"Your child's behavior has meaning," Dawn said. "You have a choice in how you see it, how you understand what they do. Will you see her as a bratty child? Or will you see her as a child expressing a need?" It's hard to discipline foster kids, she explained. You don't know their triggers. You don't have a history together. You haven't developed trust. You don't know what works and what doesn't. Foster children move from one home to another, and every placement has a different set of rules. They don't know if they're allowed to eat while they watch television. They don't know if they're supposed to clear their plate from the table. They don't know the bedtime routine.

"What will you do when they break your rules?" Dawn asked. She explained that even if you spank your biological children, you are not allowed to spank your foster children. *No corporal punishment*, she wrote on the board. "If you violate the state's discipline policy, your foster kids will be removed from your home," she said. "Sometimes these kids are very difficult. You'll need patience."

No withholding of visits with their biological parents.

No soap or tobacco on tongues.

No restraining.

No doors that lock from the outside.

"We know we're not going to get a perfect little baby who follows all of our rules," one of the women in the class said. "We didn't get that from God. Why would we think we'd get that from the state?"

Dawn walked around the room and placed a piece of candy in front of each person. Three Musketeers. Snickers. Peanut M&M's. Reese's Peanut Butter Cups. Twix. "Look at the kind of candy at your seat," Dawn said. "That will be your group." She sent us to different parts of the room to gather with the people who had the same candy. She handed each group a slip of paper. "Given what we've been talking about today, discuss the statement you see on your slip of paper," Dawn said.

Ours said: *You said to treat biological and foster children equally, and I spank my biological children.*

Every parent in the group with me said they spanked their kids. "It's in the Bible," one of the men said. "Spare the rod, spoil the child."

"I know we're not allowed to do it," said another man. "But it works."

compartmentalization of decay

To guard against invaders like bacteria and fungi, trees generate chemical barriers, a living protective force. Trees work hard to keep invaders out; invaders work hard to get inside the tree. Wounds make their infiltration easier.

Most trees are wounded many times during their lives. They endure fires and weather. Branches die and break. Insects, birds, and small and large animals peck or tunnel or claw or burrow or nest. When the wounds are small, the tree can close them quickly. When the wounds are large, there is the possibility of decay, which can lead to trouble for the tree.

A tree is made of many trees. Each growth ring can be considered a tree. And every one of those trees within the tree is divided into compartments. Think of each compartment like a room with walls. The tree's many-roomed structure allows the tree to stop decay from spreading. It works like this: When a wall is injured, the tree will form a new wall, confining the damage and protecting any new growth. The decay is isolated in its own room by a barrier zone that separates wood formed before wounding from wood formed after wounding. This is called the compartmentalization of decay.

irreversibility

Sometimes children in foster care have developmental delays. "Let's say a child comes into care at the age of two," Dawn said, "but she doesn't get a forever home, what we call *permanency*, until the age of four. You lose development when you're scared as a child. Your mind is busy worrying about other things. Will I be safe? Where will I sleep? When can I go home? You can't think about learning to walk or speak.

"Close your eyes," Dawn said, "and I'll tell you the story of Baby Sam and Baby Andrew."

We closed our eyes. Someone turned off the lights.

Baby Sam and Baby Andrew are born on the same day. Baby Sam is brought home to a house with a room that's been set up for him. When he cries, one of his parents holds him or feeds him, gives him whatever he needs. When Baby Andrew cries, no one holds him or feeds him. No one gives him what he needs. His parents leave him in a playpen in the other room while they get high. Baby Sam's parents read to him. They place him on a blanket in the living room and wind the mobile so he can hear music and watch the animals twirl over his head. Baby Andrew's parents sleep through Andrew's cries. They sleep all day. They invite friends over at night and hope the noise won't wake Andrew. They close his bedroom door in case it does. Andrew cries and cries and no one comforts him. He stops crying.

Dawn explained that attachment works like this: A child experiences discomfort and expresses that discomfort by crying or acting out or yelling, and that expression reveals a need, and a parent meets that need by comforting the child, and the child feels better and learns to trust the parent. But if a child doesn't get their needs met, no trust, no attachment. "It changes their brain," she said. "It can't be undone."

We took a pizza break. "It can be undone," Eric said between bites of cheese pizza.

"What can?" I asked.

"Children's brains are plastic. They can recover," he said. "The brain can be rewired. New connections are being made all the time."

convining one plant to take care of another

To graft is to join the root system of one plant and the upper part of another so they appear to grow as a single plant. The root system is called *rootstock;* the upper part is called *scion,* which means "sprout" or "shoot" and can also refer to a person's descendants or heirs.

Splice, bark, saddle, whip, tongue, bridge—there are many grafting techniques, but the basic practice is to cut both plants' cambium (the layer of actively dividing cells between the xylem and the phloem). The wounded tissues of one plant are placed in intimate contact with the wounded tissues of another, and they are wrapped together with cloth or string or wax or masking tape. The injured parts then form masses of cells that heal the wounds.

Grafting is used to repair injured trees, to strengthen resistance to disease, to adapt to adverse soil and climate conditions, to ensure pollination, and to produce trees that bear more than one kind of fruit or plants that bloom more than one kind of flower. In theory, any two plants that have a continuous cambium can be grafted. Though it is not necessary for them to be the same species, the rootstock and the scion should be related— for example, you can graft a plum tree on a peach tree's rootstock, while apple grafted on oak fails immediately. Apple grafted on pear sometimes grows well for a year, even two, but eventually, it weakens and dies. It's best to graft apricot on apricot, but in moist soil in cooler regions, apricot trees can thrive on plum rootstock. After two plants are grafted, whether they flourish and grow, whether they remain compatible, is mediated by complex physiological and environmental factors.

Many years ago, Eric walked through a garden with his cousin, a botanist. "Most simply put," his cousin said, "grafting is convincing one plant to take care of another."

family tree

Part of Idaho's mandated curriculum in public schools includes an assignment requiring elementary students to make family trees. "This is a hard activity for foster kids," Dawn said, and I thought of my brother-in-law and his sister's son, who came home from school charged with making a family tree that traced his family's history all the way back to the person who arrived first in this country. My brother-in-law and his nephew are Black. Their ancestors were stolen, kidnapped, brought here chained in the holds of ships. Most of their names were not written down. To create the illusion of bodies without kin, to make humans appear to be marketable, sellable, disposable, property, children were separated from parents. Sisters from brothers. Husbands from wives. Aunts from cousins from grandparents. Dropped on different continents.

"My son will not be making a family tree," the child's mother told his teacher.

gone

I woke up one morning at a writing residency to the sound of chainsaws. I looked out my window and watched a man roped to a pine tree cut off branch after branch. Other men retrieved the branches and put them into a chipper. When nearly all the branches had been removed from the trunk, the roped-up man cut off the top of the tree, and a crane lifted it away. Piece by piece, the trunk was cut down, the logs loaded into a truck.

After the men left, I walked outside and counted the rings on the stump that remained. The tree must have been more than two hundred years old. The day before, there was a tree whose top I'd had to crane my neck to see; now, with no ceremony, this being older than all of us, older than our grandparents, older than our great-grandparents, was gone.

That afternoon, I watched a man use a machine to grind down the stump. Men raked the pieces into trash cans, dumped them into the back of a truck to be hauled away.

I called Eric and told him about the tree.

"I don't want to hear any more," he said. One of his earliest memories is of watching his grandfather cut down a tree. Eric cried so hard he nearly threw up. We never have a Christmas tree because Eric doesn't see the point in killing a living thing so we can bring it into our house and decorate it and watch it slowly die until we drag it to the curb and leave it there. He refuses to look out the car window at the thrown-out trees lining our town's streets after New Year's.

Before I'd left for the writing residency, we'd been watching a robin build a nest in the crook of the maple outside our bedroom window. The day before I left, she'd settled onto her nest. Eric texted me photographs of her while I was away. She'd rubbed off her chest feathers so she could better regulate the eggs' temperature, and Eric collected the fallen feathers. The nesting mother bird and her partner, who moved from branch to branch in the yard watching for danger, had become a symbol of our preparation for the child, our own vigilant waiting.

"How's Mama Robin?" I asked after I told him about the cut-down tree.

"I have some bad news," he said. "She abandoned her nest."

VI

HOMESICK

blond hair, blue eyes

I went to the police station to be fingerprinted for the background check Idaho requires for foster parent certification. A sign in the lobby said if you were there for fingerprints, you should pass through the lobby and enter a room at the back of the building. In that room was a black telephone. A sign said to pick it up. I did. It rang. A woman answered. "Yes?"

"I'm here for fingerprinting," I said.

"Did you fill out the form?"

"Yes," I said.

"How many cards?"

"Two."

"It's five dollars per card," she said. "Cash."

"I have a twenty," I said.

"We can't make change," she said. "Come back when you have the exact amount."

A few weeks later, Eric and I returned to the police department. Between us we now had four cards that needed to be fingerprinted, two each. I'd brought twenty dollars.

I picked up the black phone again. "I'm here for fingerprinting."

"How many cards?"

"Four cards, two people," I said.

"That's ten dollars each."

"I have a twenty," I said.

"I can't make change."

"You don't need to make change," I said. "Four cards, five dollars each. That's twenty."

"You can't give me a twenty," she said. "You have to give me two tens."

Eric looked in his wallet. He held up two tens.

"We have two tens," I said.

A deputy opened a door and wheeled a cart into the center of the room. She did my prints first. "Relax your hand," she said. "Don't try to help." She placed each finger in ink, rolled it onto the card.

"Why do you need to be fingerprinted?" she asked, and we explained we were in the process of getting background checks so we could be certified to adopt.

"How generous," she said. "International?"

"Domestic," I said. "Right here in Idaho."

"I thought about doing that," she said. "But I only wanted to adopt from Ireland or Russia, because, you know, I have blond hair and blue eyes."

I looked at her dyed blond hair. I looked at her dark roots.

"But they're too strict over there," she said. "I'm not going to do it."

i'm going to get real ethnic

"Let's turn to the section of your binders on racial, ethnic, and cultural identity," Kate said and waited for us to find the right page. Kate joined Dawn as our teacher for the rest of the PRIDE sessions. "We've been fostering for ten years," she told us. "We started when our son was four months old and our daughter was two. Now we have numbers fifteen, sixteen, and seventeen in the house. And we're getting number eighteen from the NICU next week." After they bring home the newest foster baby from the hospital, they will have seven children in their three-bedroom house.

Most of the students in PRIDE identified as White. There were a few Latinx folks, including one woman named Maribel, who didn't speak English, but there wasn't a translator. Her husband, Joel, appeared to be about three thousand years old. He spoke English, but he couldn't hear, and he wasn't wearing hearing aids. He never spoke in class, didn't ask or answer any questions, didn't participate in the group activities the facilitators made us do.

"Joel is really on the ball today," Eric whispered to me one morning at the start of class, and I looked across the room and saw that Joel's nametag was upside down and he was asleep.

Kate talked about the importance of having books about different cultures in the house, stories with protagonists of every color. She told us to sign our foster kids up for dance classes and cultural activities. "Make sure you have a doll that looks like your child," she said. "But don't tell them, 'You only get Brown dolls because you're Brown.' You should have a variety for them to choose from."

There was one person in the class I couldn't stand. John dominated, mansplained, talked all the time, spoke over his wife. He rolled his eyes while Kate talked.

"How do you celebrate what everyone looks like?" Kate asked. "How do you help your child if they don't like how they look?"

When no one spoke she answered her own questions. "You say things like 'What beautiful eyes you have,' or 'You smile just like your mama,'" she said. "You support what makes them special."

Kate changed the slide on the projector, put up a quote from Toni Morrison's *The Bluest Eye.*

"Let me give you an example of how I messed things up," Kate said. "One of the foster kids who came to our house was part Navajo and part Hawaiian. Beautiful. Gorgeous skin. Long dark hair. So I'm thinking, I'm going to get real ethnic. I made Navajo fry bread to show her I respect and celebrate her culture, but she had no idea what it was."

John shifted in his chair, crossed his arms.

"Sometimes you'll think there's nothing to worry about," Kate said. "We had two kids come into care, ages three and nine, both White, and I'm thinking, no big deal, we're all White. For Easter at our house, the Easter Bunny doesn't hide the eggs the kids have dyed, because I don't want any hard-boiled eggs lost in my house and stinking the whole place up. Instead, he fills the kids' baskets with eggs and candy. So when we got home from church, one of the little girls started to cry when she saw the dyed eggs in her basket. 'The Easter Bunny didn't like my eggs,' she said. 'He didn't hide them.' In her house, the Easter Bunny always hid the eggs. She thought she'd done something wrong because her eggs were still in her basket. The point is: You never know where kids are coming from. Your assumptions about what holidays look like, even for White kids, will be wrong.

"Really," she added, "kids just need someone to listen to them."

I was ever the good student, raising my hand, participating in every activity, turning in my homework on time. I took so many notes I filled a notebook. Eric didn't talk much during our classes. He rarely raised his hand, but he had something to say now. "Kids don't just need someone to listen," he said. "They need trusted adults who can help them sort through the complicated experiences of racism and microaggressions. They need to talk about what it feels like to live with White people who may or may not understand what they're experiencing."

"Give me a break," John said. "We wouldn't have a problem with race if people would just stop talking about it."

"That's not how racism works," Eric said.

"People need to stop acting so different from one another, stop insisting on separate identities. But if you're in favor of assimilation, like I am, you're seen as a racist," John said. "Look at Clarence Thomas. This is a man at the pinnacle of his career, and his own people call him Uncle Tom."

The room was quiet.

"We're all the same," John said. "It's a problem if you tell people they're not Black unless they're a Black Panther."

"I couldn't disagree with you more," Eric said.

"Let's take a lunch break," Dawn said. "Tacos!"

jane crow

Black and Brown parents, especially when they are poor, parent in public, under suspicion, in ways White parents of means don't have to. Money allows you to abuse your children in private. The criminalization of parenting choices by poor women of color is being called the new "Jane Crow." Lawyers say the system assumes their clients—predominantly poor Black and Latina women—"don't have the ability to make decisions about their kids." They are always and already suspect.

When I was in the ordination process to become an Episcopal priest, I worked at a church in a rich, mostly White suburb of Boston. I remember talking with a member of the church about the hidden violence in that big-lawn, big-house community. Spousal abuse. Child abuse. "Guess the most common reason why the police are called in this neighborhood," she said.

"What?" I asked.

"Parents taking out restraining orders against their own kids."

I never heard about Child Protective Services being called. I don't remember learning that any of the children in the church school, which I directed, had ever been in foster care.

Thirty-seven percent of children in the United States experience a CPS investigation by the time they are eighteen. That's more than one in every three children. "But for Black children, that number skyrockets to 53 percent," Trey Rabun writes in an article about confronting the racial disparity in foster care itself and about the need for more Black foster parents. "African-American children are placed in foster care at twice the rate of white children." What's more, once these children of color are in foster care, they receive fewer services and are at a higher risk of being harmed by people in the system who are supposed to help them.

Black parents don't abuse or neglect their children more than other parents. There is "no difference in the actual incidence of child abuse or neglect among different ethnic groups." Nevertheless, many professionals in the foster care system "routinely contend that Native American and African American children are the most at-risk for child abuse and neglect." Based on this racist misperception, "the system removes these children from their families at rates higher than children of any other race." Racism means that if you're Black or Brown, your children are more likely to be taken from you than if you're White. And they're also more likely not to be returned to you.

Landlords use the threat of foster care to bully their tenants of color. If they want to kick a family out of an apartment before their lease is up, they tell them they have to leave or they'll report them to CPS, say they abuse their kids. If a tenant complains about water damage or rats or black mold or roaches, landlords call CPS rather than make the repairs. And when CPS arrives and finds the water damage or rats or black mold or roaches, they declare the living situation "unsafe" and take the children away.

filled with my love always

I visited the Smithsonian National Museum of African American History and Culture in Washington, D.C., and rode a packed elevator to the lowest level of the building. When the doors opened, we entered a small room, our bodies joining the bodies already in that place. I could hear the sound of water.

On the walls hung manifests, name after name after name, and images of ships with holds designed to carry kidnapped people from one country to another, moving bodies by water, by force, leaving a mother on one continent and her children on another, throwing people overboard with cannonballs locked to their ankles whenever more money could be made by claiming loss than by sale.

Next to an auction block hung a cotton sack with these words stitched on it:

> My great grandmother Rose
> mother of Ashley gave her this sack when
> she was sold at age 9 in South Carolina
> it held a tattered dress 3 handfulls of
> pecans a braid of Roses hair. Told her
> It be filled with my Love always
> she never saw her again
> Ashley is my grandmother
> Ruth Middleton
> 1921

Mark Auslander, an associate professor of anthropology at Central Washington University, searched for the family who had owned the sack. He determined that the fabric was from the mid-1800s and the embroidery floss was from the early twentieth century. Rose was the most common name for enslaved women in the 1800s, and Ashley was one of the most unusual. The stitched words said that Ashley was nine when she was sold, and Auslander knew that "young children were usually sold with their mothers or in large groups at estate sales" after the death of their enslaver. He searched records online and in courthouses until he found a woman named Rose who was enslaved by Robert Martin, Sr., in South Carolina. When Martin died in 1852, the people he'd enslaved were sold to someone a hundred miles away. Among them was a child named Ashley, Rose's daughter.

Auslander then looked for Ruth Middleton, the woman who had stitched the story on the cloth sack. He studied the 1920 census and found sixteen African American women with her name. Eventually, he found a Ruth Middleton with roots in South Carolina. She had a daughter named Dorothy; Ruth had stitched her family's history on the bag so Dorothy would know it. Dorothy died in 1988 in a nursing home in Philadelphia, her possessions probably taken to a thrift store, "which is how the bag must have ended up at a flea market twenty years later."

Auslander called the sack a national treasure. "We have to remember the narratives of resilience, of courage and of family continuity," he said. "You can't imagine a family being more terribly torn apart than by a slave auction of a nine-year-old little girl, but this family story continued."

trash bag

When children in the foster care system are moved from home to home to home to home, they are given a trash bag in which to carry their belongings.

this is your bed

"Though physical abuse can be just as traumatizing to children as sexual abuse," Dawn explained, "sexual abuse is often more traumatizing to us—the caretakers, the adults. It also makes it harder to work with birth parents."

"You still have to work with the birth parents when there has been sexual abuse?" the man next to me asked.

"The goal is reunification," Dawn said.

"What?" several people said at once, but Dawn ignored us.

"Seriously, what?" someone asked in a louder voice.

"What should you do if your foster child reveals abuse?" Kate asked.

The room was quiet.

"How you react is important," she said. "If you react with anger, the child will think you are angry with her."

"What should you say?" someone asked.

"There should be no shame, no guilt," Kate said.

"But what should you say?" someone else asked again.

"You can say, 'I'm sorry that happened to you,'" Kate said. "You can say, 'You're safe here. Let's get you help.' Do not ask any questions about what happened, because later that will be understood as you putting ideas in the child's head, leading her, offering suggestions. Say, 'I'll be with you all the way.' Say, 'We'll get someone to help you.'"

Kate explained that if a child tells us she's been abused, we're supposed to call the social worker as soon as we can. The social worker will make an appointment with a person who is certified to handle cases like this, who is trained to get forensic evidence.

"This is called a 'Cares Interview,'" Kate said. She turned away from us, wiped her eyes. "I'm sorry. I've just gone through this with one of the littles in our care."

Before bedtime the child would shake. Before bath time the child would shake.

Dawn set up an easel at the front of the room, and on the easel she placed a large diagram of a house. Living room. Kitchen. Master bedroom. Bedroom. Bathroom. Another bedroom. "How do you prepare your home to take care of a child who may have been sexually abused?" Dawn asked.

Again the room was quiet, waiting.

"I don't understand what you're asking," I said.

"Here's an example of what I mean," Dawn said. "Every child in your home needs a private space where she can go to feel safe, where she can change clothes by herself."

Respectful nurturing, she wrote on the board.

"I'm talking about ways to make your homes safe, rules you should have," she said. "And what this really means is preparing your home to take care of all children. Six percent of children in foster care have experienced sexual abuse, but chances are you won't have any idea at first whether the child in your care has been abused or not. In fact, you might never know which of your foster children has or has not been abused. So you should set up a safe home, just in case."

"Can you give us some examples about how to do that?" someone in the class asked.

"Yes," Dawn said. "Only one person in the bathroom at a time. When you watch a movie on the couch as a family, everyone should have their own blanket. If your child is uncomfortable at bath time, let them wear a swimsuit. Don't ever have them sit on your lap. Bedroom doors stay open if there is more than one child in the room. Bedroom doors stay open if there is an adult in a bedroom with a child. No foster kids allowed in the master bedroom. No foster kids allowed in the master bed. No one allowed in the foster child's bed."

"But what if it's bedtime?" someone asked.

"Stand next to the bed," Dawn said.

"What if it's time to read bedtime stories?" I asked.

"Sit in a chair beside the bed," Dawn said.

It wasn't until Dawn laid out these safe practices that I realized what a role physical closeness played in my imagined interactions between our child and me. Hugs and shared naps and stories. I love reading bedtime stories to my nephews, love the feel of their small bodies nestled under my arm.

"This raises important questions," Dawn said. "How do you nurture a child who does not want to be hugged? And how do you nurture a child who knows only touch as affection?"

She recommended weighted blankets. She recommended cooking together, standing side by side in the kitchen, washing lettuce, measuring flour, stirring cookie batter. She recommended chores, clearing the table, sweeping the floor, helping fold laundry, unloading the dishwasher, making the bed.

"Chores are nurturing," she said. "Participating in household activities makes children feel they are contributing to the home. It makes them feel like they're part of the family."

Dawn lowered the lights and started a video. In the film, it's a child's first night in a foster home. The foster mother says, "This is your bed. No one else will ever get in your bed."

She says, "These are your dresser drawers."

She says, "This is your closet."

We watched her hand the child pajamas, watched her leave the room so the child could change in private, watched her give the child choices, agency, a feeling of control.

"Do you want me to read you a story?" she asks.

"Do you want me to leave the light on?" she asks.

"Do you want me to close the door?" she asks.

Dawn brightened the classroom lights and handed everyone

a few Post-it notes. She instructed us to write on the Post-it notes things we could do to make our homes safe for children who've experienced sexual abuse.

"Stick those notes on the appropriate rooms in the diagram," she said, and we wrote ideas about love and boundaries and safety and stuck them all over the house. *We'll keep you safe here and here and here,* we promised.

no one could hear

The first elephant arrived in North America in 1795 from Cal-
cutta, chained in the hold of a ship. They called her Old Bet.
Once on land, the captain tied her to a stake on the corner of
Broadway and Beaver in New York City so people would pay to
see her and turn his $450 investment into a fortune. She was the
first elephant on the continent of North America. She was
alone.

When Hackaliah Bailey saw the elephant, her broad shoulders, her enormous feet, he was entranced, enthralled, in love,
not with the elephant herself, but with what she might make
possible, with the quick work a yoked animal that size could
make of his fields. After several visits, he bought her and took
her home to live on his farm.

But an elephant in the countryside draws a crowd, and
Hackaliah soon realized he could make more money by selling
tickets than by plowing a field, so he and his elephant toured the
country. For over a decade they moved from town to town
under cover of night, so no one could catch sight of the elephant without having first paid to see her.

*See her curved tusks. See her magnificent trunk. See her gigantic
ears. See her bulletproof hide,* Bailey cried, and some say a gang of
men took this last descriptor as a challenge. Others say it was a
young boy, who hid himself, then shot the elephant in the eye.
Still others say it was a neighboring farmer who killed her, believing it was a sin to charge people good money to see an animal.

She was twenty years old when she died, though elephants
can live to be seventy.

Elephants remember. They can find distant watering holes
still full in drought, even when the last drought was decades
ago. They recognize one another as family even when they

haven't seen one another for more than twenty years. Elephants are social animals, eating and breeding and finding water and protecting their young by working as a group. Elephants talk among themselves. They secrete decipherable odors through their skin. They growl. They trumpet. They stamp their feet. Some sounds they make are at frequencies too low for human beings to hear. They vibrate through the ground, seismic signals picked up by the toes, by the inner ears, by the tips of the trunks of elephants as far as six miles away.

This first elephant, chained, alone, lifted one leg and put it down. Lifted another, then put it down, again, again, and people clapped, people laughed, delighted, thinking she was dancing for them, but she wasn't dancing, and there was no one who could hear that trembling earth.

one in three

In the exhibit *The Hampton Project,* the artist Carrie Mae Weems engages photographs made by Frances Benjamin Johnston at the Normal and Agricultural School in Hampton, Virginia, "a boarding school established for the education of African American and, subsequently, Native American children." The school was founded at the end of the Civil War by General Samuel Chapman Armstrong, who wanted to "educate and elevate" the enslaved who were newly freed.

Johnston intended his images to show the success of the school's assimilationist agenda, but Weems reveals its violence. Weems enlarged a photo of the school's founder and his family and printed across the image these words: *With your missionary might / you extended the hand of grace / reaching down & snatching me / up and out of myself.* Weems then hung two photographs of Native American men on either side of the picture of the founder's family, a *before* and an *after.* In the image on the left, the men wear traditional dress, their hair long; in the image on the right, taken two years later, the men wear suits, their hair short. So much lost.

Though most of the boarding schools closed in the early twentieth century, "the rupture of Native American families continued in other ways," primarily through foster care and adoption. Racist perceptions of Native families and homes resulted in taking Native children from their parents and placing them with White families at an alarming rate. By the 1960s, between 25 and 35 percent of all American Indian children had been placed in adoptive or foster homes or institutions, and 90 percent of those children were being raised by people who were not Native American. Many would never see their biological families again.

humanity in question

My friend adopted two children. He is White; they are Brown. "People used to come up to me in grocery stores when I had my kids with me, and they'd say, 'They're so lucky,' and they meant my kids were so lucky I'd adopted them," he told me. "They'd say this right in front of my children. They could hear them, could understand these strangers were acting like I'd done my kids some kind of favor, like parenting them was a good deed, an act of service or charity or something. I always had to correct these people in the grocery store. I'd say, 'You've got it all wrong. I'm the lucky one.'"

In *The Undercommons*, Fred Moten writes, "The coalition emerges out of your recognition that it's fucked up for you, in the same way that we've already recognized that it's fucked up for us. I don't need your help. I just need you to recognize that this shit is killing you, too, however much more softly, you stupid motherfucker, you know?"

It was never our humanity that was in question, the enslaved person said to the people who thought they owned her. *It was yours.*

what we don't talk about

Indian Child Welfare Act: If a child who has entered the foster care system is Native American, the tribe or tribes to which that child belongs must be notified. They will be involved in the case and will have some control over what happens. They will help determine the best permanency options for the child.

After Dawn explained how ICWA works, Kate told a story. A friend of hers, a foster mom, had been caring for a girl for more than a decade. The woman is White, the child is Indigenous, and the tribe to which the child belonged would not let the White woman adopt the child. She could be the legal guardian, the tribe said, but not the adoptive mother. "She's cared for that girl for twelve years," Kate said.

"That's ridiculous," John said. "I mean, seriously? That's what I'm talking about. This country has gone insane. All this PC nonsense."

When I was teaching at the art school in Portland, one of my students was Native American, and she'd been adopted by a White family with whom she'd first been in foster care. Growing up, she thought she was White. In the Thanksgiving Day play at her elementary school, she asked to be a pilgrim, but the teacher wouldn't let her. "You'll be an Indian," the teacher said. They braided her hair. Dressed her in a brown paper bag cut with fringe. Put a feathered band on her head.

Eric hadn't spoken in class for hours. "Let's try to remember a little history, man," he said to John. "How about hundreds of years of genocide? How about 'Indian Schools'? How about children being taken away from their parents, from their communities, banned from speaking their own language, banned from wearing their own clothing?"

Dawn put her body between the two men.

"Come on now," she said. "The one rule we have in this class is we don't talk about religion and we don't talk about politics."

VII

FAMILIES BELONG TOGETHER

what children deserve

"Reunification, reunification, reunification," Dawn said during our training. "That's our goal. It's what children deserve. It's the safest and most successful way."

The assumption at Idaho's Department of Health and Welfare is that it's best for children to live with their biological parents. Second best is for children to live with a relative. Low on the list of good outcomes is foster care with a nonrelative, and adoption by a nonrelative might even be considered a failure. Though DHW asks foster parents to care for and love children they did not birth, in practice the system values the biological relationship between parent and child more than any other relationship. Every support is designed to ensure the return of children to the parents who made them. And I can see why. Some of the greatest harms we inflict on one another look like forcing families apart, rupturing communities. Yet sometimes biology does not guarantee care or well-being or protection. Sometimes the love of one stranger for another is what keeps us safe.

Dawn told us that DHW first offers resources to families in trouble so they can keep their children at home. They provide money for rent or medicine or food, whatever might be needed. But if a judge decides a child should be taken away, DHW shifts their approach. They design a case plan and place the child in foster care until it's safe for the child to return home.

"Only two groups of people can take a child from their parents in Idaho: police and judges," Dawn said. "They wreck the puzzle. We put it back together."

ice

In my small town, police pull Brown people over for having snow on their license plates, for having their windows tinted too dark, for failing to signal in time, and if they don't have driver's licenses, or if the officer suspects they might not have documentation, they are taken to jail and ICE is alerted.

Soon after we moved to Hailey, I helped found a group to support immigrants and refugees and families left behind when someone is deported. We hosted events that taught people their constitutional rights, how to tell the difference between a fake ICE warrant and a real warrant signed by a judge, what to do when ICE knocks on the door. We hosted workshops to help families prepare should a parent or a sibling or a cousin be deported. We helped parents complete forms that designated guardians for their children, that indicated who would pick up their kids from school should the parents get detained on a school day.

In that first winter after the inauguration, news spread about an ICE raid in our valley, and families fled to the hills, slept outside in subzero weather, in the wind and snow and ice, night after night after night.

robins

The snow melted and the sun stayed longer, and Eric and I sat in the backyard and watched robins. Two robins, in particular, an adult and a fledgling—a father and his child. When baby robins hatch and then grow big enough to leave the nest, the mama robin stays in the nest to warm a second set of eggs. The papa robin is primarily responsible for feeding the newly fledged birds. He teaches them to fly.

The papa set the fledgling in the protected crook of a low branch near our fence line. We watched the father land on the grass, tilt his head, then beak the grass and pull an enormous worm.

"Can he smell the worms?" Eric asked.

"Does he hear them?" I asked.

With the worm in his beak, the robin flew to the crook of the branch and fed the fledgling. He did this again and again. Sometimes, the papa robin would leave the yard—for ten minutes, for half an hour—presumably to feed his other children, which we imagined he'd stashed in different trees on our street. The fledgling would wait on the branch for his father's return, as still as could be.

maneuvers too risky to try above land

A social worker based in Twin Falls called to schedule a home visit with Eric and me so she could complete our home study. Twin Falls is the closest city to Hailey, the place we all go to shop at the big box stores you can find in every American town. To get to Twin, you have to cross a bridge that stretches over an enormous gorge—deep and wide, dark rocks and yellow grasses on the walls of the canyon carved by the Snake River. To get a good look at that beauty, you have to be in the passenger seat. The lanes are too narrow, the cars too fast, for the driver to look at anything other than the road. I've seen BASE jumpers leap off the bridge, a sport with no margin for error. Miscalculate, and you slam into a rock or a tree or the ground. I once walked to the center of the bridge, clinging to the railing, my knees shaking, heart pounding, everything in my body telling me to go back to land. The bridge shook whenever cars drove across it, which was all the time.

"The social worker's name is Rolayne," I told Eric when we compared calendars to find a time for her visit.

"Rolaid?" he asked.

"Rolayne," I said.

The next month, Rolayne rang the doorbell, her hair cut in a neat bob with bangs. She wore black pants and a white blouse and a turquoise jacket, sunglasses on her head.

I offered her tea or coffee. "No, thanks," she said. "This will be quick." She seemed to be in a hurry. Kay, our Portland social worker, always gave me the feeling that she could stay as long as it took to break me, but Rolayne acted like she had about fifteen minutes. She'd driven nearly two hours from her office to our house. She wanted to make the drive home before dark.

I thought I was better prepared for her visit than I'd ever been for Kay's, but as soon as she started talking, I realized I'd prepared as if Kay 2.0 were coming, as if it were an opportunity to play the same game better now that I understood the rules, now that I knew to be delightful, to avoid sweating or crying or offering cookies too many times, now that I knew I shouldn't talk about therapy or tequila. But I hadn't prepared for Rolayne.

"What do you two like to do for fun?" she asked. This is a question people ask in Idaho. It's not a question people ask in other places I've lived, like California or Massachusetts or Oregon. Where do you work? What do you study? Where did you go to college? Where did you go to graduate school? Those were the kinds of questions I was ready to answer.

"I paraglide," Eric said, and I thought, *Really? You're going to tell this woman who will decide if we're responsible enough to be parents that you like to attach yourself to a nylon wing and step off mountains and rise into the air?*

"My husband paraglides too," Rolayne said.

"I'm about to take a clinic in Salt Lake next month," Eric said. He'd signed up for a five-day course during which, in class after class, the instructor would use a boat to pull Eric high above a lake while wearing his wing, so he could learn how to do maneuvers too risky to try above land.

"My husband took a clinic in Salt Lake," she said. "But the teacher was terrible. I can't remember his name. I hope it's not the same clinic." Rolayne looked down at her phone and began to text her husband. "I'll ask him for more details," she said.

"Thanks," Eric said.

"In the meantime, let's get started," she said. "Happy childhoods?"

We nodded.

"Romantic history?" she asked, and I told her about my high school boyfriend, mentioned he'd gone to West Point, as if his military service might help our cause, told her about my college boyfriend, left out that he'd grabbed me, shaken me, yelled, left out everyone else I'd slept with.

"Wait," she said. "He's texting me back." She told Eric the name of her husband's instructor, the one he didn't like.

"Different clinic," Eric said.

"Whew," she said.

Rolayne wanted to know how we'd met, where we'd lived, how we'd been disciplined as children, our parents' names and occupations, our siblings' names, whether they had kids, how we'd decided to adopt.

"How will you nurture a child?" she asked. She wanted to know if we were willing to make sure the child had the support they'd need, whether we were willing to take them to the doctor and physical therapy and therapy-therapy.

"Yes," we said. "Yes" and "Yes" and "Yes."

"What kind of kid do you want?" she asked.

"Kind of kid?" I asked.

"Racial or gender preference?" she asked.

"No," we said.

"What are your limits?" she asked. This was Rolayne's version of the "list" conversation we'd had with Kay and Renee in Portland based on that fifteen-page form that listed everything from defiance to wiping excrement on the wall. Kids with major medical needs? Babies with drug addictions? Kids with physical disabilities?

She looked out the living room window. "You can't have a water feature," she said. "If you do, that raises the age of child you can get to six and up."

"We want a baby," I said.

"We get lots of broken babies," she said.

Broken babies, I wrote in my notebook as if its pages were a shield. When I heard information I couldn't process, facts too traumatic to take in all at once, I wrote them down.

"There's one woman in particular who helps take care of the broken babies," she said.

"Broken how?" I asked.

"It's different baby to baby," she said. "Could be a shaken baby or a baby with broken bones or a baby that needs major medical interventions."

Shaken baby, I wrote. *Broken bones.*

Rolayne explained that doctors can test to see if a baby has drugs in her system, but there's no test for fetal alcohol syndrome. "We ask the mothers if they drank while pregnant," she said. "But they will often lie."

Rolayne was tasked with writing our home study. She'd be the person to certify us, to determine whether we could provide a safe home for a child. "You're a writer," she said. "You both went to a lot of graduate school. Maybe I'll just send you the home study form and you can fill it in? That would save me a lot of time."

I laughed. I thought she was joking, but the next day she sent me a blank form and suggested I write the home study, and I ignored her email. When she sends us the completed home study to review months later, the first line will read, "Sarah and Eric desire to foster a child with the idea that adoption might be an outcome." The document will be riddled with errors. For several pages, she will call us by someone else's names (Heather and Tom). She will get our birth cities wrong, the names of our colleges wrong, make mistakes in our family histories. I will fix any errors I find, and though she will have told me to make all changes in red, I won't because I don't want to embarrass her.

Rolayne stood. "That's about it," she said. "Let's take a look at your house."

We took her on a tour, showed her every room, and she told us what we needed to do to get the house ready so she could certify us. "You'll need to lock up all vitamins and medicine," she said. "Cleaning supplies, too."

"What about alcohol?" Eric asked. He's a homebrewer. In our garage, we have a kegerator with three beers on tap.

"No need to lock that," she said.

"Knives?" I asked and pointed to the magnetic strip in our kitchen.

"Those are fine," she said.

We took her into the kid's bedroom, which was empty, no furniture at all.

"You sure you only want one?" she asked.

"One," Eric said.

"It's a hard line?" she asked.

"Hard line," Eric said.

"How about twins?" she asked.

"One," Eric said.

She walked to the window. "You'll need a rollout ladder," she said. "In case there's a fire."

We showed her our offices. "You both work at home?" she asked.

"Yes," we said.

"So you won't need daycare?" she asked.

"We'll need daycare," Eric said.

I explained I had a book coming out that summer, so we thought the best time to welcome a child into our home would be October. It was April.

"When does your book come out?" she asked.

"July 4," I said.

"I'll call you on July 5," she said. "But it's too bad you're not certified yet. I have a baby right now for you. He's with the woman who likes broken babies, but there's nothing wrong with him."

We walked her to the front door. "How many times will you come back?" I asked. "Should we schedule the next visit now?"

Whenever I'd complained about how invasive the Portland social workers were, Eric would say, "The state is entrusted with a *child*. Don't you think they should be as invasive as possible?"

"I only have to come back once," she said. "I need to make sure you've locked up all the medicine and gotten that fire ladder."

Walking to her car she turned and waved. "I'll call you when I get a baby," she said.

kinship everywhere

For several weeks in early summer, Eric and I ate lunch together on our back porch and watched the robins. The papa robin guided the fledgling to a different part of the yard every day. First the crook of a lilac, then the low branch of a spruce, then a protruding knot of a maple tree, then a fence post. The father's worm-getting skills were mind-blowing. He never missed, his beak emerging from the grass with a worm every time. The fledgling's belly grew rounder and rounder.

"Is the baby too heavy to fly?" Eric asked, and as if in answer, the fledgling flew from fence to lilac, from lilac to maple.

Then one day we brought our lunches outside, but the two birds were gone.

A flock of robins spent time together in the chokecherry tree in our front yard. I heard robins singing in our neighbor's pine tree, too. But I could not pick out the papa and the fledgling. I missed them.

I researched robins, their mating habits, their migratory patterns. I learned that the first hatched fledglings will help the father take care of the next group of eggs to hatch, and the third brood, too, should there be one. And when all the birds can fly and feed themselves, the siblings and parents continue to spend time together, a flock, a family. I'd never thought about birds that way before. Father, mother, sister, brother. I'd been taught to disregard family structures in animals that weren't humans. But now, kinship everywhere I looked.

families belong together

The Associated Press reported that migrant children separated from their parents at the border have been placed in American "sponsor" homes, and the administration doesn't want to reunite them with their parents. Too much time, too much money, too much staffing, too much effort. And even if they could reunify them, even if they could be bothered to locate the parents again, the people in charge of such efforts insist reunification would likely cause the children to "be emotionally harmed."

It's not the original separation officials are worried about—taking children by force from their parents at the border—it's this secondary separation: taking children from their American foster family. Removing children from sponsor homes to rejoin their parents "would present grave child welfare concerns," officials insisted. It would be "traumatic to the children."

A woman from Guatemala who lived in Missouri was arrested in an ICE raid and put in prison. While in prison, she sued to try to stop her one-year-old son from being adopted by a family in the United States. But the judge ruled in favor of the adoptive family. About the child's biological mother, the judge wrote, "Smuggling herself into the country is not a lifestyle that can provide any stability for the child."

wet nurse

Enslaved women were often forced to breastfeed the children of the people who enslaved them, to deny their own children breast milk and nurse White infants instead. Sometimes White women used Black wet nurses to supplement their milk supply. Other times it was vanity that drove this practice; White women didn't want their breasts to go flat, so they'd make enslaved women nurse their infants. They'd separate Black women from their just-born babies, forcing those new mothers to move into the plantation house so they could nurse White children through the night. Sometimes the enslaved women's infants would die, and with breasts still full of milk, they'd be forced to feed White women's babies. And the White women would write in their journals about what a wonderful opportunity it was for their children to have that new milk supply. The White mothers did not see the Black women who nursed their White children as mothers, much less as grieving mothers. They saw them as sources of nutrition.

Visitors to the American South commented on the sight of Black women nursing White infants. They were shocked by the practice. Not because of its violence, but because of the proximity it encouraged between the slavers and the enslaved. Because of the intimacy. White children cried when the women who nursed them were whipped.

In an 1848 interview in *The Emancipator*, Charity Bowery explained that her enslaved mother had "suckled all [her master's] children." Her mother's reward for that labor? Her "mistress made it a point to give one of my mother's children to each of hers," Bowery explained. Children given as gifts to other people's children, children you'd nursed, a brutal reminder of slavery's ability to turn anything into a commodity—body, breast, mother, child.

children of the group

"The Convention on the Prevention and Punishment of the Crime of Genocide, signed in 1948, defines genocide as including not only massacres of ethnic groups but also 'forcibly transferring children of the group to another group,'" Rachel Nolan writes in *Harper's*.

childproof

I spent my forty-fourth birthday in the Salt Lake City airport. Though Salt Lake's skies were clear, an early October snowstorm in the valley where I live delayed my plane. Friends texted me: *No way you're getting in today.* They sent pictures of snow-covered roads and windowsills, snow-covered cars and rooftops. Eric sent pictures of trees. He'd spent hours outside with a broom knocking the heavy snow off branches that still had their leaves, trying to keep those limbs from breaking.

We boarded the plane. The pilot said he'd do his best to get us home, but low visibility might make him have to turn around. The flight between Salt Lake and Sun Valley is short, less than an hour. As we neared the landing zone, I looked out the window and could see my town below. "We're going to make it," I said to the woman sitting next to me. I felt the landing gear emerge from the plane, the nose of the plane angle down, but then the pilot gunned the engines, and we rose. "I can't see well enough to land," the pilot said. He flew us back to Salt Lake.

Our flight was canceled. The woman at the desk told me she could get me home on a flight the following night. "But I have a social worker coming to my house tomorrow morning," I said. "We're trying to adopt."

"I don't know what to tell you," she said.

"Want to rent a car?" I asked the woman behind me in line.

"Yes," she said.

"So do I," said the woman I'd been sitting next to.

Together we made the five-hour drive, which gave us plenty of time to get to know one another. One of the women was fifty, the mother of a five-year-old. She'd done IVF, used a donated egg and her husband's sperm.

"There are lots of ways to make a family," I said.

"Yes," she said. "But the kid's blood is still mine."

The other passenger had adopted both of her children. She'd adopted her first daughter twenty years ago from a relative who couldn't care for her. Her first child had addiction issues, so the woman in the car with me was now raising her daughter's daughter too. "I'm the mother of a four-year-old and a twenty-four-year-old," she said.

We arrived home at midnight. I'd missed my whole birthday.

"We'll have a do-over," Eric said when he picked me up from the rental car lot at the airport.

Rolayne was due to arrive at two-thirty the next day, but she knocked on the door at two. There was a second woman with her. Eric was still on a conference call for work. "I couldn't read my own handwriting," Rolayne said when I opened the door. "Were we scheduled for two or two-thirty?"

"Two-thirty," I said. "Eric is still on a work call, but he'll come downstairs as soon as possible."

"I don't even need to see him," Rolayne said. "This is Jen. She'll take over when my part of this process is done."

Rolayne told us the home study had been her assignment, and it was finished. Someone else would call us when a child came into care, maybe that would be Jen, maybe it would be a different social worker. "Social workers are assigned to the child, not to the foster parent," Rolayne said. "Kid by kid by kid by kid."

I offered both women tea, water, juice. I offered cookies, crackers, cheese. I offered the bathroom (they'd driven nearly two hours). They wanted nothing.

"I just need to see all the child locks," Rolayne said. "That's about it."

I overprepared for every social worker visit, treated it like a holy thing. These were my prenatal yoga classes, my early visits to the doctor, my baby shower. I cleaned the house. Meditated. Imagined our child arriving at our door.

But my preparation for the social worker visits didn't match what the visits were like at all. Many of the social workers in the foster care system are traumatized people who don't understand themselves as traumatized. They see terrible things every day. They witness the violence people do to children, to babies, and they've seen it for so long, it's no longer out of the ordinary. They aren't interested in my meditations, in the dreams that tell me my child is in Idaho, in the visions I have of my ancestors cutting through my bedroom walls to hand me the child they've chosen for us.

If I had ever shared those experiences with them, I imagine they would have said, "What the fuck are you talking about?" Though most of the social workers are Mormon, and they don't swear.

To prepare for Rolayne's visit, Eric and I had spent the previous weekend locking up toxic substances: laundry detergent, toilet bowl cleaner, chemicals of all kinds. We'd put vitamins in a tackle box with a padlock. We'd put medicine in a locking toolbox Eric's grandfather had given him. This was what Rolayne wanted to see.

I led Rolayne and Jen around the house, showed them the mudroom's locked closet where cleaning supplies were stored, showed them the medication and vitamins in locked boxes, showed them the childproofed drawers. I pointed out child lock after child lock—on kitchen cabinets, on bathroom cabinets, in the laundry room. Rolayne didn't open anything. She didn't look inside.

"The fire ladder is in the kid's room," I said and opened the bedroom door. During Rolayne's first visit, that room had been empty, but now there was a crib with whale-patterned sheets, a twin bed, a changing table, a stack of children's books. "I'm driving to San Francisco next week," I told Rolayne. "My friends are giving me all their old baby stuff."

"Uh-huh," Rolayne said. I never felt like she was listening. She didn't take many notes, didn't write anything down when we talked. I was afraid she'd forget we wanted a baby. I thought my best strategy was to say the same thing over and over again so it might sink in, so when she heard about a baby she'd think of us.

"I want a baby," I said.

"I'm looking forward to picking up our baby from the hospital," I said.

"Thanks for finding us a baby," I said.

I must have sounded insane.

"I thought of you this summer," Rolayne said. "We have this crazy woman who's had her kids taken away before. She had another baby. Didn't even name him. Everyone just called him Baby Boy. You all weren't certified yet, so I couldn't call you. A couple took him home from the hospital. They wanted to keep him."

"Oh," I said. Baby Boy. I imagined what our lives might look like now if we'd been certified.

"But the social worker did her due diligence," Rolayne said. "She found Baby Boy's two half siblings, who were living with another family. The department decided the baby should be with his siblings. It was heartbreaking for the parents who'd taken the child home from the hospital. They'd had him for three months."

"They had to give him back?" I asked.

"Yes," she said. "They do what they think is best for the child."

Reunification, reunification, reunification.

"We want a baby," I said.

"We want to adopt a baby," I said.

"We can't wait to pick up our baby from the hospital," I said.

"We have another girl who might be just right for you," Rolayne said. "She's not a baby, though. She's four. She was put into care with her grandmother, but her grandmother says she's having night terrors, and that the terrors are going to ruin her marriage. We need to find her another home."

"How do night terrors ruin a marriage?" I asked, but what I meant was: *What kind of person gives her granddaughter to strangers because she screams in the dark?*

"The little girl is challenging," Jen said. "Though she's not the most difficult kid we've ever seen."

Eric's conference call ended. He came downstairs, met the second social worker, signed the papers Rolayne wanted him to sign, and then the social workers left.

what makes us sick

When in flight, a group of vultures is called a kettle. When feeding, a group is called a wake. When roosting, a committee.

A committee of more than three hundred vultures has been roosting for six years on a 320-foot radio tower at Kingsville Station in Texas, near the U.S.-Mexico border, disrupting communication between Border Patrol agents, making maintenance and repair of the tower nearly impossible. The Kingsville Station's primary task is the operation of the Border Patrol checkpoint at Sarita, Texas, on U.S. Highway 77 North, one of two major routes of egress from the Rio Grande Valley.

Vultures migrate across borders, ride mountain ranges, find thermals, anything that gives them lift so they might conserve energy and avoid having to flap their wings. The Migratory Bird Treaty Act makes it illegal to kill a vulture, so Border Patrol agents can't figure out how to get rid of them. Agents know that vultures avoid areas where other vultures have died, so they are considering constructing a decoy. They have proposed hanging the freeze-dried or taxidermied body of a vulture from the tower.

The roosting vultures drop flesh and bones and fur on the buildings that house Border Patrol employees and equipment. The tower's railings, catwalks, and supports—the parts workers must touch to climb the tower—are coated with urine, feces, and vomit so corrosive they're eating away at the metal. Vultures' stomach acid is toxic. What they regurgitate is strong enough to kill dangerous bacteria on their bodies and on the bodies of the dead they eat, allowing vultures to consume what would harm other scavengers.

To call a person a vulture is considered an insult. It implies she has taken what does not belong to her, stolen what he didn't work for. Someone who is a vulture gains from another's trouble, preys on them, bloodsucker, vampire, predator. But this name-calling reveals a misunderstanding of vultures' work. Vultures are raptors who rarely kill. They eat what is already dead. If left to rot, dead bodies spread diseases. Vultures remove those poisons from the environment. They protect us from what makes us sick.

declared

Kate—the facilitator at PRIDE who was married to Ben—called to schedule a "nuts and bolts meeting" with Eric and me at our house. During the meeting, she encouraged us to write a weekly email to our caseworker and to the social workers who did our home study (Rolayne and Jen), and who would also be the people who helped process an adoption, if there was one. "This week I had to write to my team and to the bio mom about a bite mark one of my littles came home with, the four-year-old," Kate said. Born addicted to meth, her foster daughter has trouble self-regulating. "She screams most of the day," Kate said. Another child had bitten the girl on her back, broken the skin, the bite mark red, bleeding, but none of the daycare teachers had noticed. "She's upset all the time, so they couldn't tell the difference between regular upset and upset because of being bit." Kate took a picture of the wound as soon as she found it, sent the picture to her social workers and to the bio mom. "I don't want anyone to be surprised during our next visit."

Kate put a chart on the coffee table between us. "This document you can keep," she said and explained that we're required to complete ten hours of continuing education every year. Kate offers some of the classes—the ins and outs of parenting a child born addicted to meth, for example, or how to deal with withdrawal or surviving colic—and she posts announcements about the classes on Facebook.

"It's also important that you two practice good self-care," Kate said. "Make time for what makes you healthy and happy."

"What are the chances that we'll get a baby?" I asked.

"I can think of a lot of examples of a baby being declared," Kate said.

"Declared?" I asked.

"Sorry," she said. "That means coming into care. Babies will be declared if their mothers test positive for drugs at birth. There are other ways you might get a baby, too. I heard about one time that police showed up to arrest someone, and they were surprised to find a baby in the apartment, too. The poor little guy was sick, just lying on the floor, no one paying attention to him, clearly no one planning to take him to the doctor."

I wrote this in my notebook.

"I can think of another example," she said. "A baby was taken into care because of an unsafe living environment. There was feces on the floor."

"Human feces?" I asked.

"Yes," she said. "Clearly there were some mental health issues for the parent. There was so much grease behind the stove that someone had stuck a Tonka truck into it."

"That reminds me," Kate said. "You get insurance for any damage a foster kid might do to your home. It covers up to two thousand dollars per year with a fifty-dollar deductible."

we don't want to hope

It was hard to wait for the certification process to be finished, for the phone to ring.

"Relax," my therapist, Juliana, told me. "Let's trust it's right and perfect timing for everyone involved." She reminded me that for us to get a call about a baby who needed a home, it would mean something hard and scary and even violent had happened to someone else.

I'd made a list in my head of the situations that would make the adoption of a baby in foster care a more likely outcome than reunification. The biological mother would most likely have had to use drugs during her pregnancy. She would have to have no relatives willing to take care of this baby. She would have to have other children in the foster care system, children who would not be returned to her because her parental rights to them had already been terminated. Those other children would also have to be living with families who didn't want to foster the new baby. And the biological father would have to be out of the picture—in jail or unknown or uninterested in parenting.

"We don't want to hope for something bad to happen to someone else so we can get what we want," Juliana said.

bonding

Kate pulled from her stack of documents a piece of paper filled with tiny print. Eric put on his reading glasses and still couldn't read it. I turned on every light in the living room. I had to squint. "I put all of the court dates on one page because I always have trouble remembering the order, and I thought it might be useful for other people, too."

"Court dates?" I asked.

Kate explained the series of court dates scheduled for every biological parent in the foster care system. She urged us to attend if our schedules allowed us to be there. Court will be the only time we will get full disclosure from the parents about what happened, about what they did or did not do, what they are doing or not doing now, about whether they used or are still using drugs. "The first court date, the Shelter Care Hearing, is your chance to meet the birth parents right away," she said. "You can ask them questions about the child in your care. You can ask the bio mom, 'What do you want me to know about your child? What helps her sleep? What's her favorite story?'"

Kate told us that we should be prepared to address the judge if we attended court. "The judge will ask you an open-ended question," Kate said. "Something like, 'Is there anything you want to tell the court?'"

One of the challenges presented by the courtroom, she explained, is that foster parents have to decide where to sit. Do you sit on the side of the defense (the birth parents) or the prosecution (the state's lawyers and social workers)? Kate usually sits by her social worker for the first few court dates. "That way you can also pass information along to them," she said. But after a few sessions in court, she sits behind the birth parents. "I want to show them I have their back," she said. "I want them to know I'm rooting for them."

But what if I'm not rooting for them? What if I want to keep their child?

"It's best to frame things in terms of the child if you're asked to speak," Kate said. "You can say things like, 'After visits with her mom, the child has nightmares.' Don't make it accusatory. Voice issues as a safety concern rather than as a judgment about the parent."

If we got an infant, Kate explained, we'd be required to do visits with the biological parents at least twice every week. "For bonding purposes," she said.

We live in a valley where very few children come into care. It's likely a child would be placed with us who came from two or three hours away. We'd need to drive the child to these twice-weekly visits.

"If you can transport the kid, it's better," Kate said. "Otherwise they'll have to ride with a tech they don't know."

Sometimes the child will be clingy after the visits. Sometimes she will want to be held because the mother's voice, which the child heard in the womb, will cause the child distress.

"Sometimes the tech can bring the birth parents to you," Kate said. "You can meet at the library or go to a park. If you're comfortable, and if it's safe, the parents can come to your house." Seeing your house can be good for the birth parents, she explained. It can be comforting for them to know the child is in a place that's safe.

"Share what you've learned about the child when you meet with the bio parents," Kate said. "You can say things like, 'He's starting to coo,' or 'If you tickle her here, she laughs.'"

Kate explained that there are things foster parents have to get permission from the birth parents to do. Some are small, like how or whether to cut the child's hair. "The bio mother might be making bad choices," Kate said, "but I saw her child walk for the first time. So if she gets to choose his haircut, it's really no big deal."

"When do you think we might get a call?" I asked.

"Any day now," she said. There is usually an influx of kids who come into care right after the school year starts, and then another influx after Christmas. "Parents have overspent," Kate said, "and they can't keep it together." January is the highest intake month.

"But this summer was wild," Kate said. Seventy-two children came into care in one month, including ten siblings. Their parents were going door to door, pretending to be salesmen. The mother would say she needed to use the restroom, and she would take prescription drugs from the medicine cabinet. "It was all over the news," Kate said.

That night, I picked up a friend from the airport. We'd gone to college together, and she flew into town to drive to San Francisco with me, to retrieve my friends' hand-me-down baby stuff—bouncers and infant car seats and toys and books and clothes—what they thought I'd need to welcome a baby.

The year before, this friend's house had burned down, a fact that now feels strangely fitting, as if she'd already understood before Eric and I did exactly what we were about to do.

VIII

FLESH
AND BLOOD

landline

Our landline rang. *State of Idaho,* the caller ID said. Eric was upstairs. "It's a kid," I shouted from the living room.

I answered the phone.

"This is Leah with the State of Idaho," she said. "Are you ready for your first placement?"

"Let me get Eric," I said and raced upstairs. He was taking a nap, his head under a pillow to block the light. "It's them," I shouted. "It's a kid!"

"What?" he said.

On the refrigerator we'd posted the list of questions we planned to ask when we got this call, so I ran downstairs to get the list, then I ran upstairs so Eric and I could be in the same room, but instead of the list I'd grabbed grocery store coupons so I ran back downstairs. I was already unmoored.

I heard Eric get on the line. "Okay," I said. "We're ready."

"I don't have much to tell you," Leah said. "We found a one-year-old."

"Found?" I asked.

"I don't even know if it's a boy or a girl. A maintenance worker found the child alone this afternoon. He heard crying through the door. Inside the apartment was this child, alone, diaper extremely full, the place filthy."

"Where is the child now?" I asked. I expected her to say the name of a town at least an hour's drive from us, Twin Falls, Jerome, Burley, Carey, someplace miles away. We'd been told by our social worker that very few children come into care in our valley, and that when they do come into care, there are family members able to pick up the pieces.

"The child is at the Hailey police station."

The Hailey police station is less than two miles from our house. I'd been there the week before to make sure I'd installed the infant car seat correctly. The woman working at the front desk had climbed into the backseat of my car, put her knee on the base of the car seat, put all of her weight on it, pulled the seatbelt tight.

"Oh, wait a second," Leah said. "I'm getting more information. It's a boy."

How was she getting more information? By text? Email? I didn't even know where Leah was.

"And he's not one. He's two," she said. Then she told us his name.

"How do you know his name?" I asked.

"He's in the database," she said.

"What database?"

"His family has been involved with the system before," she said. "He has a sibling, who's a year or so older. Apparently, the parents separated, and each parent kept one child, and this is the result of that."

Eric and I looked at each other, each of us holding a phone.

"We need to talk," I told Leah. "We'll call you back to let you know."

"That's fine," she said. "Take your time."

skin to skin

The baby books stacked on my bedside table, on the coffee table, on my desk, say the same thing: Human babies are born too early. Horses give birth to foals able to walk and run the day they're born. Dolphin babies can swim right away. But newborn humans can't do a thing. Treat the first four months of an infant's life like a fourth trimester, the books advise. Wear the baby in a sling all day. Don't attempt to schedule their sleep. Feed on demand. Focus on skin-to-skin contact.

The vulnerability of infants, their need for others who are willing to tend and hold and feed them, reveals something about human vulnerability in general, Judith Butler proposes in *Precarious Life*. We are as dependent on one another for survival as newborns are. Though we pretend we are self-sufficient, we are, in fact, radically reliant on one another. Our bodies connect us. They allow us to tend and to be tended, to love and be loved. Yet they put us at risk of both experiencing violence and committing violence. "Although we struggle for rights over our own bodies," Butler writes, "the very bodies for which we struggle are not quite ever only our own."

looking for signs

I was sitting cross-legged on our bed, and when I hung up the phone after our conversation with the social worker about the child they'd found in an apartment, I folded over my legs, cried, hit my fists on the mattress. A two-year-old who looks like a one-year-old, left alone for hours, in an apartment close enough I could walk to it.

We'd moved to Hailey from Portland a year before, and Idaho's mountains, the big sky, the lakes and forests, the elk and moose and nighthawks, had been good medicine, but all that time, while I'd climbed hillsides and watched the moon rise, there had been a boy, close, alone, afraid.

"I need you to think out loud," Eric said. "I need you to tell me what's going on."

"He's right there," I said and pointed south, out our bedroom window and through the branches of the maple tree.

"I know," Eric said.

"How do we make a decision like this?" I asked.

"I don't know," he said.

The phone rang, a number I didn't recognize. "It's me again," Leah said. "I'm not calling to pressure you, but the office phones shut off at five, and I wanted to give you my cell number so you can call when you're ready."

"Thanks," I said and wrote her number on the back of our list of questions.

"Talk to me," Eric said. "Tell me what you're thinking."

"How can we say no?" I asked. My longing for an infant felt small in the face of this child's suffering. How could I refuse a two-year-old because I wanted a baby? Because I had a room full of baby stuff? Absurd. Selfish.

"Let's look at our list," Eric said. Some questions we knew the answers to—*How did the child come into care? Why did the child* come into care? Why were they removed? How far away are the birth parents?—but most of the questions we didn't: *Do you anticipate the child will need any services? Do they have any special needs? Do they need physical therapy? Do they have fetal alcohol syndrome? Have they been sexually abused? Do they have developmental disabilities? Were they born addicted to drugs?*

We needed more information. We called Leah.

"I've told you everything I know," she said. "But here's the number for the social worker assigned to the case. He might have things to tell you."

She told me his name, Zal, and it was my grandfather's name, my uncle's name. I was looking for signs.

you are what you eat

In some communities, it is not birth that creates the bonds of kinship but names. On the Alaskan North Slope, for example, Iñupiat will name children (and sometimes adults) after the dead. The newly named become members of their namesakes' families.

In other communities, family is formed by food. For the New Guineans of the Nebilyar valley, kinship "is produced by the transmission of *kopong*," which means "grease" or "fat." *Kopong* is "the essential matter of living organisms, whose ultimate source is the soil." It is carried by the father's semen and the mother's milk, but it is also carried by sweet potatoes and pork. The "substantial connection" between a child and her parents can be accomplished by sharing food grown on the same land.

In the New Guinea Highlands, burying bodies allows this grease to flow back into the land from the dead. Their bodies nurture the plants that grow from the land and the animals who eat those plants, and it is then returned to our bodies when we eat those animals and those plants.

"Take, eat," Jesus says and hands his followers pieces of bread. "This is my body."

you are not alone

Eric dialed the number, and Zal answered. "What else do you know about the child?" Eric asked.

"I don't know much," he said. "But I do know this family has been involved with the system before. A couple years ago the older child came into care because of a broken femur."

The femur is the strongest bone in the body.

"The child we found in the apartment wasn't born then," Zal said. "But his mother just called the police station now, all upset, crying."

"You found his mother?" Eric asked.

"She told the officer that the boy's father wanted to play more of a role in the child's life. She says she was trying to support that relationship. The apartment is in her name, but she says she doesn't live there, that only the father lives there. She says she had no idea it was a pigsty. She says she has texts on her phone to prove her case. She lives with the other kid and her sister-in-law. She's on her way to the police station now."

"So the child will go home with her?" Eric asked.

"A resolution like that would be good for everyone involved," Zal said.

"Yes," Eric said.

"Look," he said. "I've been doing this for a long time. My gut tells me she's legit, but we won't know until we see her. It might just be that we all want her to be legit. This is a person who has already had a kid taken away from her, and who worked to get that kid back, so if she's lying now, this is terrible. We just have to wait and see. This could be a situation in which we'll have rapid reunification, or this could be total bullshit."

I wrote what I heard, took notes on the back of our list of questions. *Broken femur*, I wrote. *Mom crying. Mom coming to get child.*

"We want to believe people," Zal added. "But given that this is her second interaction with the system, even if the best case turns out to be true, there will probably be at least twenty-eight days of protective supervision."

I pointed to our list of questions—drug addiction, developmental delays, physical therapy. "Are there health concerns we should know about?" Eric asked.

"He didn't have any clothes on. His diaper weighed about a hundred pounds. The place was filthy," he said. "But other than that, there don't seem to be any other health concerns we know about."

"We'll talk and give you a call back," Eric said.

A two-year-old abandoned in an apartment, for hours, maybe days. An older sibling who'd had bones broken, who'd been taken away and returned. A mother on the way to the police station to claim her child.

My hands shook. I couldn't stop crying. I wanted someone else to make the decision.

Earlier that day, I'd driven to a copy shop to pick up two thousand yellow cards on which were printed the number for a hotline a group of people and I had worked for months to get up and running. Twenty-four hours a day, seven days a week, free, confidential, answered by bilingual people, designed to support people in our valley whose family members have been detained or deported. *You are not alone,* the cards said. *No estás solo.*

"You need to breathe," Eric said. "Tell me what you're thinking."

"I want a baby," I said.

"I know," he said.

"But how can we say no?"

"It's our community," he said. "Our neighborhood."

"If the mother dropped him off, why didn't he have any

clothes?" I asked. "If she's been involved with the foster care system before, why didn't she check out the dad's apartment before she left her child there?"

"Maybe she was working," Eric said. "Maybe she didn't have time."

"Why is the apartment in her name if she doesn't live there?"

"People's lives are complicated," he said.

I went into the bedroom Eric and I called "the kid's room." Bins of baby clothes were stacked on the floor. On the bedside table were candles, a children's book titled *You Belong Here,* a painting of the moon. The room wasn't ready for a child. Breakable things everywhere. Scissors. A glass jar of pushpins. A lamp without a bulb. But there was a crib, its fitted sheet patterned with blue whales. A two-year-old could sleep just fine in that crib.

I sat on the floor. *Yes.* I closed my eyes. *Yes.* I heard this word from the four directions. *Yes.* We can do this. *Yes.*

Eric walked into the room.

"I think we should say yes," I said.

"I think so too," he said. He handed me the phone.

all the possible ways

Kinship is not something you *are*, Elizabeth Freeman writes in her essay "Queer Belongings." Kinship is something you *do*. It is a practice. It is all the possible ways one human's body can be vulnerable to and dependent on that of another. It is all the possible resources one body can gather to take care of another.

turned off the light

"Yes," I told Leah. "We can take the child."

"I'll text Zal and let him know," she said.

I didn't want to wait for her to text Zal. It seemed an unreliable way to communicate such a big decision, so I called him. "We'll do it," I said. "We'll take the child."

"We still need to get some things figured out," he said. "We need to talk to the mom and find out what's going on. The night social worker is driving from Twin Falls to Hailey right now. She'll call you when she knows if the child is coming into care."

I was wearing leggings, a sweaty workout shirt, a vest stained with beans I'd spilled at lunch. I hadn't washed my hair in days. Could I welcome a child looking like this? Our house wasn't clean either. Dust bunnies in the living room. Dishes in the kitchen sink. Kitty litter on the floor of the mudroom.

We had to get ready. We went first to the kid's room—our child's room. I put everything breakable in a bag, took the bag to my office. We covered outlets, plugged in lamps, plugged in the sound machine next to the crib, turned up the heat, shelved the children's books my friends from college had mailed us, stored the clothes in the closet. Then we went to the basement. I'd removed the car seat cover so I could wash it. I googled *Chicco Keyfit 30 install car seat cover* and watched the YouTube video, followed the man's instructions. We turned on the hall light. We turned on the porch light.

"What do two-year-olds eat?" Eric asked.

"Regular food, I think," I said. I'd only been reading about babies—what they eat, when they eat, when they sleep. I'd ordered organic formula. I'd ordered unbleached newborn diapers. *What do two-year-olds eat*, I googled.

"They eat what we eat," I said, reading the results.

"I'll cook something," he said. "You pick out some toys, and you should probably text people and let them know we won't make it to dinner."

We were supposed to meet friends for pizza and beers that night. *We just got a call from a social worker,* I texted. *We might be getting a kid.*

From the boxes of toys people had given me, I picked just a few. We didn't want to overwhelm him. A wooden bead maze. Two small cars with wheels painted blue. A soft book. Stackable cardboard boxes. I put a booster seat on the bench of our breakfast nook. From the basement, I carried the puzzle-shaped pieces of a brightly colored rubber mat we could use to make our floors more comfortable when we sat to play with our child.

We were deciding whether to build the mat on the kitchen's tile or on the living room's wood floor when the phone rang.

"This is Cindy, the night social worker Zal told you about," she said. "I'm about half an hour away. Do you have any questions for me?"

"Do you know anything more about the child?" I asked.

"He's actually almost three," she said. "But he can't walk. He can't crawl. He doesn't speak."

Doesn't walk. Doesn't crawl. Doesn't speak. I wrote these words on the back of an envelope inside of which was a bill for life insurance, something foster parents are required to have.

"He's severely malnourished," she said.

Malnourished.

I looked at Eric. I pointed to the words I'd written. He turned off the stove. He read over my shoulder.

"These are just the law enforcement officer's observations," Cindy said. "I haven't seen the child yet. But this appears to be a case of severe neglect. He has not been taken care of properly."

Severe neglect.

"What about the mom?" I asked. "Zal said the mom might be coming to pick up the child."

"The mother has been arrested," Cindy said. "She's in jail. It seems she had a lot to do with how the child has been cared for. She's the cause of it."

Mother is the cause.

"What about the father?" I asked.

"The dad is not in the best state," Cindy said. "That's all I know. The officer said the father is not able to care for the child."

"Oh, Cindy," I said. "This is more information than we had before. Eric and I need to talk. We'll call you back in ten minutes."

I hung up. I cried. Eric cried. We held each other.

"Breathe," Eric said.

I paced the kitchen, back and forth, back and forth. I looked at our list of questions, what we were okay with, what we'd agreed in advance we'd say no to.

This child had severe developmental delays. Maybe from neglect. Maybe from drugs in utero. Maybe from something else altogether. He was almost three. My nephew had just turned three, and when he visited us that summer, he'd hiked two miles through aspen groves, thrown rocks into the river, raced trucks up and down the hill in our yard. One of the baby books I'd been reading said the first three years are the most important years. Brain development. Attachment. How a child learns what the world is like.

I knew we would say no.

Shame. Shattering.

I was not the person I'd imagined myself to be.

"We need to call her," Eric said. "We need to let her know."

"I can't," I said. "I'm ashamed."

"I can call her," he said. "I'm willing to call her. But I feel like it might be important for you to do it."

"I can't," I said. I was still pacing, crying.

"You have nothing to be ashamed of," he said.

"I can't," I said. "I can't."

"You need to get grounded," he said. "You need to pull yourself together." He handed me the phone.

I dialed Cindy's number. She didn't answer.

"Should we leave a message?" I asked.

"I don't think so," he said.

I picked up the toys we'd chosen, the maze, the cars, the book, the stackable boxes. I carried them back to the basement.

I called again. Still no answer.

"She's probably on the phone with the police," Eric said.

I turned off the lamps in the child's bedroom. I turned off the porch light.

I called again. This time she answered.

"I was out of cell range," she said.

"I'm sorry," I said. "We don't think we're the right home for him. We think he'll need more support than we're prepared to give."

"Okay," she said. "Thank you for letting me know."

"I'm sorry," I said.

"I know this is your first placement," she said. "This little guy would be a hard first placement."

"I'm sorry," I said. "I'm so sorry."

many are the ways

For the Ilongot of the Philippines, "those who share a history of migration and cooperation 'share a body.'"

For the Malays, people can "acquire the same 'blood' by living in the same house and eating from the same hearth."

In some Inuit groups, people born on the same day are kin.

For some people who live in Amazonia it is not blood but "affinity" that produces kinship, and affinity can arise not just between people, but between people and animals and strangers and gods. Plants are the children of the Amazonian women who cultivate them; animals are the kin of the Amazonian men who hunt them.

The Trukese use the category "my sibling from the same canoe" for people who have survived a life-threatening experience at sea.

Feasting at the same table, reincarnation, living under the same roof, sharing memories, working side by side, friendship, common suffering, adoption, eating from the same land, experiencing the same fortunes of migration, surviving shipwreck together—there are lots of ways to make a family. If everything descends from the same creators—if we are all made of the same material—then everything is kin: house, tree, whale, person, canoe.

i saw her picture

In the local paper I saw a picture of the boy's mother, a mug shot. I read the story below her photograph and learned more about the boy. He has two siblings, one a year older, one a year younger. Aged one and two and three. In the apartment where the maintenance worker found the boy there were no diapers, no food. The only thing in the refrigerator was spoiled milk. The boy was crying, lying near the door in a puddle of what appeared to be urine.

Neighbors reported that the middle child—the boy who would have been ours—was left alone for long stretches all the time. The mother's sister—who was only eleven years old—had made the mother take the boy to the hospital in the spring, more than a year ago, and doctors reported that the boy was malnourished, reported they'd seen injuries all over his body resulting from "lack of supervision."

What do neglect-caused injuries look like?

Why did the doctors let the boy go home?

I showed the article to Eric, and he said, "I can't stop thinking about the maintenance worker. He's the only person in this situation who seems to have done the right thing. I wonder if he has anyone to help him process what he witnessed."

Saying yes and then saying no had left me reeling. When I looked in the mirror, red-rimmed swollen eyes looked back at me. I could not welcome a child in this state. I needed to learn to answer these phone calls without losing my shit.

Friend after friend assured me it was okay to say no, that it was important to know your limits, but I was ashamed. I'd been studying and writing about violence and torture and photographs of suffering for fifteen years, insisting we needed to do something to make the world better for the most vulnerable among us, for people in pain, but I said no to caring for a boy in pain, a boy living less than two miles from my house.

"I feel terrible we said no," I told Eric. "What kind of people are we?"

"We're all saying no all the time," Eric said. "Just look at the news."

"But I had to actually say no," I said. "To someone who called our phone number and asked us to help a little boy right down the street."

For Eric, the phone call and our response to it confirmed his worldview. The universe is indifferent. Humanity is a cancer. We fail to respond to those in need, be they beasts or birds or trees or refugees or children. "It's a hard world for little things," he said. "And I'm failing here to make it any better."

But I'd imagined it could be different. I'd let myself hope that maybe, just maybe, love might transform us, might reveal our essential kinship, might help us remember we're always already home.

how a body heals

When a woman is pregnant, cells from the fetus cross the placenta and enter her body, transforming her into what scientists call a *microchimera,* named after the mythological beast Chimaera, that fire-breathing, two-headed lion-goat-snake. Part herself and part her child, the woman carries genetic material from her fetus for decades.

Scientists don't yet understand what work fetal cells do in her body. Like stem cells, fetal cells are *pluripotent,* meaning they can become any type of tissue. Chemical cues from neighboring cells guide their transformation. If they land on breast tissue, they become breast cells. If on the thyroid, they become thyroid. If on the brain, brain. And it seems these three sites are often where they go. Scientists suspect fetal cells travel to organs that support the fetus in the womb and the baby when it's born—breast for milk production, thyroid for metabolism and heat transfer, brain for maternal attachment. The fetus bends the mother's body to its own needs.

Sometimes fetal cells migrate to injury sites within the woman's body. If, for example, she has liver damage, they travel to the liver and work to heal her. Scientists have also found evidence that fetal cells protect the mother from autoimmune diseases, those illnesses in which a body turns against itself.

But sometimes the cells are not salve but disease, working not to heal injury but to cause it. Fetal cells have been found in cervical cancer, in lung tumors.

I imagine the boy's cells inside his mother's body. They travel from arm to leg to shoulder, find home in bone, in lung, in blood, wreak havoc, make her sick, those cells able to do to her what he could not do, because he was so small, helpless, abandoned, those cells meting out punishment, retribution.

I imagine the harshest consequence might be love, his cells finding her heart, or it might be memory, his cells finding her brain so she cannot forget, his cells finding her eyes so she sees him everywhere, no matter where she goes, grocery store, sidewalk, classroom, car, bedroom, even when she closes her eyes.

but this time

After we said no to the child, I struggled to fall asleep for many nights, and if I did fall asleep, I'd wake up screaming minutes later, convinced someone was breaking into our house, convinced I was being tricked, my life an elaborate setup, a trap.

Where was he?

Who was caring for him?

What was he feeling?

What had we done?

I closed the door to the room. I didn't want to see the crib with the whale sheets. The changing table. The mobile with the black-and-white shapes. The banner of blessings from my friends. The shelf of books. The walls painted sky blue.

"Any news?" people asked in aisles of grocery stores, in parking lots, at parties.

"No news," I lied.

"Waiting must be hard," they said.

"Yes," I said.

"But exciting!" they said.

They assured me the way I was feeling was how they felt while trying to get pregnant, while waiting for their children to be born. Frustration. Impatience. Fear. Lack of control in the face of mystery, of the unknown. I'd nod as they insisted on our sameness. But I didn't believe a word they said.

another call

Now when I saw *State of Idaho* on my landline's caller ID, I wanted to ignore the call, let it go to voicemail, refuse to listen to the message. Calls sometimes came in the middle of the night, the landline ringing, then Eric's cellphone ringing, then my cellphone ringing.

"I can't do it," I said to Eric. "I need you to answer."

"It's okay to say no," Eric said.

We said no a lot. To sibling set after sibling set. To older child after older child. To child in need after child in need after child in need.

"These phone calls really mess with you," Juliana said. "You need to tell Rolayne you only want to be called when there is a baby."

I called Rolayne. "Would it be possible to ask people to call us only when there is a baby who needs a foster home?" I asked.

"It doesn't really work like that," she said. "I'll make a note in your file, but when social workers are trying to place children in foster homes, they just go down a list of possible foster parents. It's usually an emergency."

When our landline rang again, I answered.

"We have a baby in care," the social worker said. "Are you available to house her?" The biological mother and her sister had recently moved to Idaho from California. They'd been in and out of jail, in and out of rehab. The baby had come into care with broken bones. She was living with foster parents now, but she needed to be moved to a different home.

"The baby won't stop crying," the social worker said. "Screams all night long. The foster parents can't take it. Maybe it's the broken bones, maybe it's an ear infection."

"How can they not know what's wrong with the baby?" I asked. "Why don't they take her to the doctor?"

"The baby has an appointment next Wednesday," the social worker said.

"That's a week away," I said.

There was a grandfather who wanted the baby. "He's taking PRIDE classes now, but who knows if he'll follow through," the social worker said.

I wanted to adopt, and if there was a relative expressing interest in taking care of the baby, adoption would be unlikely.

"No," I said. "We can't take her."

shelter

Eric and I spent all morning cleaning our house. We swept. We cleared the kitchen counters. We folded laundry. That afternoon, we had an appointment with Jen, a social worker, who would recertify us as foster parents. It had been a year since we'd first been certified in Idaho. We had to meet with her to keep our license up to date.

Eric and I had assembled an outdoor couch for our patio the day before, and it had rained during the night, soaking the cushions. We laid the cushions in the sun to dry. Before Jen arrived, Eric went outside to put the couch back together.

"Sarah, come see this," he said through the screen door.

An ant colony had taken up residence under the cushions in the few hours they'd been drying on the pavers, and the ants had laid hundreds and hundreds of eggs. Without the cover of the pillows, the eggs were exposed to the sun. It was early August and hot. "I don't want their babies to burn," Eric said. He rested two of the couch pillows together to create a triangular shelter for the eggs, protecting them from the heat. He checked on them every hour, made sure the eggs were still shaded, watched the ants disappear the eggs between the pavers. "There must be an underground network beneath our patio," he said.

To be recertified as foster parents, each of us had to complete ten hours of continuing education. Before Jen arrived, we typed up the list of articles and books we'd read and a description of the two workshops we'd attended on whiteness and racism.

"I wish everyone would give me lists that looked like this," Jen said when we gave her the document. She didn't mean the content of our list; she meant that it was typed, legible, organized. She didn't read what we'd written. She didn't ask us any questions about what we'd learned, what fears we had, why we kept saying no to placement after placement after placement.

She did ask to see the smoke detectors and the carbon monoxide monitors, and Eric used a broomstick to press the button on each alarm to make it beep. She took pictures of our driver's licenses, our car registration, our car insurance.

"Do you still have life insurance?" she asked.

"Yes," we said.

"Are you open to an older child?" she asked. "Or do you still only want to be called for an infant."

"Infant," I said.

Jen arrived at our house at two o'clock, and she left by 2:11. "I've been telling everyone we have a great family waiting for an infant," she said on her way out. "When they get a baby, they will call me, and I will call you."

IX

BIG LOST

big lost

At the end of the summer, Eric's friend Derek visited, and we drove over Trail Creek Pass and into the Big Lost Wilderness to hike into the Pioneer Mountains and up to Betty Lake. We made camp a hundred feet from the water's edge and lived in that gorgeous basin, without cell service, without other people, for three days. Every night, I sat on an enormous rock and watched the sun set, watched the sky go pink then blue then black, watched the moon relight the landscape and sparkle the lake, no headlamp needed. We saw moose and elk, chipmunks and a peregrine falcon. When it was time to go, we hiked out through fields of cows. "We're vegetarian," I shouted at them when they blocked the trail, as if their knowing we would never eat them might allow us easier passage through their fields of shit, their howling.

We followed the Big Lost River home, driving through a valley then back over the pass. We went straight to Grumpy's, where we drank beer and ate baskets of French fries. My parents met us there, and then my sister and her husband and my two nephews joined us, all of us on the patio in the sun.

The next morning we planned to take paddleboards to Silver Creek, a nature preserve less than an hour from our house. Before we left for the preserve, I had a phone call with a writer to discuss a chapter of her manuscript she'd asked me to read. While we talked about her pages, my cellphone rang. I ignored it. Another call clicked through on my landline. I ignored that, too. Eric came to my office door, which is mostly glass, and knocked on one of the clear panes. I hate it when he tries to talk to me when I'm on the phone, so I glared and pointed to my headset. He walked away, but he had a strange look on his face.

His aunt was very sick. I worried he'd received news she'd died. I texted him: *You OK?*

Baby, he texted back.

When?

Now.

due date

In the second and third centuries, people argued about what happened to Mary's body in childbirth. Some insisted she felt no pain, that her body did not split open, that her hymen remained intact. Mary gave birth so quickly and with such ease, others insisted, that the appearance of the child startled her.

Think of the paintings we see of Mary kneeling by the manger, the New Testament scholar Jennifer Glancy writes. She's not lying in bed or on the floor. She's not squatting or sitting on the lap of a midwife. She's not tired or pale from loss of blood. She shows no pain, no weakness. Her body bears no sign that she has just given birth. Maybe she never even looked pregnant.

Though I thought a lot about my unchanging body, about the invisibility of our preparation, I didn't think about the changing body of the woman who would have given birth to the child we would bring home. But then, after the phone call, I thought of nothing else. Did people stand to give her their seat on the bus? Did they congratulate her when they saw her swelling belly? Did they nod and smile? What does it feel like to give birth and then have your baby taken away, either by choice or by force?

Some feminists try to reclaim Mary's birthing body as holy— the bloody mess of it, the stretch marks, the scars—and in rendering Mary's body holy again, they hope to sanctify the bodies of all birthing women. Pain teaches you how to become a mother, Glancy argues.

But what about people who give birth but do not become mothers?

And what about people who become mothers without giving birth?

The Mary story I like best, because it reads to me now like an adoption story, is found in *Ascension of Isaiah*. In this telling,

Mary is pregnant for just two months. One day, out of the blue, an infant appears in the room with her. Mary is surprised. One minute she is alone, and the next minute, there he is. Mary's womb is unchanged, the story says, and her child doesn't need milk to live, but Mary breastfeeds him anyway, so no one will know he is special, so she can keep him safe.

how soon

I ended my call with the writer. Eric and I listened to the messages a social worker named Grace had left on my cellphone and our landline and his cellphone. The same voice said the same thing: There was a three-day-old baby girl at the hospital in Twin Falls.

I called Grace. We asked her our list of questions. Eric and I talked. Then we called again and asked a few more questions, heard her use words like *imminent danger* and *premature* and *declared*.

"Does the baby have a name?"

"Coco," Grace said.

"What about the bio mom?" I asked.

"Evelyn," she said. "And she's a poor prognosis."

"Any relatives who want to take care of the baby?"

"No," she said. "Not that we've found."

"One minute," I said. I covered the phone, told Eric what Grace had told me about the baby, about the mother, about the likelihood of adoption. He nodded.

"Yes," I said. "We'll come get the baby."

"How soon can you be here?" Grace asked.

It takes almost two hours to drive from our town to Twin Falls. It was already eleven. "Two o'clock?" I said.

"See you at two," she said. Grace told me the name of the hospital's social worker, told me where to park, told me to go to the front desk when we arrived and ask them to page her. It was Friday, the start of Labor Day weekend. They wanted to get things squared away before the department's office closed for the holiday, she explained. "Bring a car seat," she added.

Eric and I changed out of what we were wearing to paddle Silver Creek and into regular clothes. We found the car seat in the basement and packed a bag of things we imagined we'd

need. Water bottles. Potato chips. Clif Bars. Baby blankets. Diapers. Wipes.

We didn't know how long we'd be gone. I showed Derek a
map of Silver Creek, explained how to inflate my paddleboard,
where to leave the car, where to hide a bike in the bushes.

"Take our picture," I said before we left, and Eric and I put
our arms around each other and stood by the kitchen table.

"Last image with total freedom," Derek said.

stranger in my arms

Driving to Twin Falls, we passed the now familiar lava fields, signs directing visitors to ice caves, sunlit hills, migrating cranes. In the rearview mirror, we could see the Pioneer Mountains, where we'd camped the day before. Later, people will fixate on this. "What if they'd called you one day earlier?" they will ask.

"We would have been out of cell range," we will say.

"What if you hadn't answered the phone?" they will ask.

"They would have called someone else."

The drive between our town and Twin Falls is beautiful but dangerous, single lanes on either side of the highway with no barrier between, people driving too fast, too tired. Crosses mark the landscape, wreaths of flowers, names of the dead.

"We're going to get a baby," I said over and over again. I didn't know how else to talk about what was about to happen, what we were on our way to do.

When we reached the bridge across the gorge, one side of the road was shut down, lined with ambulances and police cars. Someone had either jumped or fallen. I saw two BASE jumpers folding their parachutes on a patch of grass. Everything felt like a sign, but of what?

We found the hospital and wandered through parking lot after parking lot, looking for the nonemergency entrance Grace had told us to use. We parked, lifted the car seat out of the trunk, and carried our bag of random stuff inside.

I said the name of the social worker, and the woman behind the front desk paged her. I needed to use the restroom, which I should have done before they paged the social worker.

"Hurry," Eric said.

I ran, and when I returned to the lobby, Eric was in the middle of a circle of women—Grace, an intern who was shadowing her, the hospital social worker, and some other people whose names and roles I don't remember. They explained there was a mountain of paperwork for us to do. "But would you like to see her first?" the hospital social worker asked.

We took the elevator to the NICU. We must have walked through doors we had to be buzzed through, down long hallways lined with patients' rooms, then down other hallways, but when we left, hours later, I didn't recognize anything, not the elevator or the hallways or the security desks.

A nurse was feeding the baby when we arrived, sitting in a rocking chair, holding her tiny body on her lap, supporting her head. "Want to hold her?" she asked and handed her to me.

Love.

This stranger in my arms already familiar.

I'd never held a baby so small. Coco weighed less than five pounds, her legs and arms like sticks, her body thin. The nurse explained how to feed her, that we'd need to give her a bottle every two hours, encourage her to eat by unwrapping the blanket around her, even unsnapping the top of her onesie because she might eat more if she was a little bit cold. She was dressed in a pink onesie with the words BEST LITTLE SISTER stitched across its front.

Every nurse who came into our room to teach us something— infant CPR, what to expect with low birth weight and early birth, signs to look for that would indicate withdrawal—clearly loved the baby. "She's beautiful," one of them said. "Not all babies are so beautiful," said another. In other NICU rooms were infants with oxygen tents, with feeding tubes, but ours was just small, a month early and strong.

Grace and the other social workers talked with Eric while I fed Coco. Then I heard Grace say, "I have to go, but don't take this as a sign of anything. Just take this as a sign of how many other cases I have."

"You're leaving us?" I asked, my voice too loud for that small room. I barely knew Grace. We'd been together for maybe ten minutes, but her departure scared me, as if the fact that she was on the other end of the phone when we received the call meant she'd shepherd us through this process in some way, as if her leaving meant we were now on our own.

On her way out, Grace said, "There won't be any visits with the bio mom over the holiday weekend."

A few weeks before, I'd received another call about a different baby, a three-week-old boy. He'd been found in a home where drugs were being manufactured. Police went into the home because of the drugs and found the baby. I'd asked the social worker the questions on our list—how exposed to drugs the baby had been, what other substances he'd been exposed to, how long he'd been in care.

"I literally do not know any of that," the social worker had said. "I just know the police declared the baby in imminent danger. They're about to give him a drug test. There are six potential family members who want to keep him. We're working with three of them."

During that phone call the social worker talked only about visits with the bio mom—how important they were, how they made bonding between mother and baby possible, how I'd need to drive the baby to Twin Falls twice a week to see the bio mom.

"Are you willing to do that?" she'd asked. "Because there are other people who are."

"Of course," I'd told her. "I'll drive to Twin twice a week." I hung up and waited for her to call back to tell me what would happen. Fifteen minutes, an hour, two hours. I called her. "We found someone else to take the baby," she said. "Someone who lives much closer."

But this time there was no talk about visits with the bio mother. No talk of bonding. No talk about driving to Twin.

Eric doesn't like babies. Any time we've been in a room with one I've tried to hand him the baby to hold, and he's kept his arms at his sides, shaken his head, but when the social workers asked me to complete some paperwork, he took Coco like he'd always known what to do, and for the next two hours, he held her, fed her, changed her diaper, rocked her.

I left the room once to use the restroom, and to get back into the NICU, I pressed the buzzer on the side of the big locked door.

"Yes?" a woman's voice asked, and I said the baby's full name.

"Who are you?" she asked. "The mother?"

"The foster mother," I said, and she opened the door.

what a mother's body does

We stayed in that small room at the hospital for hours, long enough to watch a video on infant CPR, long enough for a second feeding so we could learn to do it ourselves, long enough to talk with the doctor who had delivered Coco. "If you wait, he'll be able to tell you more about the birth," Grace had said before she left.

I liked the doctor in his blue jeans and plaid shirt, with his kind face. He answered my questions about what the birth was like, about whether the baby had had any breast milk, about the state of the mother.

Later we'll learn that Coco's biological mother drove hours and hours from the state where she used to live to Twin Falls the day before she gave birth. We'll learn that the time from her check-in at the hospital to delivery was six minutes. We'll learn that a friend drove her from that other state to Idaho, and when we meet that friend, she will tell us that Coco's mother came to make a new start, but the social workers will tell us she came to avoid Child Protective Services in her hometown because she already had a child in foster care there and she didn't want them to take this baby too.

The doctor explained Coco was still learning how to swallow, how to breathe, how to eat. "Because she was born early, her body is having to learn how to do what the mother's body would be doing for her if she were still in the womb," he said.

Though we'd brought our own car seat, they made us use a car seat that had been approved by the safety staff at the hospital. It was pink with a leopard-skin pattern and in the seams were crumbs and pet hair. One of the nurses handed me a bag of clothing. "The birth mother brought this with her," she said.

On the drive, I sat in the backseat next to Coco, watching her, making sure she was breathing. She held my pinky finger and didn't let go.

love

"What did you feel when you held her for the first time?" Eric asked me that night.

"Love," I said.

"But what did it feel like?" he asked.

"I can't explain it," I said.

"Did you have an overwhelming need to protect her?" he asked.

"What?"

"For me, it was visceral, primal," he said. "I felt, *If you come at her, I will fuck you up.*"

We use the word *vulnerable* to describe susceptibility to attack or disease, to highlight our precarity. But *vulnerable*—from the Latin noun *vulnus* (wound) and verb *vulnerare* (to wound)—used to mean both "capable of being physically wounded" and "having the power to wound." That second meaning—the ability to cause harm to others—has fallen out of popular usage, but it was exactly what Eric understood when he held Coco for the first time. He knew, in his bones, how defenseless she was, how exposed, and he also knew he'd do anything to shelter her.

"It was like all the indifference and harm in the universe collapsed onto the being I was holding, and all I wanted to do was protect it, protect her," he said. "I've never felt that before."

what the mother brought

I wanted to document the contents of the bag of clothes the nurse handed to me when we left the hospital, treat them like the holy objects they were, sacred, because they might be the only things Coco ever had from her mother.

In the bag were two new outfits on hangers, still with their price tags, everything pink and peach, clearly intended for a girl, which meant her mother must have had at least some prenatal care if she knew she was having a girl. There was other pink baby clothing, too, onesies and T-shirts. At the bottom of the bag was an adult's lacy black and pink strapless bra.

Later, I will thank Evelyn for the bag of clothing, and she will have no idea what I'm talking about.

which parts poison

Years before she moved to Idaho, Coco's biological mother lived near an open pit copper mine. When the mine stopped yielding copper, it was shut down, abandoned, and it filled with rainwater so acidic nothing could live in it or near it, no fish in the water, no plants along its shore. Its runoff turned a nearby river red. If you were to drink this water, it would kill you, corroding your body from the inside out. Sometimes, a fog hovers above the water, a mist, and residents of the town worry it is poisonous, though it can't be contained. When birds are migrating, people stay close to the pit, shoot fireworks, shoot guns, fly drones, all to try to scare the birds, to make them land somewhere else, or to encourage them to leave the pit as soon as possible after a short rest, but it doesn't always work. One November, thousands of migrating snow geese stopped to rest at the mine, some staying for more than a week, and several thousand of them died. Hunters who killed geese anywhere near the mine around that time were warned to process and freeze the birds, but not to eat them until tests determined which parts of the birds were edible and which parts poison.

written on her body

We brought Coco home on Friday night and had a doctor's visit Saturday afternoon, a holiday weekend. The office staff behind the desk couldn't figure out who we were or whose insurance to bill or who was financially responsible for the baby. I had a blue folder of paperwork from DHW, and I showed them various pages that explained our relationship.

The nurse had us undress Coco and place her on the cold table with no blanket, no cover, while she looked for what she needed. She opened cabinet after cabinet, every drawer in the room, to find thermometer, diapers, measuring tape. When she measured Coco, she wrote on her body with a permanent marker.

When people learn Coco is not our biological daughter but our foster daughter, they ask the same questions. "The mother must be young?" they ask.

"Drugs?" they ask.

"She didn't want her?" they ask.

And Eric and I give the same response: "We're not allowed to say."

Our answer, which we give to friends and family and strangers alike, is in part because of our legal obligations. As foster parents, we are agents of the state, bound to keep confidentiality. But we also don't share information about Coco—not the circumstances of her birth, not why she was taken away, not what substances she was exposed or not exposed to, not what her mother did or did not do to her—because we don't want people to impose their ideas about what's possible or not possible on her. We don't want anyone to see her through any kind of filter. She deserves a fresh start.

But as soon as the doctor walked into the room, I could see how she was seeing Coco. She had access to her medical records, to her mother's medical records, to all the information we block from other people. The doctor rolled her eyes, talked about the challenges Coco would face, her disadvantages. She opened the mother's file. "What do you want to know?" she asked, as if it were a juicy tabloid magazine.

"I don't like her," I said to Eric as soon as the doctor left the room.

"That was obvious," he said.

"We're never coming back here," I said.

"I know," he said.

her breath from our breath

My cousin gave us a round pillow with a hole in the middle that she nicknamed *the donut*. Coco didn't like sleeping in the pack-and-play bassinet—too flat, too much space around her—so in those first few days she slept in the donut instead, right next to our heads. But Eric and I couldn't sleep that way, each of us waking the other up with sudden movements, each afraid the baby was going to die. So we took turns, breaking the night in half, one of us awake for our allotted hours with Coco in the donut in the twin bed in her room, not risking closing our eyes, in case in that moment of blindness she were to stop breathing.

I called my sister who has two small boys, one still a baby. "How do you sleep?" I asked. "I'm too afraid she'll die."

"She's stronger than you think she is," my sister said.

We watched Coco breathe, put our ears to her tiny mouth, our hands to her tiny chest, and rose to feed her every two hours, carrying her five-pound body carefully down the stairs.

Her body learns to regulate her breath from the sound and feel of our breath, I read. *Her heart learns to beat from the sound and feel of our heartbeats.*

shelter care

We'd been taking care of Coco for about ten days when Grace called to tell us it was time for the Shelter Care Hearing. Court would start at nine on Thursday, she explained, and "start at nine" meant that everyone on the docket for that day had to be present at nine, but no one knew when their case would be called, so we would all wait together in the hallway outside the courtroom, maybe for a few minutes, maybe for hours.

"Bring Coco," Grace said. "It will be okay to let Evelyn hold her."

The night before court, my parents called. They had googled Evelyn and found her Facebook page, and in her profile picture, she's holding a baby. "She wants her back," my mother said.

While we talked, I, too, googled Evelyn and found her Facebook page, and another Facebook page, and another, and I looked at the photograph of her holding a baby, in a hospital bed, soon after birth, medical bracelets on their wrists. "Is that Coco?" I asked Eric. The baby in the picture didn't look like her and wasn't wearing the hat she was wearing when we picked her up at the hospital and wasn't wrapped in the same blanket, either. In the other photographs in Evelyn's Facebook feed, she's in a bar or standing near a convenience store's refrigerator of beer. In some of the photographs, she's beautiful, smiling.

"How do you know the court won't just give her the baby tomorrow?" my dad asked, and though he tried to hide it, I could hear he was crying harder than I'd ever heard him cry.

That the court might give the baby back had not occurred to me, but then, it did.

she needs your in-loveness

My friends brought food, knocked gently on the front door or texted to let us know dinner was waiting on the porch. They brought onesies. Her first pair of overalls. A pink-and-purple snowsuit. Cozy blankets. Swaddles. Slings. Toys. Lovies. Teddy bears and ducks and lambs and elephants.

Sometimes my friends came inside, and together we'd stare at Coco, wait for her to yawn, wait for her to open her dreamy blue eyes. We'd study her red lips, her upper lip in the shape of the letter *m*, her well-defined chin, her cheeks that grew plumper and rosier every day.

"Cute baby," strangers said when they saw her, and because Eric and I didn't make her, because how she looked had nothing to do with us, we could say, "I know!"

"Your first?" they asked. And when we told them she was our foster daughter, that we might have to give her back to her biological mother, I watched them step away.

"I'll pray for you," they said.

"I couldn't do that," they said.

I didn't know if I could do it either.

But I also knew it's what we do every time we choose to love another mortal being. Someday we will have to give them back too.

My friend Katie, a poet, gave birth at twenty-four weeks to an impossibly small girl and for months they didn't know if her daughter would live or die. She told me that one night she left the NICU and asked herself, "Am I in or am I out?" She knew her baby would probably not survive. For an entire day my poet friend didn't go back to the NICU because it made her weep to see her child. Then she understood: She had to love her whether the baby was with her forever or just for a few days. "No matter what happens," she told me, "Coco needs your full-on in-loveness, so you aren't making a mistake to give it."

It's never wrong to choose love, she texted a few hours later. *I'm starting to make her a quilt.*

X

FLIGHT RISK

love you too much

We woke before the sun and drove to Twin Falls for the Shelter Care Hearing. I sat in the backseat with Coco, watching the same landscape we'd watched when we drove to the hospital to bring her home, the sunrise turning everything pink.

We arrived early and fed her a bottle in the car and watched people enter the courthouse. I loved the sounds Coco made when she drank her formula, loved supporting her chin and head in one hand and patting her back with the other to burp her as she sat on my lap. She didn't mind being fed in the backseat of the car, didn't mind being burped, didn't mind being loaded into or out of her car seat, loved having her diaper changed while watching the bright shapes on the mobile above the changing table, loved taking baths and the feel of the water pouring over her head. We could take Coco anywhere—middle school volleyball games, restaurants, the grocery store, court— and she was a delight. Coco was easy from the beginning, as if she knew her situation brought a different kind of challenge and she wanted to ease whatever she could. Sometimes I'd look at her and feel that I was looking at a sage old woman filled with the wisdom that comes with lifetimes and from stars, and then she would let out a long string of farts, like a tiny machine gun, *pop pop pop pop pop.*

On the sidewalk in front of the courthouse, a young man, maybe sixteen years old, carried a baby in a car seat with one hand and smoked a cigarette with another. An even younger woman trailed behind him, dragging her feet, eyes down.

Grace texted us to meet her outside the courthouse's main doors. We put Coco's car seat in the stroller and covered the opening with a blanket, a kind of tent.

"You made it," Grace said, and then, behind her, we saw Evelyn. We recognized her from the photographs we'd seen on

Facebook, but she looked so different in person we weren't positive it was her.

"You must be Evelyn," I said. I raised the blanket so she could see her daughter, the baby she'd birthed just two weeks before. Evelyn's body still carried signs of pregnancy, her breasts tender with milk she wasn't allowed to share.

She leaned close to her baby. "I love you," she said.

After we went through security, in the hallway outside the courtroom, Evelyn asked, "Could I please hold her?" I lifted Coco from her car seat, wrapped her in a blanket, and handed her to her mother.

Evelyn was tender, cradled Coco's tiny body, cooed. She cried, held the baby close to her chest. "I love you too much," she whispered, again and again. Evelyn sat on a bench, her friend June next to her, and I sat in a chair across from them under a ficus tree whose leaves kept brushing against my head, whose branches got caught in my hair.

"I should have been the foster mom for the baby," June said. "But I had to choose whether to take care of the baby or take care of Evelyn. I chose Evelyn, and she feels guilty about that, but the baby will be living with us soon enough."

I waited a few minutes. "I'll be right back," I said to everyone in the hallway and to no one, and I found Grace sitting on a different bench around the corner. I told her about June, about how she said Coco would soon be living with her.

"That's not going to happen," Grace said. "We have concerns about that relationship. We're monitoring it. And we have no plans to move the baby. Remember, June is the person who drove Evelyn from the other state. They drove here one day, and Evelyn gave birth the next." Grace then told me why they had taken the baby away, what the doctors saw, what their tests showed.

I had a notebook in my lap, and in it I wrote everything

Grace said, everything June said, everything Evelyn said, which was only *I love you I love you I love you.* I also recorded people's names when they introduced themselves to Eric and me or to Evelyn and June. Social workers, attorneys, CASA (Court Appointed Special Advocates) volunteers, the judge. I didn't know it then, but DHW will never give us a handout with everyone's names and phone numbers and email addresses, no contact list of any kind.

Evelyn's lawyer, assigned by the state, introduced herself to Evelyn. "What a cute boy," she said.

"She's a girl," Evelyn and I said at the same time.

"How old is he now?" the lawyer asked me.

"She," I said.

"Gray," she said, "is for boys," and pointed to Coco's clothes, to her blanket.

June asked when the next doctor's visit was, and we told her, and a woman in the hall who heard us told Evelyn she had a right to attend the doctor's visits, so I shared the date and time of the appointment with her, then June suggested we exchange phone numbers so we could text, and I texted them the appointment date and the doctor's office address. I looked at Eric, and he raised his eyebrows.

You really want her to have your phone number? he texted.

"What are your names?" Evelyn's lawyer asked Eric and me, shuffling a stack of papers. "Sarah and Aaron?"

"Eric," he said.

I walked down the hallway and around the corner to talk with Grace again, to ask about the doctor's visits, to see if Evelyn was allowed to attend. "Yes, it is her right to come to all doctor's appointments," Grace said. "But you should know she is a flight risk. Watch the doors."

"Did you just say *watch the doors?*" I asked.

"Put your body between her and the door whenever she is

holding the baby," she said. "Do not let her hold the baby in the hallways. Only let her hold the baby in places where you can close the door."

The bailiff called Evelyn's name, and we walked into the courtroom. The state's attorney sat at a table on the left side of the room and Evelyn sat at a table on the right side of the room with her lawyer. Eric and I sat behind Evelyn. "Show the bio mom you have her back," Kate had told us. "Sit right behind her, on her side of the room."

A court stenographer sat to the judge's right. In a voice so quiet I could barely hear him, the judge named the people in the room—the prosecutor, the public defender, Evelyn, the social workers, representatives from CASA. "Who are you?" he asked Eric and me, and we said our names, told him we were the foster parents, and he said, "Thank you so much for being here."

"Do you agree with the state that the mother cannot at this time provide a stable home for the child?" the judge asked Evelyn's lawyer.

"Yes," she said. "She cannot at this time provide a stable home for him."

"Her," Evelyn said.

"And the father?" the judge asked.

"He is in prison," her lawyer said.

"Right," the judge said. "I see that here. And his name is not on the birth certificate?"

"No," she said.

"The parents are not able to provide a stable home for the child at this time," the judge said. "Do you agree with that?" he asked Evelyn.

She nodded.

"The child will remain in shelter care," he said and explained there would be another court date in two weeks.

all they do

At the courthouse, Grace gave us vouchers to use for clothing and formula and diapers, so we drove to the big box store in Twin Falls we'd been told accepted the vouchers. No place in our town would take them. We walked in and the first person we saw was the wife of the racist man from our PRIDE class, waiting in line for customer service.

"We were in PRIDE together," I said and introduced myself. "I remember your husband's name, but I'm sorry I don't remember yours."

"I remember you," she said and told me her name. "How many placements have you had?"

"This is our first," I said and pointed to the stroller.

"We've had nearly a dozen so far," she said. "Right now, I have two meth babies, one nine months old and one ten months old. All they do is scream and drool."

The customer service representative called her by name, waved her to the front of the line. "They know me here," she said. "Good luck."

Eric and I wandered the aisles. All the baby clothes were too big for Coco. We loaded our cart with formula and diapers and wipes.

"What a cute boy," everyone said when they peeked into the stroller.

"She's a girl," we said.

"Gray is for boys," they said.

two birds

The day after court, two birds flew into our living room window. One was a warbler, bright yellow, beautiful, and dead, her body right below the window. The second hit the glass, then landed between the cranked-open window and the screen, trying to recover. When birds hit their head and get a concussion, they puff up their body to try to get blood to circulate to their brain, but they need to be warm for this to work. We locked our cats in the mudroom so they wouldn't bother the bird at the window, and we watched her through the screen. She seemed to be doing better with every passing minute, but then the sun went down, and the temperature dropped.

Eric went outside holding a thin soft cloth and gently wrapped the bird and placed her in a shoebox I'd lined with a towel. We put the box in my office under the lamp we'd bought fifteen years ago at Ikea that gives off so much heat my cats lounge under it while I write. We let the bird warm for hours. Then, when we could hear her moving around, stretching her wings, hopping up and down, we took the shoebox to our front porch and opened the lid and she was gone.

that one is mine

Coco had her first doctor's appointment with her primary care physician, who was also my doctor and Eric's doctor. When we checked in at the front desk, the receptionist could not figure out how we were connected to Coco or who would pay, but then a woman sitting at a different desk popped up. "I know them!" she said. She had checked us in at that first doctor's visit over the holiday weekend the day after we brought Coco home, and for the next few months, every time we visit the doctor's office, she will come out from behind her desk to look at Coco, to *oooh* and *aaah* and ask how much she weighs.

I'd called our doctor in advance to let her know we'd be at the appointment with Coco's biological mother. I wanted her to have some background about Coco's birth and medical history so she could ask the right questions to get the information needed for Coco's best care. I also told her Evelyn was a flight risk and we'd been told to keep our bodies between her and the door whenever she was holding the baby.

We were called from the waiting room before Evelyn arrived, so I texted her: *We're in room 6.* When she found us in room 6, she wanted to hold the baby right away. The doctor asked her all kinds of questions about prenatal care and her addiction history and other things she might have done or used or experienced while Coco was in her womb. Evelyn's answers were vague, and when the doctor pushed, when she said she needed accurate information to make sure Coco got the right and necessary care, Evelyn was still evasive. When the doctor listed the possible consequences of her behavior on Coco, Evelyn stood in the middle of the small room and cried.

"But, really, the biggest predictor of Coco's health and well-being is a stable and secure home life," the doctor said. "It is possible she may never experience any of these symptoms."

I wrote this in my notebook.

"Is this your first child?" the doctor asked.

"No," Evelyn said.

"How many children do you have?" the doctor asked.

Evelyn counted on her fingers, touched her thumb to her index finger, then middle, then ring, then pinky. "Four," she said.

"Do any of them live with you?"

"No," she said.

"Are they with relatives or in foster care?" the doctor asked.

"Kind of," Evelyn said.

We'd brought the car seat we'd been given at the hospital to the doctor's office. The buckle was nearly impossible to latch, and Eric and I both hated it. We had a different one we wanted to use, but we'd been told at the hospital we had to use the one they gave us. "Can you give us approval to use a different car seat?" I asked the doctor. I pointed to the one with the pink leopard-skin cover. "I don't like this one," I said.

"That one is mine," Evelyn said. "I want it back."

"We're going to weigh her and measure her now," the doctor said, "which means we have to take her into the hallway."

"I'll carry her," Evelyn said.

"I'm going to carry her," I said, "and you can have her right back when we return to this room."

Evelyn glared as she handed Coco to me. I carried the baby into the hallway and followed the nurse to the scale. Evelyn followed me. Eric followed Evelyn.

"She's gaining weight," the nurse said. "Good job, everyone."

When we were checking out and scheduling the next appointment, a woman carrying a car seat that had a baby inside who had oxygen tubes in his nose asked, "How old?"

"Two weeks," I said.

"Wow! You look amazing!"

"Thank you," I said, "but I didn't give birth to her." I pointed to Evelyn, who was sitting next to Eric on a bench, crying, collapsed. "She gave birth to her."

"Oh," the woman said. She turned to Evelyn. "You look good, too," she said.

flight and flock

Robbed of both flight and flock, parrots kept as pets are "twice-traumatized beings," I read in an article by Charles Siebert in *The New York Times*. In the wild, parrots move through the air the way whales move through the sea, Siebert writes. "Long-time pairs fly wing to wing, within extended, close-knit social groupings." Each member of the group has their own call, like a name, which they are taught to speak soon after birth "during a transitional period of vocalizing equivalent to human baby babbling known as 'subsong.'" This is what makes parrots good mimics.

But humans keep parrots alone. In cages. They bring parrots home because their feathers match the living room. They keep parrots in drawers. Clip their wings. Though parrots separated from their flock attach—deeply, fiercely—to their keepers, people abandon them when they no longer want a bird as a pet.

At Midwest Avian Adoption and Rescue Services—a parrot sanctuary and rehabilitation facility in Minnesota—scientists studied an umbrella cockatoo, bred in captivity, Siebert writes. The parrot had had multiple caregivers, none of them stable, and had been exposed to domestic violence, substance abuse, addiction. He was diagnosed with complex PTSD. Giving a parrot this diagnosis, looking through a trauma lens at parrots' distress behaviors—cage pacing, screams, self-mutilation, aggression when touched, nightmares, insomnia—allowed scientists and psychologists to see, in the words of Dr. Gay Bradshaw, that "the symptoms of many caged parrots are almost indistinguishable from those of human P.O.W.s and concentration-camp survivors."

At Serenity Park in Los Angeles, veterans with PTSD work with parrots with PTSD. Pacing, rocking, screaming, cowering in corners—behaviors that would usually be dismissed as "bird-brained" or "mindless mimicry" or "mere parroting," Siebert writes, "are recognized as classic symptoms of the same form of complex post-traumatic stress disorder" afflicting veterans.

Every day at Serenity Park, flight lessons. Siebert watched a woman set a parrot on a perch and then gently take hold of each wing tip, moving the wings "up and down a few times as though priming a pump." The parrot then perched on her index finger, and the woman thrust her finger up and let the bird fall free. Flailing, Siebert explains, will become "firmer flaps," and then, eventually, the bird will fly again.

she knows you

For the second court date in Twin Falls, I went by myself, left Eric and the baby at home. We were new parents to an infant, and we hadn't slept for weeks. Eric made me an enormous thermos of coffee, and I drove through those lava fields and watched the sunrise and the valley turn pink then purple then blue. I'd been told to arrive by 9:30, but so had everyone else involved with a child who had been taken into care in our district: foster parents, bio parents, social workers, CASA volunteers, lawyers, children. We all waited together in that narrow hallway that smelled like an ashtray and felt like it might ignite.

"Where's Coco?" Evelyn asked when she saw me.

"They told me not to bring her," I said, which was what Kate had advised on the phone when I called her to ask what to expect in court.

The people waiting with us—most of them women—were on the losing end of all of our oppressive systems. Poverty. Abuse. Neglect. Addiction. Racism. Sexism. Lack of healthcare and housing. In that hallway lined with vinyl-covered benches and a few chairs, nowhere near enough seating for all the people waiting, fury and shame, indignation and resignation simmered. Emotions were volatile and strange. Every time I used the restroom that morning at the courthouse, there was always someone in one of the stalls crying.

I watched one woman who had a young girl—four or five years old—hiding in her skirt. The woman was tender to the girl, handed her ziplock bags of Goldfish then apple slices then Cheerios. Next to the woman with the child hiding in her skirt was the woman's daughter, a teenager, and from what I overheard of their conversations, the child was the teenager's biological daughter.

Earlier that week, Grace had called to tell us she would no

longer be our social worker. We'd meet our new social worker, whose name was Camilla, at court. "It's good cop, bad cop," Grace explained. "One of us—that's me—takes the child away from the biological mother; the other one of us—that's Camilla—tries to help her get the child back."

A woman with short blond hair and high-heeled black boots leaned against the wall next to me. When she saw me scanning the hallway, she asked, "Who are you looking for?"

"Our new social worker," I said. "Her name is Camilla."

"She's my social worker, too," she said and pointed to a woman at the other end of the hallway.

"How is she?" I asked, and the woman shrugged.

Evelyn sat on one of the benches. On her lap she held a calendar with a thin vinyl cover. Every biological parent who'd had a child taken away held a version of that calendar. It was the giveaway, revealing who was a parent and who was a social worker or foster parent or CASA volunteer.

"Can I sit next to you?" I asked Evelyn.

"Yes," she said. "Want to see some pictures?"

"Yes," I said, and she showed me photos on her phone. Pictures of her other children. Pictures of birthday parties, of herself sitting in a folding chair on the sidelines of someone's baseball game, of herself standing with family all around. Pictures of her holding someone else's baby, their noses touching, both of them smiling.

"My life before," she said. "Can I ask what you do for work?"

"I'm a writer," I said.

"The only thing I'm writing now is letters to Coco's father," she said. "Want to see his picture?"

"Yes," I said, and she showed me a picture of him in prison, on the other side of the glass, wearing orange, holding a phone.

"I know how to pick them," she said.

We waited in the hallway for nearly two hours, until the

woman who'd pointed out Camilla for me stormed out of the courtroom. We learned there had been a trial no one knew would be held that day. The biological mother and the biological father disagreed about what should happen to their child who was in foster care, so they'd brought the father to court from prison, and when there is a prisoner involved, that trial always goes first.

The bailiff called Evelyn's name next, and we entered the courtroom, and I sat behind Evelyn again, on her side. The same quiet judge sat behind his enormous desk and whispered at us.

"Who are you?" the judge asked me after all the other people in the room had been identified for the record, and I said my name, said I was Coco's foster mother, and the judge again thanked me for being there.

The judge said the mother could still not provide a stable home environment. He said the father could not either because he was in prison.

"We'd like to request unstable visits, your honor," Evelyn's lawyer said. "I mean, *unsupervised* visits." Her lawyer laughed.

"No way," the judge said and listed the reasons the child had been taken into care in the first place. "She's only three weeks old."

Then the judge said, "No stable home environment is available for this child with either parent at this time." He determined it was in the best interest of the child to remain in foster care. "Such custody is ordered," he said.

The whole thing took three minutes.

"See you in three months," the judge said.

I watched Evelyn turn to her lawyer and say, "Three months?"

I walked out of the courtroom with Evelyn and through the hallway still lined with people waiting their turn.

"That sucked," she said.

"Waiting two hours for three minutes?" I asked.

"No," she said. "All the terrible things I did to make this happen."

From the car, I called Eric to tell him about court, but I saw Evelyn walking alone on the sidewalk, crying, so I hung up and got out of the car. "Are you okay?" I asked. "This is hard. I'm so sorry."

"She doesn't even know me," she said, and I thought of my friend Emily, whose son had died before he turned three, who'd gone blind, who could barely move, and how when I visited Emily before Ronan died, I'd held him for hours, and he'd turned his head to follow Emily's voice from room to room.

"When he hears your voice he turns his head," I'd said to Emily.

"Do you think he still knows me?" she'd asked.

"Yes," I'd said. "He knows you."

I looked at Evelyn, standing on the sidewalk outside the courthouse, crying. "She knows you," I said.

My heart broke for Evelyn. The work ahead must have felt insurmountable. But there was another part of me, a bigger part, that lifted. *We're going to get to keep the baby*, that part whispered. *She's ours.*

lasana

That night Eric and I googled the father and found his Facebook page. His name was Cody, and he hadn't posted for months, probably because he was in prison. *A woman running for president is as useless as the g in lasagna,* his last post said.

"Lasana?" I said. "Lasana? Seems like the *g* is pretty fucking important."

We found his arrest records, read about a car chase with the police and a stolen motorcycle, read about him breaking into houses in a lakeside town. We found a photograph of him fishing, standing in a river, cottonwoods along its banks, willows, cradling a rainbow trout in his hands. In that photograph holding the fish he looks happy, like a completely different person than the man in his mug shot, his skinny face and hard eyes unrecognizable.

"That's not him," I said.

"It is," Eric said. "Look at his ears."

I looked at his ears in one photograph and his ears in the other photograph, and they were the same.

In a different picture on his Facebook page, he's wearing a black T-shirt emblazoned with a skull and crossbones. DADDY IS A BAD INFLUENCE, the T-shirt says.

icarus

The king needed a place to cage a beast. The beast was the queen's son, a love child made with someone who was not the king. The king wanted to hide the child, banish him, lock him away, so he hired an artist to build a labyrinth deep underground, beneath the king's court. The king would trap the beast.

When the maze was finished, the king didn't want the artist to tell anyone how to escape—especially not the beast—so he imprisoned the artist and the artist's son in a high tower. The artist understood his imprisonment as deserved punishment. He'd built a cage for someone else's child.

To pass the time, the artist and his son studied clouds. They learned the names of constellations. They kept time by the waxing and waning of the moon. And they watched birds. Great flocks. Murmurations. Migrations. Sparrows and herons, finches and gulls, bluebirds and meadowlarks, peregrines and golden-crowned kinglets, ruby-throated hummingbirds and cedar waxwings, robins and bald eagles and tanagers. The artist and his son fed the birds from their hands. They learned their songs. Soon the birds grew to love the artist and his son. The birds landed on their shoulders and left feathers on the windowsill, day after day after day.

The artist collected the feathers, and inside that tower, he dreamed and drew, imagined and drafted. He built two elaborate sets of wings with those feathers, glued them together. The father and son stood on their beds to practice, flapping their winged arms, lifting their knees to their chests as they skimmed the floor.

The artist watched the winds, measured their speed. He knew which cloud formations signaled lift, knew when each dark rock outcropping on the cliffs along the edge of the water warmed the air. When the conditions were right, they stood on the window ledge. The artist reminded his son not to fly too close to the sun, for fear the wax would melt, and not to fly too close to the water, for fear the salt would render the feathers useless. Then, they leapt.

XI

NO OTHER WAY

first visit

I answered my phone and the voice on the other end said, "What time should I pick up your foster child tomorrow?"

"What?" I asked.

"For the visit," she said.

"Who is this?"

"I'm an intern at the department," she said. "They told me to pick up the baby and drive her to Twin Falls to visit the mother."

"No one told me about this," I said. "And I'm not putting a weeks-old infant in a car with someone I don't know."

"Someone was supposed to call you," she said.

"No one did," I said.

"I guess you should call your social worker," she said.

I called Camilla. "No one told you?" she said.

"No one told me," I said and then explained I didn't think it was a good idea to have an infant—barely a month old—driven in a car for nearly two hours each way with a stranger. "I'll drive Coco myself," I said.

"If you want to drive her, that's up to you," Camilla said.

Before we were certified as foster parents, we'd been told by social worker after social worker that the future foster child in our care would have regular visits with their biological parents, if and when those visits were determined to be safe for the child. They might take place in your home or at a therapist's office or in a restaurant or in a park, social workers told us. You need to prepare your foster child for the visit, tell her what to expect, what will happen, try to ease her fear, they advised. You should say something like: *You can hug your mom if you'd like to and then you'll play for an hour and then I'll take you back to our house again.* Make sure to leave time for whatever emotions arise at the end of the visit, the social workers warned. You might need to sit in the backseat with the child. You might need to let him cry all the way home. You might need to give her a pillow to punch. Use the visits to learn as much as you can about the child in your care. Take photos, which you can put in a frame and place in the child's room. Ask the biological parents questions about their child. What is her favorite movie? Favorite food? Favorite book? What is his bedtime routine? Ask the parents to tell you stories from the child's life before you were on the scene.

"Here's an example," one social worker said, the woman who had adopted eight of her ten children. "One of our kids has a scar on her face, and I wanted to know how she'd gotten it, so I asked her bio mom. It turns out she got that scar when her brother hit her with a sledgehammer and she went through a glass door." The social worker laughed. "You see? You can find out good stuff like that."

How do you prepare an infant for a visit with her biological mother? Coco still kept her eyes closed most of the time, held her limbs close. She slept with her right arm alongside her ear, and even asleep, she smiled. She rarely cried, though she sometimes squeaked, the gentlest, smallest sound, making us laugh every time. I spent hours on the couch with her tiny body on my chest, all five pounds of her, her head on my heart, her diapered bottom in the air, her body curled into the shape of a bean, which is one of the many names we called her. *Bean, Butterbean, Squeaks, Frog.*

The day after the phone call, I drove Coco to Twin Falls to be with Evelyn at the department offices. I sang to her on the drive. She slept most of the way.

While Coco slept, I thought about how we'd been told that our relationship with the biological parent is just as important as our relationship with the child. One of the social workers told us to remember that every parent wants to be the best possible parent, even if it doesn't always look like that's what they're doing. "For example," the facilitator said, "we worked with a parent who often did meth, who was addicted to meth, but she smoked it while she held her child on her lap, and in this mother's mind, she was being a good parent because instead of leaving the child at home alone while she went out and got wasted, she did her drugs at home, keeping her child close, making sure she was safe."

"I'd rather be beaten than have meth blown in my face," one of the students in the class said.

Another social worker led us through an exercise during which she asked us to brainstorm the emotions a child taken out of his home and placed in a foster home might be feeling. She wrote words on a poster at the front of the classroom as we shouted them: *fear, confusion, shame, guilt, relief, anger.*

"That new foster child will be thinking, 'You're the one who took me from my mother's house,'" she said. "They won't be thinking, 'You're the one who saved me from abuse.' Remember: A child wants their mother to be different, but that doesn't mean they want a different mother."

She put a second piece of poster paper on the white board. "Now let's imagine the emotions the biological parent will be feeling," she said. "What might it feel like to have your child taken from you and given to people you don't know?" Again, she wrote down the words we said.

She put the posters side by side so we could compare them. "What do you notice about these two lists?" she asked.

"They're basically the same," Dan said. Dan was a long-haul trucker who dressed in camouflage from head to toe, and my favorite person in the class. He and his wife were getting certified as foster parents because Dan's friend had asked him to take care of his child because he was in no shape to parent. "I'll crawl through broken glass to help anyone who needs it," Dan said. "Once."

"These biological parents love their children," the social worker said. "We have to remember it's possible to love somebody completely and still not do the right thing."

"If you can't love the children's biological parents," she added, "then the children will think you can't love them, either."

I parked in the lot in front of the DHW offices. The visitation room was behind locked doors, the visit supervised by someone from the department because it had been determined it was not safe to leave Coco alone with her mother.

let's make today amazing

A woman named Fiona called to schedule Coco's next visit with Evelyn. "I've been told it's not safe to bring her to your house because she probably shouldn't know where you live," she said. "So where should we meet?"

I remembered a bank that had just been built at the south end of town with meeting rooms they let people use for free. Fiona called the bank and reserved a room. She texted to tell me to meet there at our agreed-upon time.

I brought everything I thought Coco might need during the visit—diapers, wipes, bottles, formula, pacifier, blankets, lovies—and was ready to tell Evelyn everything I thought she needed to know about Coco for the ninety minutes she'd get to spend with her—how long it had been since she'd eaten, how much formula to feed her, when she might need a change of clothes, what her different sounds meant. I wanted to show my fitness, my expertise. I wanted to assure Evelyn that Coco was being well taken care of. But Evelyn didn't ask any questions, didn't want to know a single thing.

"All of a sudden she has eyelashes," I said. One day they were barely there. The next day they were long and curled, delicate against her nearly translucent cheek. "She ate about half an hour ago," I added.

"This isn't my first baby," she said.

"She's probably sleepy," I said.

"Her fingernails are too long," she said. "You need to cut them."

"I'm scared to cut them," I said.

"Then you should bite them," she said. "That's what I always did."

The bank became our usual meeting place. I'd park, then

carry Coco in her car seat inside and hand her to Evelyn. Several bankers sat in the open central area of the building and watched us, trying to figure out what was happening, who was who. That Evelyn loved Coco was clear—she was tender, gentle, and spent most of the time she had with Coco holding her. But Evelyn also did what she wanted to do with Coco, not necessarily what Coco needed her to do. Coco's needs—for sleep, for food, for play—were secondary to Evelyn's need to express her love, her desire to mother. I'd tell Evelyn that Coco had just had two ounces of formula, and Evelyn would feed her again anyway, and sometimes Coco would throw up because she'd been given too much to eat.

"This is hard," I said to one of the women at the bank on my way out.

"I know, honey," she said.

Evelyn looked different every time I saw her. One day she'd look put together—newly dyed and straightened hair, a shirt that read LET'S MAKE TODAY AMAZING, high-heeled boots, a leather jacket—and the next time I'd see her, sometimes the very next day, she'd be wearing baggy sweatpants with holes in them, an even baggier sweatshirt, and a jacket that was ten sizes too big, her hair uncombed, her face exhausted. On those days, right after I'd load Coco back into my car, she'd sit on the curb and smoke Marlboro Reds.

When Evelyn looked good, I thought, *We'll have to give Coco back.*

When Evelyn looked bad, I thought, *We'll get to keep her.*

"You need to detach," Juliana said. "This is going to go on for a long time."

my heart

A friend gave me the name of a woman who might be available to help take care of Coco for a few days a week while Eric and I worked. I called her references—all positive, glowing—and then invited her to our house for an interview and to meet Coco.

I knew Claudia was the one when she held Coco. She cradled her, put her cheek to Coco's cheek. She had three children. The youngest was two, and he was very social, she explained, and needed to be around other kids during the day. She'd just signed him up for daycare, so she now had time and was ready to go back to work.

We offered her the job, but we had to explain the situation—how Coco was our foster daughter, how we might have her for years, for forever, or she might be reunified with her biological mother in a few weeks or a few months.

"I would like to be with her for as long as she's with you," she said.

Claudia brought light to our house, joy. "Good morning," Claudia would sing when she came through the front door. Eric or I would be playing with Coco on the floor or feeding her a bottle, and Coco would stop whatever she was doing and look for that voice. When she saw Claudia, she'd open her mouth wide, swing her feet, bounce up and down, wiggle her body. Claudia would pick her up, and Coco would put her open mouth on Claudia's cheek—a kiss—the only person Coco did that with.

Claudia taught us how to take care of Coco. How to swaddle her with a blanket. How to dress her. How to put her down for a nap. How to use tiny rubber bands to put tiny pigtails on top of her head. How to feed her solid food. How to get her to fall asleep for naps, for bedtime. How to let her have time alone when she woke up in the morning—to play, to explore, to learn to be happy by herself.

Sometimes I'd be in the kitchen pouring a cup of coffee or making myself lunch, and through the monitor I'd hear Claudia talking to Coco. "My love, my love, my love," she said. "My heart, my heart, my heart."

how to pass the time

I was not allowed to be present during Coco's visits with Evelyn, so I experimented with what to do during that time away from her, which felt like a rehearsal for our future separation. I read. Meditated. Grocery shopped. Wrote thank-you notes. Ran errands.

During one of Coco's visits, I drove to the town just north of Hailey to look for long-sleeved onesies. I arrived at the baby clothes shop at ten-thirty, but the sign on the door said they didn't open until eleven. The store owner saw me outside and waved me in. "Come in, come in," she said as she unlocked the door. "I'm here."

She asked if I was shopping for anything in particular. "Long-sleeved onesies," I said. "Zero to three months."

"Is it for your baby?" she asked.

"Yes," I said. "Actually, our foster daughter."

She put her hand to her heart. "I was raised by a foster mother," she said.

"You were?" I asked.

"Yes," she said.

"For how long?"

"My whole life," she said. "I loved my foster mother. I loved my family. My biological parents didn't want me, and I'm so glad they didn't want me, because I had the most wonderful life."

space place

At the last minute we were told there would be a Family Group Decision Meeting and that Eric and I should attend and bring Coco. The meeting gave Evelyn an opportunity to have a voice in developing her own case plan—the plan she'd need to complete to be reunified with Coco. The Family Group Decision Meeting was in Twin Falls on a weekday, a workday, so Eric and I rearranged our schedules. Since we were already taking Coco to Twin, our social worker scheduled a visit for Evelyn and Coco there before the meeting, saving Evelyn a drive to Hailey later in the week.

Fiona texted to tell me she was double-booked that morning, so there would be a different supervisor in a different room near the department's offices called *space place*. I thought the name was a typo. I thought she meant *safe place*.

Where is the room located? I texted.

Left side of front of building last door, she texted.

When Eric and I arrived at the department's offices *left side of front of building last door* made no sense. I entered the building and walked to the left to the last door, which brought me to the social workers' offices, where Coco had her first visit with Evelyn. I stood at the receptionist's desk for a few minutes while she ignored me.

"Can you tell me where a room called safe place is?" I asked, but she continued to act like I wasn't there. In the waiting room was a woman who looked like she'd been crying.

"I'm looking for safe place," I said.

She didn't respond.

"Or maybe it's called space place?"

"Why?" the receptionist said.

"Fiona told me I was supposed to meet my foster daughter's bio mom in space place, but I can't find it."

The receptionist pointed to the woman in the waiting room. "There's your bio mom," she said.

"That's not my bio mom," I said.

"Yes, it is," she said. "There's your bio mom."

"I've met our foster daughter's bio mom several times, and that woman is not her bio mom," I said.

"Yes, she is," she said, her voice louder. "There's your bio mom right there."

"I'm sorry," I said, "but she is not my bio mom." The woman was Latina. Evelyn is White.

"Yes, she is," she said. "She's waiting for a visit with her child with Fiona; you're waiting for a visit with your bio mom with Fiona. That's your bio mom."

I made eye contact with the woman in the waiting room. We both rolled our eyes like, *Can you fucking believe this shit?*

"That is not my child's foster mom," the woman said.

At that moment a side door opened and Fiona came out, holding this mother's son, who was three or four, and the woman went through the door and hugged her child for a long time.

"Can you please tell me where space place is?" I asked the receptionist.

"Go outside," she said. "Walk all the way around the building, and there will be a locked door. Wait there."

Eric drove the car around the building to a back parking lot and a door with no label on it. We stood outside holding Coco in her car seat. A woman opened the door, Evelyn just behind her. We carried the baby through what looked to be a storage area and into a small room that was filled with furniture, two couches, several chairs, all mismatched, seemingly abandoned, waiting for the dump. I handed Coco to Evelyn.

"See you in an hour," I said.

"It's never long enough," Evelyn said.

recovered their own habitat

The wild inhabitants of damaged lands show humans how to heal them.

In March 2018, a fire set on Santa Cruz, one of Southern California's Channel Islands, burned 260 acres of invasive fennel, but then the out-of-control fire scorched scrub oaks. Scientists had noticed that when the islands' scrub jay populations increased, the scrub oaks increased, too. Could they induce the jays to help replace those burned trees?

Scrub jays are "scatter hoarders," storing thousands more acorns than they will ever eat. Scientists loaded platforms with scrub oak acorns, and the jays came. The birds carried the seeds in their beaks, winged them away, then buried the seeds in the ground. The jays gardened; they recovered their own habitat. When the scientists returned months later, there were green shoots in that burned land. "Our children," they called the baby oaks.

idaho joe's

We retrieved Coco from space place an hour after we'd dropped
her off and drove to Idaho Joe's for the Family Group Decision
Meeting. Idaho Joe's is a restaurant, so when we walked in, the
hostess said, "Three for lunch?"

"No," I said. "We're here for a foster care thing?"

"It's in the back," she said.

At the back of the restaurant, we found a door to the rest-
rooms and a door to the kitchen. The only other door was labeled EXIT, but we opened it and entered a small room with
tables arranged in a U, a hamburger and fries in a see-through
plastic box at every seat. A waiter brought a high chair and
turned it upside down so we could rest Coco's car seat on it.

Evelyn was sitting at the table with her friend June. Two
CASA workers, Alejandra and Carrie, also sat at the table, along
with our first social worker, Grace, and our second social
worker, Camilla, and Evelyn's counselor.

At the center of the U were a screen and a projector with a
loud fan. Once everyone was seated, the facilitator explained
that the goal of the meeting was to work together to develop a
case plan to support a safe and stable home environment for
Coco. The gathering was designed to allow Evelyn to name her
problems and to determine what the solutions would be, to give
her some agency. What we decided in that meeting would become part of the case plan that would be finalized by the judge.
It would be a list of the things Evelyn had to do to get Coco
back.

"Let's go around the table," the facilitator said, "and everyone will say something they like about Evelyn, something she's
good at."

Evelyn went first. "I'm a good mom," she said. "I'm proac-
tive."

"She's loving to Coco," I said when it was my turn. "And she's really good at putting her in the car seat."

"I don't know what to make of the fact that you fled one state to run away to another," Grace said when it was her turn. "Were you trying to hide? Were you trying to escape? Were you trying to get well? I don't know. But taking that long drive the day before you gave birth to try to make a different life means you must be pretty strong."

Evelyn cried when the people around the table spoke about her. She rocked back and forth.

When we were done, the facilitator projected a document on the screen. "We forgot to print this for you," she said, "so you'll have to look at it on the screen." The print was small, the focus blurry. *Assault charges*, I read. *Anger management*.

Then we looked at Evelyn's family tree, a box of text for every member of her family, listing addictions and prison time, listing causes of death and histories of violence. "This is the one page of the packet you're not allowed to keep," the facilitator said. The family tree was incomplete, blank spaces where information should be, because Evelyn didn't know some of her family members' last names or how to spell them, didn't know their birth dates or when they'd died or where they lived.

I'd imagined foster care as somehow ethically cleaner than private adoptions or fertility treatments, but it became more complicated, and I became more complicit, by the day. Children taken from parents who want them. Children taken from parents who struggle with addiction. Children taken from parents who are poor. Children taken from parents who abused them because their parents abused them, and their parents, and their parents, and on and on and on. "There's no innocent space," my professor would say when I was in graduate school. "Nowhere to stand but right here."

"Now is the time of the gathering when we list what your

challenges are, our areas of concern," the facilitator said to Evelyn, and the people in the room created a list, and it was long.

"Now is the 'what if' part of the plan," the facilitator said. "If, for any reason, reunification isn't possible, where would you like Coco to live?"

"It's called Plan B," Grace said.

"I don't see that you would fail," Camilla said, "but this is planning we do just in case."

"June," Evelyn said. "She'd live with June."

The facilitator announced that there would be a break and that everyone would leave the room except for Evelyn and anyone she wanted to stay with her. This was Evelyn's chance to determine what she needed to do to get Coco back. Evelyn asked everyone to leave except for June, but when I got up to leave the room, she said, "You can stay, Sarah."

"Thank you," I said.

"Go figure out how we become Plan B," I whispered in Eric's ear as he stood to leave.

"Fill out this roadmap," the facilitator said and handed Evelyn a piece of paper that was mostly black. It seemed there used to be a road that curved through the paper, and at each bend of the road, Evelyn was supposed to write a challenge and how she planned to address the challenge, but the quality of the copied page was so bad it was impossible to figure out what to write where.

"Give me the paper," June said. "I know what to do."

Challenge: *No housing.* Solution: *Housing.*

Challenge: *No car.* Solution: *Car.*

Challenge: *Mental health.* Solution: *Counseling.*

"They want you to go to AA or NA," June said. "But that's not a good idea. What if you meet your next hookup there?"

While we waited for people to return from the break, June said, "I'm going to ask if we can keep the baby for Thanksgiving, take her on a trip to see my family. I'll also ask if I can do the supervised visits instead of a social worker."

When everyone was back in the room, the social workers talked about what Evelyn needed to do to regain custody of Coco. They started most of their sentences with *When Coco comes home,* or *When Coco returns to her mother,* or *When Evelyn gets her daughter back.* I sat on my hands. I bit my cheek. I put the tip of my tongue on the roof of my mouth, which I'd read somewhere was a way to keep from crying.

bridge

Though grafting most often brings two different plants together as one, it can also be used to allow a tree to repair itself. When trees are harmed by cars or lawnmowers or rodents or cold temperatures or disease, it takes years for the tree's wood to close over the injury. A large break in the bark interrupts the tree's ability to transport food from its root system to its leaves, sometimes causing the tree to die. Bridge grafts help support the broken pipeline, allowing water and nutrients to move across the damaged areas, saving the wounded tree. Bridges are most often made from the injured tree's own new growth.

glitter and unicorns

In the car in the parking lot of Idaho Joe's, I texted Camilla. *Can you call us when you have time, please?*

While we waited for her call, Eric and I made a list of questions to ask her.

"I'm rooting for Evelyn to relapse," I told Eric. "I'm rooting for her to fall in love and run away again. Does that make me a terrible person?"

Camilla called, and we asked our questions, and she answered them.

"What's the timeframe?" I asked. "If Evelyn can complete her case plan, when would Coco be returned to her?"

"Look," Camilla said. "If everything is all glitter and unicorns, if it all goes perfectly, according to plan, it will take nine months. That's the quickest timeframe possible. I'm going to go slow. She's a baby. I'm not going to take any risks with a baby. I'm not going to let a baby die or get hurt on my watch."

"We were told that if Coco is in our care for fifteen of twenty-two months, then we get to keep her," I said. "Is that right?"

"Yes," she said. "And even if Evelyn relapses, the clock will keep ticking."

"Do you think Evelyn will be able to do what's being asked of her?"

"No," Camilla said. "Honestly, I don't."

pull it together

Coco loved taking baths. One of my mother's friends sent us a bag of sea-themed bath toys—octopus, oyster shell, crab, turtle, dolphin, whale—and in the tub Coco chewed on the toys, held her hands in the stream of water I poured from a cup, spread her feet against the sides of the baby bathtub to make them squeak, splashed, laughed, babbled.

If we got to keep Coco, would the keeping ever feel clean?

I couldn't stop thinking about having to give her back to Evelyn, couldn't stop picturing people coming to my door, making me hand her over, watching them drive her away. We'd been told from the beginning that the goal was reunification, and now I could see that everything was designed to support Evelyn, to protect her rights, to make sure the state would not be sued for stealing someone's child. The process was not child-centered. It was biological-family-centered. It was get-this-case-off-your-desk-centered. It wasn't about Coco at all.

"I've never seen you like this," Eric said. I was leaning over the kitchen island, my cheek resting on the butcher block countertop. "I'm worried about you."

He was right to be worried. I didn't know how I would survive this. I didn't know if I wanted to survive.

I called Juliana.

"You don't have to keep doing this," she said.

"I know," I said.

"You can stop at any time," she said.

"I know," I said.

"Do you want to keep doing this?" she asked.

"Yes," I said.

"Then you have to pull it together for your child," she said.

another court date

I didn't bring Coco to court, and when Evelyn saw I didn't have the baby with me, she had no interest in me. She sat a few benches away. I watched Evelyn's lawyer talk to her.

"Who are you?" her lawyer asked, flipping through a stack of papers and manila folders. "Emily?"

"Evelyn," Evelyn said.

The lawyer apologized, and Evelyn's response was generous. "I know you have a lot of cases," she said. "It's okay."

Evelyn talked with Alejandra, the CASA representative assigned to Coco.

"How's it going?" I heard Alejandra ask her. "Want to ask for unsupervised visits?"

"Yes," Evelyn said.

"I'll ask Camilla," Alejandra said.

The woman who'd first pointed Camilla out to me, the woman who'd shot out of the courtroom like a flame, like a rocket, sat across from me, her blond hair now dyed black. The bailiff called her name first, and she marched down the hall in her black high-heeled boots, the hallway becoming her runway, our bodies lined along the benches, along the floor, her audience.

I ate a chocolate-covered granola bar and pieces of chocolate fell on my white pants and when I tried to brush them off I made the stain worse. One of the biological mothers—the mother of the young girl who hid in her grandmother's skirt—passed the time by writing down birthdays in her calendar.

"When is Uncle Joe's birthday?" she asked her mother.

"He was a day late for Valentine's Day," her mother said.

"February 13?" the girl asked.

"A day *late*," her mother shouted.

"How about my brother's birthday?" the girl asked.

"Your brother's is the day after your father's," her mother yelled, which wasn't useful to the girl at all.

I looked away. I was afraid of those lost dates, of what it's possible to forget, the threads that connect us so thin that any sharp object (a needle, a knife, a piece of paper) can sever them. I hadn't known that in this age of social media it was still possible to lose someone.

Months before, I'd heard an art historian say that failed perspective in medieval paintings—the fact that the world in those paintings looks flat—was a form of prayer. I didn't know what she meant, didn't know if the prayer was for the viewer or for the artist, and I had no idea what an answer to that kind of prayer might be. But I liked the idea that painting a collapsed world could be an invocation, a plea. In such images, instead of size revealing distance—what is closest to you is biggest, what is farthest from you is smallest—size was based on importance, on holiness. Hierarchical proportion: sacred figures are large; human beings are small. Time was irrelevant. God was not bound by time, so events from different eras could be shown side by side. Realism was not the goal. Human experience didn't matter. Only religious experience did. The settings were flattened to remind viewers that the paintings were otherworldly.

The world of that courtroom was flat too. In the hallway, I understood it was possible to fall off the edge of it.

the hero

Idaho loses foster parents at a rate faster than they can train and certify new ones. "Most of our foster parents stop being foster parents after only one placement. They take care of those first foster kids and realize foster care isn't anything like they imagined it would be, and they quit," a social worker said during one of our training sessions, and I remembered a story I'd read that goes something like this: One day, a kindly man came upon an injured bird. The man saved the bird's life, and to thank him, the bird gave the man a seed to plant. The man planted the seed, watered it, and the seed grew into a plant bearing cucumbers that were filled with gold and silver. A neighbor, watching the man harvest the cucumbers, this windfall of riches, decided to save a bird too. But he couldn't find an injured bird, so he injured a bird so he could nurse it back to health. The bird he'd injured and then nursed back to health offered him thanks and a seed. And the neighbor planted it, but his cucumber plant grew so tall it reached the moon. Thrilled, the man who'd injured the bird climbed up the plant to the moon to seek his reward of gold and silver. But when he reached the moon, the plant vanished, stranding him there forever.

not worth more

"I've never been worried about you like this," Eric said nearly every day. "You have to promise to tell me what you're feeling."

"I want to die," I said.

"Do you mean you're suicidal?"

"No," I said. "I'm afraid I'll die if we have to give her back."

I called Juliana. I was crying so hard I could barely talk. "I want to keep her," I said. "I think I'll die if I have to let her go."

"I need you to listen to me. You're not going to like what I'm about to say," she said. "The best and most enlightened thing to do is to be hoping and wishing and praying that Evelyn gets her shit together to get Coco back."

I had not been hoping and wishing and praying that Evelyn would get her shit together. I had been hoping and wishing and praying she would disappear. I had been hoping and wishing and praying she'd relapse, hoping and wishing and praying she'd flip her truck.

"She is exhibiting the desire to raise this child, to change her life," Juliana said. "We have to root for that. If we don't root for that, we'll be doing harm to another person. And we can't do harm to another person to get what we want. That's not who we are."

"But what if it is who I am?" I asked.

She reminded me Evelyn had had a difficult life. "We can't wish her more ill," she said.

I couldn't speak.

"There is no other way," she said.

I still couldn't speak.

"Your life is not worth more than her life," she said.

But that was exactly what I'd been thinking. I'd been judging her for her addiction, for her multiple kids with multiple men in prison, for having other children taken away.

"You have to take the high road, or you will perish," Juliana said. "You need to radically shift your thinking. You need to stop rooting against her and start cheering for her, for this human who has suffered so much. Then, if she makes it, if she gets her child back, you will walk away clean. Will you be sad? Yes. But you won't be sad and mean."

"I'm paying you for this?" I asked.

"Our goal is right human relations," she said.

"What if I can't do it?" I asked.

"Think about it this way," Juliana said. "If you get to keep Coco, someday in the future she will ask you about her biological mother, and you will have to be able to look her in the eye and say these words, and they will have to be true: *Coco, I was so in love with you, and I was so rooting for your mom. She was beautiful and kind and caring and nurturing toward you. She tried and did her best.* Those are the words you will want to say. You won't want to have to say to your daughter, *I wanted to keep you so badly that I wished harm on your mother.*"

I knew she was right, but I still couldn't speak.

"You need to be the person Coco thought you were when she chose you," she said. "This child might save Evelyn's life, and you don't need your life saved."

XII

A TALE OF TWO MOTHERS

pink

On nights before Coco's scheduled visits with Evelyn, I bathed Coco, imagined what I'd be looking for if someone else were taking care of my child: clean bib, clean diaper, fresh diaper cream, short fingernails, warm hat, soft blanket, toys. I sent her to visit Evelyn wearing gray or yellow-and-white-striped or blue onesies that matched her eyes. Most of the baby clothes we have are from friends or relatives, inherited from nephew after nephew after nephew. But no matter how I dressed Coco, Evelyn sent her back to me in pink. Pink hat. Pink shirt. Pink onesie. Pink pants. Pink jumper. Pink hoodie. A proxy war, both of us marking her body, that small territory, *mine mine mine.*

I LOVE MOMMY, her onesie said when I undressed her at home after a visit.

Sometimes Evelyn would bring bags of clothing—a duffel or a trash bag—and in the parking lot of the bank, she would hand me the bag and I would hand her the baby, a suspicious exchange for the security cameras. "I'll have to change her every hour of every day for her to wear all these clothes," I said and laughed as I lugged the bags to my car.

Evelyn did not laugh. "If you don't use them now," she said, "you can use them for the next baby you foster."

Next baby?

I stored the clothes in their own drawer in Coco's room. I said I did that so I'd remember what was from Evelyn in case she ever wanted it back, but the truth was I kept the clothes apart because it hurt my heart to see them, pink dresses and pants and shirts from another woman with a bigger claim on this baby than our claim, which, it turned out, was no claim at all.

wire mother, cloth mother

In the early twentieth century, government pamphlets used to warn parents not to touch their children, not to rock them or play with them or hold them too much. More than one kiss per year was too many, psychologists insisted. Love was "a dangerous instrument," a menace. Doctors had observed that the children most often held by nurses got more infections. "Don't pick up your child," they warned. But by the 1940s, healthcare workers in hospitals and orphanages realized that children who were never picked up, who were never loved, withered and died. But the field of psychology ignored them—until Harry Harlow did his experiments with rhesus monkeys.

In the 1950s, Harlow, a psychologist, wanted to prove love makes a vital difference, to prove infants need more than just food to thrive. He took infant monkeys away from their mothers immediately after birth. He kept the baby monkeys isolated in cages. Then he provided each infant with two substitute mothers, one made of wire and the other made of cloth.

I imagined the substitute mothers enormous, gorilla-sized, but when I looked at photographs of his experiments, I saw the mothers were small, nearly the same size as the infants. A cylinder of wire formed one mother, her head a white rectangle, like a robot's head in a child's drawing. A triangle of terrycloth formed the other mother, her head round, a smile on her face.

The wire mother had milk, a bottle inserted below her head. According to previous theories, it was food that bonded babies to their mothers, and if that were the case, the infant monkey should spend most of his time with the wire mother. But in Harlow's experiment, the baby spent less than an hour a day with the wire mother and spent seventeen to eighteen hours a day on the cloth mother. The infant cuddled with her and ran to her when he was scared. With the cloth mother near, he was confident and secure.

I watched a video of Harlow's experiments, listened to him explain his work to another man in his laboratory. "Here is Baby 106," Harlow says. "Watch." He lifts the door at the front of a cage—one cage in a room full of cages—and the infant monkey runs through the opening and to the two surrogate mothers, who are side by side in a cage of their own. He sucks on the nipple of the bottle attached to the wire mother. "Got to eat to live," Harlow says. Then the infant sits in the lap of the cloth mother, keeping one arm wrapped around his own body, close to his chest. He looks around the room, eyes wide, tense. He returns to the wire mother, drinks more milk, then jumps back to the cloth mother, rocking, sucking his thumb.

"But is this really love?" the man in the video asks Harlow.

"What do you mean by saying a baby loves its mother?" Harlow asks. "If you had a baby who was frightened and then ran to his mother and all that fear dissipated, if you watched that, wouldn't you say that baby loves its mother?"

Harlow opens another box, and inside is a robot he designed to frighten the baby monkeys. It makes loud noises and has huge eyes and big teeth and a mouth that opens and closes.

Harlow shows the man a peaceful baby monkey inside a small cage he shares with the wire mother and the cloth mother. Harlow places the scary robot at the opening of the cage and opens the door. The baby monkey shrieks and cries and runs to the cloth mother. He clings to her.

"He's scared all right," the man in the video says. "He's running away."

"It's more than running away," Harlow says. "He's running to his mother."

The camera pans out, and I can see the laboratory where Harlow does his experiments, how big it is, how many cages there are. I can see that this experiment, designed to show the importance of nurture and the power of love, is a torture chamber.

nights

Coco slept in a bassinet next to our bed. Eric and I took turns, alternated who got to put in earplugs and sleep and who got to wake up to feed the baby, and we dragged the bassinet from one side of the bed to the other depending on whose night it was.

When it was my turn, I walked downstairs, holding the handrail with one hand and her tiny body with the other. Sometimes the moon shone through an upstairs window, and I paused and held her in that glow. "Moonlight," I whispered. I fed her bottles of warmed formula, held her against my chest to burp her, held her against my heart. I loved that time with her, the two of us awake and everyone else asleep.

But my fear of losing Coco was greatest during those feedings every two or three or four hours in the dark.

"That time of night is hard for all mothers," Juliana said when I told her about my racing mind, my fear we'd lose Coco. "You need a mantra," she said. "Imagine it tattooed on your body."

This is a gift, I imagined tattooed in black letters on my arms, on my shoulder blades.

Thank you thank you thank you, I said when I felt afraid.

really connected

I brought some art to a frame store recommended by a friend. I had Coco with me, and the woman behind the counter admired her, and when I said, "She's my foster daughter," she asked, "Are you Sarah?"

We live in a small town, and she's good friends with another good friend of mine, and it turned out she and her husband built the house where Eric and I now live. She asked questions about foster care, and when they heard my answers, the other people who'd been busy building frames came from the back of the store to see the baby, and they asked questions, too, about the biological mother, about Coco, about whether we'll get to keep her, and in response I said the line I'd practiced with Juliana: "We're rooting for the bio mom, and we're rooting that we get to keep her." And they cried, and I cried, and Coco cooed and laughed.

Her laughter was new. Now when we made funny sounds or showed her high-contrast black-and-white drawings or the cats' tails tickled her face, she'd open her mouth wide and laugh, turning her head from side to side, waving her arms. Her eyes were open for more hours at a time, and they were three kinds of blue—slate and indigo and navy. When I fed her, we'd stare into each other's eyes, and I'd feel that she could see me, but then, in the doctor's office, I looked at a chart that showed what babies are able to see, month by month by month, and I learned that what she could see when she looked at me was a black square.

The bell above the door rang, and another woman entered the frame shop. "The baby whisperer!" the frame store owner said. And the baby whisperer asked to hold Coco and offered to babysit. "She's really connected," the frame store owner said and pointed to the ceiling, which meant she was pointing to the sky, which meant she was pointing to God, but not in a way that weirded me out. "She'll put you on her prayer list," she said, "and it's a powerful one." I was glad to have her prayers. I wanted them in a way I hadn't wanted prayers since I'd left Christianity.

After the frame store, I went to the dry cleaner. The daughter of the woman who works at the front desk had died in a car accident a few months before. I'd happened to be at the dry cleaner on the woman's first day back to work after her daughter's death, and when I saw her I'd started to cry, though we barely knew each other. She'd taken me to the back room, and we'd talked about her daughter, how her daughter had called her from the road at the beginning of her drive home, what they'd talked about, what she wished she'd said. The next time I came in to the dry cleaner, I had Coco with me, and we talked about foster care and how I might have to give Coco back, and now she won't ever let me carry my own dry cleaning. She insists on walking with me, holding all that plastic-wrapped clothing, even when I'm parked blocks away.

This time, after the frame store, when I walked into the dry cleaner, she looked at Coco. "Is she yours to keep yet?" she asked. And I said that it would take time, maybe a year, that they give the bio mom a good chance to get her life together, and she said, "No. If I were the judge, I would say, You've had your chance, and I'd give that beautiful baby to you. You love her. I can see how much you love her." She rang the bell and yelled at someone in the back to come watch the front desk so she could walk with me.

Then I went to the grocery store to pick up a couple of things, toothpaste, olive oil. I was checking out in the express line, and I had Coco strapped to the front of me in her carrier, and the cashier said, "How old is your baby?"

"Three months," I said. "She's my foster daughter."

The cashier stopped pressing buttons. "I was raised in foster care," she said. "The good homes make all the difference."

We stood there, looking at each other, our eyes welling. The other people crowding the small grocery store at the lunch hour rush seemed to disappear.

store the images

After Coco had been living with us for three months, her visits with Evelyn were increased from one per week to two per week, ninety minutes each. Because of Evelyn's work schedule (nights) and her meetings and appointments (many), she was available only on Thursday afternoons and Friday mornings, so the two visits were held back to back. My work schedule and Eric's work schedule never mattered. As foster parents, we worked for the state, we were reminded, and the expectation was that we would do whatever we could to make the visits possible. They could change the schedule at the last minute. We could not.

Evelyn still wasn't allowed to drive herself to the visits or to be alone with Coco. She was driven and supervised first by a social worker and then by two women (one on Thursday, the other on Friday) who worked for Northstar, a service that contracted with DHW for exactly this kind of thing.

One morning, Camilla texted me to see if I would be willing to supervise Coco's visit with Evelyn because no one else was available.

Is that a good idea? I texted.

There have been no concerns about how Evelyn handles the baby, she texted back.

I'm not worried about that, I texted. *I'm worried about the flight risk part.*

Just make sure you put yourself between her and the door, she texted.

I talked with Juliana about whether I should agree to supervise the visit. It seemed an odd role for me to play. I wanted Evelyn to trust me. I wanted her to know I was taking good care of her daughter. What would it do to our relationship for me to sit in a room with her and watch her, take notes, write some kind of report? What if she tried to run?

"Take a picture of her license plate," Juliana told me. "If she runs, you get to keep the baby. She's not going to run."

I'll do it, I texted Camilla.

"It will be good for you to watch Evelyn being loving with Coco. Store the images of the two of them together in your mind." Juliana said. "You might need to remember that tenderness."

even when the mother is not a real mother

To prove that a mother's love is essential, Harlow subjected infant monkeys to varying periods of motherlessness. Sometimes an infant taken from her biological mother would be given a surrogate cloth mother right away. Sometimes Harlow kept the infants alone for weeks or months. Sometimes he never provided them with surrogates at all and raised them in isolation. I watched a video of one of Harlow's infants who was never given a surrogate mother. He turned his back to the room. He rocked and rocked and rocked. He fell on the floor.

Attachment can occur even when the parent is not biological, Harlow argued. Even when the parent is a doll, a wire body wrapped in cloth, even when the mother is not a real mother. You can take a monkey away from his mother, and as long as you give him another mother within ninety days, he will turn out just fine.

To further make his point, Harlow turned the cloth mothers into abusive mothers. "Evil mothers," he called them. Spikes would shoot out of the mother's body when the infant climbed on her. Or the cloth mother would shake and shake and shake until the infant's "teeth and bones rattled in unison." Or a spring-loaded cloth mother would hurl the baby away.

But when the spikes retracted and the shaking and throwing stopped, the babies returned to the cloth mothers. The babies cooed and stroked and groomed and flirted. They did anything they could to make the mothers love them again.

became a dad

I went out of town for a long weekend with friends to visit hot springs, and before I left, Coco started to cough, her cheeks flushed.

"It's nothing," Eric said. "We'll be fine."

He wanted me to have fun and knew I wouldn't go if I thought Coco was sick.

But she was sick, and her cough grew worse, became barking, hoarse, and she had a fever. I was six hours away. Eric took her to the doctor. Croup. "It will sound worse than it is," the doctor told him.

But it sounded horrible. Eric soothed Coco, held her, rocked her, played with her, stayed up through the night because she couldn't sleep, listened to her cough, watched her eyes water, her fear, because she didn't understand why her body hurt, why her throat was raw. She was surprised by her pain, scared of her cough.

"She was suffering, on my watch, and I was helpless," he said. "There was nothing I could do, and everything I could do. I was her world."

Then the sickness was gone.

"It was like she was grateful," he said. "But really I was the one who was grateful."

When I came home, his attachment to her was different. They belonged to each other.

"I became a dad this weekend," Eric told me. "She became mine, and I became hers. She isn't just a 'baby' anymore. She's my daughter."

do no harm

Before Camilla visited our house, I made sure Coco's room was just right, her play mat, her mobile, her changing area and its stack of diapers, her crib, her bassinet. I heated water in the kettle in case Camilla wanted tea. I made sure we had cookies. But Camilla didn't want tea. And she didn't want cookies. And she didn't want to see Coco's room.

I thought it mattered whether she thought we were good parents. I thought I could influence what happened next, will it, manipulate, control. That's what I'd done my whole life. Muscled things through if they didn't go my way. Studied harder. Worked harder. Paid more. This is what my privilege allowed—my whiteness, my social class, my citizenship. That was the whole point of it. I could make the world work for me even as it failed others. But that meant nothing now. All the system cared about was that our house was not a meth house. We didn't hit the baby. We fed her. She had a place to sleep.

Camilla told us that to get Coco back, Evelyn had to work her program—test clean, attend parenting classes, attend meetings, attend counseling—and to meet minimal parenting standards. Not good parenting standards. Not great. Minimal. One step up from "do no harm."

"Look," Camilla said. "There are two boys in care now who are about to be returned to their biological mother. I know they'd be much better off with the foster parents who are taking care of them now, but we have to give them back. Legally that's what we're required to do. And there's nothing I can change about that."

A government agency with the power to take children away from their parents is dangerous. What is there to stop social workers from deciding parents are too poor or too Black or too gay or too political or too feminist or too atheist to be "good" parents? You don't want social workers who think they know what's best and "best" is what looks like them and talks like them and prays like them.

"Evelyn is doing everything we've asked her to do," Camilla said. "And it looks like her son will be coming to live with her soon."

"What?" I asked.

"In time for the holidays," she said. "He's coming home."

"That's in less than a month," Eric said.

"Yes," Camilla said. "And Coco is on track for reunification, too."

Coco was on Camilla's lap when she said this, bouncing on Camilla's knee, holding a rattle that glowed red then green then blue, putting it in her mouth. "Your brother," Camilla said to her.

During the most recent conversation I'd had with Camilla, just a couple of days before her visit, she'd told us how much Evelyn was struggling, how unlikely reunification was, how far away. Evelyn still needed to move out of June's house and find her own place to live, still needed to work her case plan in the state where her son lived, still needed to have a budget, maintain sobriety, manage her anger, complete a mental health evaluation. The road ahead was long, she'd told me.

"That's good news for Evelyn," I said. "She must be happy."

"Does she have a place to live?" Eric asked.

"Not yet," Camilla said. "But she's looking for one."

"Does she have childcare for Coco while she works nights?"

"No," Camilla said. "If you have a problem with this, you should talk with Alejandra. She's the only person who can override my recommendation for reunification."

Alejandra was the guardian ad litem from CASA. Her role was to advocate for Coco. She was the one person in the system assigned that task. Everyone else—the prosecutor, the social workers, the judge, the attorneys—is charged with protecting the biological mother's rights and keeping the state from being sued. But Alejandra had met Coco just once, at Idaho Joe's during the Family Group Decision Meeting. She'd never been to our house. She'd never attended Coco's visits with Evelyn. She hadn't even called us on the phone to talk about how things were going.

Camilla left, and Eric and I stood by the front door and cried.

break every bone

"I want to keep her," I cried to Juliana. "What can I do to keep her?"

"There is no fight here," she said. "Go limp or you will break every bone in your body."

a language they didn't speak

The day after Camilla told us the plan was to reunify Coco and Evelyn—unless Evelyn relapsed, unless she majorly fucked up—the Alliance of Idaho, the nonprofit I co-founded, hosted an event to support immigrants on their path to citizenship.

All morning I listened to stories about children entering swift rivers at the border, the water up to their necks, because their parents had crossed the border first and then sent for them, about children held in cells for hours and hours, without their parents, without lawyers, forced to sign documents they didn't understand, written in a language they didn't speak, about families separated at the border, about one parent being a citizen and the other being denied citizenship and returned to a country where she had not lived for decades, without her children, and then coming back to this country because she could not stand to be away from her kids.

In our front yard we have a FAMILIES BELONG TOGETHER sign, bright yellow with orange letters, visible from the street. "Don't you think you should take that sign down when social workers come to your house?" my dad asked.

what matters most

I found myself driving to and from Twin Falls all the time—for court or to use the vouchers DHW gave us to buy diapers and formula or to take Coco for a visit with Evelyn. I love the landscape along that highway, the big sky, the fields of sage, the hawks and vultures, love crossing the bridge and peering into the deep canyon to see the river. On the way home from one of these Twin trips, I spoke on the phone with my friend Jeanne, who was also driving home from Twin Falls. Her husband was dying, and she was returning from taking him to radiation treatments.

"I am facing the fact that I have no control over what matters most to me," she said.

my baby

How's my little princess? Evelyn texted me. *How's my perfect baby girl?*

cheesecake

I delayed becoming a mother in part because I was afraid I'd resent the time I spent with my child instead of writing or sleeping or reading or hiking, but I felt no resentment with Coco. I wanted our time together to go on and on. I loved her tiny hands, the way she folded them when she slept. I loved how she loved the black-and-white images we'd taped in our kitchen so she could look at them from her swing—the smiling sunflower, the woman's face, the carrot. I loved her smile, how wide she opened her mouth, how she showed her gums and turned her head to the left, lifting her shoulders. Eric and I did everything we could to make her smile like that all the time, which was easy, because she was a happy baby. She woke up giggling every morning and after every nap, her body wiggly, delighted.

"Is she a good baby?" strangers would ask me, and I wanted to know what they meant, how any baby could be "bad."

When I complained about the recurring question, my friend Erin joked, "You should answer, 'Nope, she's racist and sexist and voted for Trump,'" which made me laugh.

One afternoon, at the grocery store with Coco, I saw a mother with two young children working her way through the aisles. "Isn't it such a pain to shop with them?" she asked and rolled her eyes. I didn't respond.

I texted my friend Emily. *I fucking hate everyone.*

What happened? she texted back, and I told her about the complaining mother in the grocery store.

I feel like punching people, I texted.

I threw vitamins at someone in the grocery store once, she texted.

I knew my fears about Coco being returned to her biological mother were not the same as Emily having to watch her son Ronan dying for more than two years. But I needed her help, needed to know what to do, what to focus on, how to live through this. We scheduled a time to talk on the phone.

"Tend your marriage," she said.

Then she told me she tried to make every day she got to be with Ronan the best possible day for him. "He loved cheesecake," she said. "So sometimes I fed him cheesecake all day long."

if you get to stay

I took Coco outside. "Snow," I said and put her hand in the snow.

"Sun," I said and held her body in the sun.

"Wind," I said and turned her face toward the breeze and watched her blink.

I took her on a walk almost every day. I dressed her in a fluffy snowsuit, put spikes on my boots, and pushed her stroller along our icy streets. She smiled on our walks or slept or sucked on her pacifier with the small moose attached to it and looked at the sky.

"If you get to stay," I said, "you'll see the leaves return to the maple trees."

"If you get to stay," I said, "this will be the park where you will play."

"If you get to stay," I said, "we'll teach you to ride a bike, to ski, to climb, to paint."

"I want you to stay," I said.

"I love you," I said.

prayers answered in three and a half minutes

Camilla and the Northstar team that supervised the visits with Evelyn decided it wasn't fair to make Evelyn come all the way to Hailey from Twin Falls twice a week. They decided one visit would be in Hailey and the other would be in Shoshone—a thirty-minute drive from Twin Falls, a sixty-minute drive from Hailey. Eric and I were informed we'd need to drive Coco to Shoshone once a week, starting that very week.

Shoshone is a tiny town, population 1,502, and the only possible location for the visit was a diner on the main street that ran along the railroad tracks.

On Thursday, I drove Coco to Shoshone, carried her into the diner where Evelyn and the Northstar supervisor sat in a booth. There was no coffee shop, no library, no place for me to wait but the gas station, which, because it was run by Mormons, was very clean. I fixed myself a green tea at the drink station in the center of the gas station. "Fifty cents," the woman working the register said.

I sat and drank my tea and worked on my laptop in a booth at the gas station until it was time to retrieve Coco from the diner.

The next time I drove Coco to Shoshone for her visit with Evelyn, my friend Erin rode with me. Erin isn't the type who says, "I'm here if you need me" or "Let me know if there's anything you need." She says, "I'm coming to Shoshone with you, and there's nothing you can do about it." When Coco's visits with Evelyn were changed from one to two per week, Erin asked me about the schedule, then blocked out those times on her calendar, though she's a lawyer, a single mother, and busy. "I'm free to hike with you during those visits if that would help," she said.

While Coco spent time with Evelyn in the diner, Erin and I walked around the town. Across the railroad tracks from the diner was a bar. The year before, a woman was shot in that bar. She was meeting with her biological father for the first time in years. He'd placed her for adoption when she was a child, and when she asked him why he'd done that, they argued. The newspaper said he took out a gun and put it against his own head. He didn't think there were bullets in the gun, but there were, and somehow the gun went off, and instead of shooting himself, he shot his daughter and killed her.

"Let's check out the bowling alley," Erin said.

Near the entrance to the bowling alley were a stand of pamphlets and a box of religious magazines. I took a copy of the magazine, and we read it in the car while we waited for Coco's visit with Evelyn to end. "Cheese: Food or Poison?" the magazine asked. Another article assured readers there was definitive proof that prayers took exactly three and a half minutes to be answered by God. That was how long it took for a prayer to ascend to heaven, to be heard, and to have an answer flown back to you, by messenger or angel or word. "There is no loitering in heaven!"

At the end of ninety minutes, I walked into the diner to get Coco. Evelyn was alone in the booth with her, the supervisor nowhere to be seen, and Coco was crying. Then the supervisor appeared. "I love that moose toy you have on her car seat," she said to me. "We're expecting our nineteenth grandchild in January, so I just ordered one on Amazon."

Evelyn and I looked at each other—a mother fighting for the return of her child, a foster mother caring for someone else's child she wanted to keep. Coco was still crying. "I think she can feel me get tense when I know the visit is coming to an end," Evelyn said.

I carried Coco to the car, and when we started the drive home, she screamed louder than I'd ever heard her cry, so loud I pulled the car over, afraid she was in some kind of physical pain. I took her out of the car and walked her up and down a snowy street on the side of the highway until she fell asleep in my arms.

kiss

During our PRIDE classes, one of the facilitators said, "It's a good idea to ask for a photograph of the biological parent." Every night when she puts her foster children or her adopted children to bed, she has them kiss their biological mother's picture good night. "We keep that photograph in a frame on the night side table," she said. "'Give your mama a kiss,' I say. It's an important part of our bedtime routine."

My neighbor adopted her daughter, and when her daughter turned four, my neighbor showed her a photograph of her biological mother, something therapists advise adoptive parents to do. My neighbor printed several copies of the photograph. She laminated them so they could be handled, loved.

I never put a photograph of Evelyn in a frame, never laminated an image of her, never told Coco to give her mama a kiss.

I did take pictures of Evelyn holding Coco—in the bank meeting room, in the bank parking lot—and I texted them to her when the visits were over. I also texted her pictures of Coco sleeping or playing on her play mat or smiling in her bouncy seat or reaching for the cat's tail or chewing on a new toy or laughing in the sun. I worried that those pictures had some kind of power, that they could make Evelyn stay sober, remind her how amazing her daughter is, how she was worth fighting for, getting better for, how her hard work would soon pay off. I didn't want Evelyn to feel motivated. I wanted her to forget her love for Coco.

And sometimes I hoped the pictures had a different kind of power. I wanted them to show Evelyn how happy Coco was without her, how big her smile was, how well fed and well loved and well tended her baby was. "You can keep her," I imagined Evelyn saying.

real mother

Evelyn attended every one of Coco's doctor's appointments. Eric and I sat in chairs on the side of the room while the nurses let Evelyn weigh Coco, place her on the table in the hallway to be measured, hold her during vaccinations or temperature taking or oxygen level measuring. Evelyn only paid attention to Coco. She didn't listen to the doctor. She didn't ask any questions or take any notes. I always brought a list of questions— how to transition her from a bassinet to a crib, what to do about her rash, how long to keep swaddling her, how many ounces a day she should be drinking—and I took notes when the doctor or the nurse answered them, told us when to introduce Coco to peanut butter and egg yolks. But Evelyn looked only at Coco, listened only to Coco. Later, when I mentioned the peanut butter instructions or what the doctor said about the rash or the crib, Evelyn got mad. "You met with the doctor without me?" she asked again and again.

"Put her on the scale, Mama," one of the nurses said during a checkup, my favorite nurse, her arms covered in tattoos. She looked at me over Evelyn's head and mouthed, "I know you're the mama."

After the appointment was over, the doctor found me in the room buckling Coco into her car seat after Evelyn had already left. "How are you?" the doctor asked, and I cried, and she cried, and she told me she'd written a letter to the judge saying it was best for Coco to stay with us.

We had a doctor's appointment on New Year's Eve, Coco's four-month checkup. Whooping cough was in our valley, and signs all over the waiting room said not to take your baby out of their car seat in the waiting room, but Evelyn wanted to take Coco out of her car seat, wanted to hold her, and Eric told her not to because of whooping cough, pointed to the signs, and she glared at him.

During the visit with the doctor, my favorite nurse administered an oral vaccine and told us it tasted like grape. "First time to taste grape," the nurse said, and I told the nurse that Coco had tasted grape before because we had given her Tylenol once, but the Tylenol's grape flavor had surprised her, and Coco had thrown up all over me, down the inside of my sweater, into my bra. In the doctor's office, telling that story about grape flavoring, I said, "So then I said, 'Thanks, baby. You threw up all over your mama.'"

I knew my mistake right away.

"I mean foster mother," I said, my face hot, sweat blooming under my arms.

Evelyn looked at me like she would kill me if she could, and I remembered a story, a fable about two women, each insisting she is the true mother of one child. They cannot solve this on their own. They visit a judge. The judge pulls out a sword and suggests the child be cut in two—that way each woman can keep half of the child.

One woman thinks this is an excellent idea.

The other woman asks for the sword to be put away. "She can keep the child," she says to the judge, and the judge knows then which woman is the real mother.

steal her child

Soon after I called myself *mama* in the doctor's office, we had another court date. In the past, other people had been the fiery presences in that courtroom hallway, ready to ignite, but this time we were the ones on fire—Evelyn and Eric and me. We were the ones who might make the whole place explode.

Evelyn's son had not come to live with her during the holidays, and Camilla had called us a few days before the court date to let us know that it turned out Evelyn's son was probably never coming to live with her, that Evelyn had made the whole thing up, that in fact her parental rights to her son were about to be terminated, that Camilla was worried about Evelyn's mental health, that she planned to ask for a second mental health evaluation.

"I made a mistake in the doctor's office," I told Camilla.

"I heard about it," she said. "Evelyn called me seventeen times."

Before we were called into the courtroom, Camilla pulled Eric and me into a side room. She told us Evelyn had found a video of me being interviewed in Australia on book tour. In the interview I talk about wanting to adopt a child. This interview happened months before we brought Coco home, months before she was even born, but Evelyn was obsessed with it, Camilla said. Evelyn thought it proved we planned to steal her child.

"She made me watch the video," Camilla said.

Camilla told us she'd explained to Evelyn that yes, we wanted to adopt Coco, that the foster care system also included the possibility of adoption, but that whether we got to keep Coco was up to Evelyn. "But you need to know that you calling yourself *mama* really hurt her," Camilla told me. "Some foster parents call themselves mama and daddy, some even change the name of the foster child, call them something else entirely. I don't care what you do in private, but don't do it in front of Evelyn."

Back in the hallway, Eric and I looked for places to sit, but there weren't any left. Alejandra, the CASA representative, texted me and told us to find her in the room where the lawyers meet. "The prosecutor wants to talk to you," she texted.

We found the room and told Alejandra and the prosecutor what Camilla had told us—that Evelyn's parental rights to her son were about to be terminated in another state. We talked about signs of relapse, about her being a flight risk, about her mental health.

"Have you visited Evelyn in her home?" Eric asked Alejandra.

"Not yet," Alejandra said. "I drove by Evelyn's house four times yesterday, but she didn't answer the door."

"Did you call to let her know you were coming?" I asked.

"I don't even have her phone number," Alejandra said.

Weeks earlier Alejandra had told us she'd been trying to contact Evelyn, but that Evelyn wasn't returning her calls or texts. "That doesn't sound like her," we'd said. "Evelyn is very responsive."

"I thought you told us you'd been trying to call and text her, but she wouldn't respond," Eric said.

"I did?" Alejandra said.

"Yes," we said.

"I must have meant I was calling Camilla," she said.

Eric coughed.

"Which house did you go to?" I asked.

"Wherever she lives now," Alejandra said.

"Where does she live now?" I asked, and Alejandra ignored my question.

Evelyn sat in the hallway with three other women—a friend from work, her counselor, and June. They wouldn't look at us or acknowledge us.

The same people we saw every time filled the hallway. Among them was the woman with the long skirt and the girl hiding in her skirt, and they had a new baby with them. There were also two children I'd never seen before, a girl and a boy. The girl talked to her foster mother, who was sitting next to me. She asked the foster mother to sit with her at the other end of the hallway next to her bio mother.

"Not today," the foster mother said.

"My mama is saying bad things about you," the girl said.

"That's okay," the foster mother said.

Earlier, at the other end of the hallway, the girl had made a loud noise, and her mother had put her hand over the girl's mouth because the bailiff had already come out to tell us we were being too noisy. Inside the courtroom was the whispering judge, impossible to hear even in the quietest room. Later, when their turn with the judge is over, the girl will stand in the middle of the hallway, her head down, her arms at her sides, and cry. "But it's good news that you're coming back home," her biological mother will say.

The bailiff eventually called Evelyn's name, and Eric and I sat on Evelyn's side of the courtroom behind June and the counselor and the friend from work. The prosecutor told the judge about Evelyn's decades-long history of addiction, about fleeing one state to avoid Child Protective Services, about her boyfriend in prison, about being a flight risk. Evelyn turned around again and again to look at her friends and her counselor. "See?" her expression said. "They are out to get me."

Evelyn's attorney pointed out how much progress Evelyn had made—she had a job, her supervisor had written her a letter of support, she had found a place to live, she'd been sober for months. "We're requesting overnight visits," she said.

The judge asked Camilla to speak, and Camilla said she thought Evelyn showed signs of imminent relapse. "She's doing well," Camilla said, "but it's not yet time for overnight visits."

The judge asked the prosecutor what the guardian had recommended, and by guardian he meant the guardian ad litem, the CASA representative, Alejandra. And the prosecutor reported that the guardian had tried to visit Evelyn at her home four times and Evelyn was never there, which we knew was not true.

"You have a lot to prove," the judge said to Evelyn. "A long history. I can see here you hotfooted it from one state to this state when you were pregnant. I will not grant overnights at this time. See you in three months."

After we left, Evelyn yelled at Alejandra in the hallway, called her a liar, yelled so loud, grew so angry, that the bailiff came out of the courtroom and asked her to leave.

"I can't believe she thinks we want to steal her child," I said in the car on the way home.

"But we do want to steal her child," Eric said.

take off your shoes

Months before we brought Coco home, I talked with audience after audience about the Jewish philosopher Emmanuel Levinas. His family was killed in the Holocaust, and Levinas dedicated his life to developing an ethical system that would make another genocide impossible. This was his proposal: When you are in the presence of the Other, a stranger, someone you don't understand, someone who scares you, someone you think might kill you, when you feel the Other is so different from you that their life might not even count as a life, then that is the sign you are in the presence of God. The life of the Other must be protected at all costs, even at the cost of your own life.

This was easy for me to talk about before Coco, before Evelyn.

It wasn't easy anymore.

I'd thought the stranger—the Other—I had been asked to care for was Coco. But the stranger wasn't Coco. The stranger was Evelyn.

"Take off your shoes," Moses hears a voice say from the burning bush consuming life as he knew it. "You are standing on holy ground."

soon it will be hard for you

Court was on Thursday, and on Friday, Coco had a visit with Evelyn at the bank. I knew I should not have called myself *mama* at the doctor's office. I knew I would act differently toward Evelyn if I didn't want to keep Coco. I'd call Evelyn *mama*. I'd say things like "Here's your girl" when I handed Coco to her during visits. I'd dress her in pink.

I needed to make things right.

"I'm sorry this is hard, Evelyn," I said when she held Coco.

"It is hard," she said.

"I know," I said. "I'm sorry."

"I know you're taking good care of her," she said. "I know you are her parents now. But it really hurt that you called yourself *mama* in front of me."

"I'm sorry," I said. "I know you are her mother."

"It's hard for me now," Evelyn said, "but soon it will be hard for you because I'm getting her back."

XIII

BE THE TREE

prey

Evelyn had to take a trip to the state where her son lived, and she didn't tell us why and our social worker didn't know, either, but it meant Evelyn would miss both of her weekly visits with Coco, so the schedule was changed. Instead of two ninety-minute visits, there would be one three-hour visit. A *supervisit,* I called it, trying to hide my fear.

I brought Coco to the bank at nine in the morning. Evelyn had been up all night working and hadn't slept, her face puffy with exhaustion. We stood at the bank's front doors, which were locked, because it turned out the bank didn't open until nine-thirty. It was winter in the mountains, cold, windy, single digits.

"Just throw her in the van," the Northstar supervisor said, "and we'll take her to McDonald's."

"Throw her in the van?" I asked. "Do you have a car seat?"

"We'll use yours," Northstar said.

"Do you have a car seat base?" I asked.

"No," Northstar said. "And we don't need it. Evelyn, you know how to install it, right?"

"Yes," Evelyn said and took the car seat from me with Coco strapped inside and opened the minivan's sliding door.

"She has to face backwards," I said.

"I know. I've had one or two," Evelyn said and laughed, and Northstar laughed with her. Evelyn pulled the seatbelt across the car seat and buckled it. The seatbelt was loose.

"That doesn't seem secure," I said, and both women ignored me. The supervisor sat in the driver's seat. She didn't check Evelyn's installation, didn't make sure Coco was safe. I watched them drive out of the parking lot.

I called Eric. "I shouldn't have let them take her," I said. "I should have driven her myself."

"Yes," he said. "We're agents of the state. Our primary responsibility is her safety."

"I'll call Camilla," I said, and Eric and I talked through what to say and how to say it. I took notes on the back of an envelope I found at the bottom of my purse.

Camilla didn't answer, so I texted her, and she texted me back, said she'd call in a little while.

Hours later, when she still hadn't called, I texted again. My phone rang. "I'm sorry for the delay," she said. "A sibling set just came into care, and I'm trying to find them a foster home. No one is willing to take them. What did you want to talk about?"

I told her about the car seat. About Northstar not checking how it was installed. About Evelyn insisting she knew how to do it even though she did it wrong. I said it was my mistake for not insisting I drive Coco. I said I'd put her at risk because I was afraid Northstar and Evelyn would get mad at me.

"Take a deep breath," Camilla said, and I could almost hear her rolling her eyes.

"They probably think we're tattletales," Eric said when I got off the phone.

He showed me a photograph on the front page of our local paper—a mountain lion standing next to a picnic table in someone's backyard. I found the street name on a map. The mountain lion had been less than a mile from our house. "Don't let your small children walk the trails alone," the sheriff advised. "Hold them close."

After the three-hour visit, I brought Coco home and dressed her in her snowsuit and a warm hat, put her baby sunglasses on, loaded her in the stroller. On the walk, with Coco sleeping, I practiced the breathing exercises my therapist had taught me. "Try this when you feel overwhelmed," she'd said. I rolled my tongue, breathed cold air through that funnel shape. I saw elk tracks on the road, through the fields, and it grounded me to know I walk where they walk. I thought of the mountain lion, could feel her coming closer, stalking.

After the walk, I put Coco in her swing in the kitchen while I cooked dinner, and every time she saw my face, she laughed.

first tooth

Look who has a tooth! I texted Evelyn. I sent her a picture of the tiny pearl breaking through Coco's bottom gum.

That makes me want to cry, she texted back.

butternut

Our pediatrician told us it was time to introduce Coco to solid foods. I put her in her frog chair and set the chair on our kitchen island. I held out a butternut squash for her to touch. The squash looked so big next to her, which made me think of those emails that tell pregnant women their embryo is the size of a pea, a bean, a grapefruit. Our baby was small compared to the butternut I peeled for her, sliced, roasted, whirled.

Her bib was green, her onesie had green frogs on it, and her hat was green, too, emerald. Eric spooned the squash into her mouth on a green spoon.

That will always be her first bite, orange and sweet. And we will always be the ones who fed it to her.

A few days before, Eric cried about the possibility of Coco's leaving us. I'd known him for nearly twenty years, and in those decades before Coco I'd seen him cry maybe ten times. Now he cried all the time. "She won't remember us," he said. "We made her trusting and open and happy, and we'll send her into a world that will not be that way. What's the point?"

"We taught her how to breathe," I said. "Her heart learned to beat because she heard our hearts beat. That means something."

After my friend Emily told me to "tend our marriage," we'd started seeing a therapist together. We wanted this experience to bring us closer together instead of driving us apart. Most marriages end when a child is lost.

"What was it our therapist told us to say when we disagree with the other person but don't want to start a fight?" Eric asked.

"She said to say, 'I hear you,'" I said.

"I hear you," he said.

not the right question

I dream a leopard circles me, sleek and growling. She closes in, pounces. She rips me apart, tears my skin to shreds. She holds my heart in her claw. "Look at your heart," she says. "Eat it."

"But will we get to keep her?" I ask the leopard.

"That's not the point," the leopard says. "That's not even the right question."

heart tree

Because Eric refused to bring a real tree into our house to watch it die over the December holidays, we had a metal version of a tree, really more of a "tree," with small curved pieces branching off its spiraling trunk. I wrapped the trunk in strings of tiny white lights, hung brightly colored balls from the branches. Coco loved the tree, loved the blinking lights, loved seeing her face reflected in the ornaments, and when the holidays were over, I couldn't bring myself to take it down. I ordered dozens of pink and red felt hearts online. I took off the green and blue and yellow and orange ornaments, left only the red and pink. The Christmas tree became a Valentine's tree. We moved Coco's play mat right next to it, so she could look at the twinkling lights, so she could see all our hearts.

caca

The only organization charged with advocating for Coco was CASA, Court Appointed Special Advocates. CASA's primary task is to support the best interest of the child. Social workers advocate for the biological parents first, the child second. Prosecutors advocate for the state. Alejandra was Coco's CASA representative, her guardian ad litem. Most CASA guardians are volunteers, but Alejandra was a paid employee. We first met her at the Family Group Decision Meeting at Idaho Joe's, and I'd seen her at court several times. A CASA volunteer named Carrie was also assigned to Coco's case. Alejandra explained that Carrie was new to CASA, so Alejandra would supervise her, attend all home visits with her. Carrie seemed well-meaning, but she was, in Camilla's words, "bonkers." The one time Carrie and Alejandra visited Coco at our house, Carrie kept calling me "mama." She crossed her fingers or winked at Eric and me whenever the possibility of Evelyn's relapsing was discussed. "She looks just like you," Carrie had said, again and again, as if likeness had any weight at all.

We'd been told CASA was supposed to visit Coco every month, but Coco had been in our care for almost six months, and Alejandra and Carrie had visited once. They'd schedule a home visit, and Eric and I would make all the necessary arrangements, changing our childcare plans, taking time off work, and then we'd wait for them to arrive, and they'd never show. This happened so often that Eric started referring to CASA as CACA.

One of my friends was in and out of foster care when she was a child and was eventually adopted by one of her foster families. When she heard me refer to CASA as CACA, she didn't like it. "CASA was the only good thing about my experience in that system," she said. "Those people are amazing."

"It's not amazing here," I told my friend.

"That is so sad," she said.

Eric and I had yet another appointment scheduled with Alejandra and Carrie on a Monday at 2:30. I emailed Alejandra the week before to confirm. She didn't respond. I texted her, and though I could see she'd read the text, she didn't text back. On Monday afternoon, we put Coco down for a nap and waited—2:30, 3:00, 3:30. I texted Alejandra. I called her, but she didn't answer. I could never leave a message because her voicemail was always full.

I called the CASA office at 3:45, explained Alejandra and Carrie had been due at our house at 2:30. Someone at the office must have reached Alejandra, because she texted me soon after. Carrie had been trying to call me all day to let me know they needed to reschedule, Alejandra explained. Alejandra had been caught up in a court case and couldn't leave.

Our landline rang. "I've been trying to call you all day," Carrie said.

"I've been home all day," I said.

"Is this your cell number?" Carrie asked and recited a string of numbers that did not belong to me.

"No," I said.

We rescheduled their visit yet again, for a different Monday a few weeks away, which happened to be a holiday. "Are you and Alejandra sure you want to work on a holiday?" I asked.

"I'll check with Alejandra," she said.

The Friday before the Monday appointment, Carrie called to confirm, but on Sunday night at nine, Alejandra texted me. *The roads are bad and icy here. How are they there?*

All clear, I texted.

"She's not coming," Eric said, and he was right.

Carrie's husband won't let her drive on these roads, Alejandra texted the next morning, and when I didn't respond, she called, and I handed my phone to Eric because I didn't trust myself to be kind.

"Tenner won't let us drive," she said. Tenner was her supervisor at CASA.

"The roads are clear here," he said.

We'd spent that Sunday in the ER. Eric had an eye injury. The ER doctor had scheduled an appointment on Tuesday for Eric with an ophthalmologist in Twin Falls, a specialist, but when Alejandra canceled, we moved the eye appointment to Monday instead.

I called Alejandra. "We're driving to Twin today for a doctor's appointment," I said. "We can meet you there so you don't have to drive here."

Alejandra agreed to meet us at the CASA offices, but a few minutes later, Tenner called.

"I can't pay my staff overtime for working on a holiday," she said.

"I didn't schedule the meeting on a holiday," I said. "Carrie and Alejandra did."

"They're not working on a holiday," she said.

"Coco is our first placement," I said. "Maybe you could help us adjust our expectations. How often should CASA be visiting Coco?"

"It depends," she said.

"So far, Alejandra has visited Coco in our home once in six months," I said. "I can never reach her by phone because her voicemail is always full. She doesn't follow through or follow up on any of the issues the court has raised. Is this common practice?"

"Look," she said. "We have a hundred seventy-seven kids we're assigned and almost no staff. We are completely overworked. I only have funding to give my staff twenty-five dollars a month for their cellphones, so I can't really tell them to make sure they have a working voicemail. If you need to talk with Alejandra, you should call the office and leave her a message there."

"I do," I said. "She doesn't call me back."

"Then leave me a message."

"I've done that, too," I said. "Several times. You don't call me back either."

"I was on vacation," she said. "I'm allowed to take a vacation."

"I understand you're overworked. I can see it's a challenge to have so many kids you're trying to advocate for," I said. "Why don't we take Coco off your caseload. We can find a new guardian ad litem for her so she can have the advocate she needs and is legally entitled to."

"The judge would not look favorably on that," Tenner said. "It would look like you're trying to game the system."

"We're not trying to game anything," I said. "We're just trying to make sure Coco has an advocate."

"Why would Alejandra need to come to your house again?" Tenner asked. "You could take it as a compliment. We know the baby is being taken care of, so there's really no reason for her to drive all the way to Hailey to see that. And what would be the point of visiting a baby anyway? Babies don't talk."

While Tenner and I were on the phone, I could hear a young child in the background. "Let Mommy work," Tenner said to him several times.

"Our job is to visit Mom now to make sure she's ready for reunification," Tenner said.

"Has Alejandra visited Evelyn?" I asked.

"I don't know," she said.

"Has she followed up about the second mental health evaluation, or the paternity test, or what's happening in the other state with the other child in foster care?" I asked.

"We're doing all kinds of things behind the scenes that we can't tell you about because of confidentiality," Tenner said.

"I see," I said.

Eric had been listening to my end of the conversation. He held up a piece of paper on which he'd written, *Do you have any advice for us as we move forward?*

"Do you have any advice for us as we move forward?" I asked.

"Thank you for asking that," she said. "I hope you know how grateful we are that you are taking such good care of that kiddo." She then suggested that I cc her on all emails to Alejandra and that I leave messages for Alejandra at CASA instead of on her cellphone.

"I know you care about this child, that's why you're even bothering to call us," she said. "But, listen, I don't know if anyone has told you this before, but if at any point anyone in the system suspects that a foster family is trying to sabotage things, trying to sabotage the biological mother, then DHS can come right in and take that baby out of your home."

"What?" I asked.

"They'll come right in and take that baby and put her in another home," she said.

"Are you threatening me?" I asked.

"I'm saying I've seen it happen before," she said. "Many times."

An hour later, Eric and I drove to Twin Falls for his eye doctor appointment. There was no ice. All roads were clear.

i'm sorry, please forgive me, thank you, i love you

I knelt in front of Coco's crib while she slept and whispered a Hawaiian prayer called Ho'oponopono, a practice of reconciliation and forgiveness. *I'm sorry, please forgive me, thank you, I love you.* To speak badly about Evelyn did harm to Coco. To think I knew what was best for her did harm to Coco. To believe she was mine mine mine and only mine did harm to Coco. *I'm sorry, please forgive me, thank you, I love you.*

Ho'oponopono means to make right, "to put in order . . . correct, revise, adjust, amend . . . ; to make ready, as canoemen preparing to catch a wave." My friend Maylen taught me the prayer, texted it to me after we'd talked on the phone about my fear of losing Coco. *I'm sorry, please forgive me, thank you, I love you.* You can say it to another person face-to-face, Maylen explained, or you can say it to that person in your mind.

I'm sorry, please forgive me, thank you, I love you. Though I tried to root for Evelyn, I failed most of the time. I wanted to keep Coco. I wanted her to wake up in our house every day, wiggly and giggly and curious. *I'm sorry, please forgive me, thank you, I love you.* I closed my eyes. I pictured Evelyn. Her smile when she sees Coco, her love whispers, the clothes she gives her, the blanket she knitted for her flecked with gold. *I'm sorry, please forgive me, thank you, I love you.*

unsupervised

Camilla was scheduled to visit Coco at our house on Monday, but at the last minute, she changed her visit to Friday, which was also when Coco had her visits with Evelyn. The new plan was for Camilla to meet with Eric and me while Coco was with Evelyn at the bank, and then Camilla would go to the bank to see Evelyn and Coco together.

On the Thursday before Camilla's visit, I drove north to meet a friend and an elk jumped in front of my car. I slammed on my brakes, and the driver behind me slammed on his, and we blinked our hazards, and the elk stood in the middle of the road. She walked toward my car, then stood still and stared at me.

I took pictures of her with my phone while cars lined both sides of the highway and waited for her to move, but she would not. The sheriff arrived, turned on his siren, tapped her gently with his car, but still she would not budge. A woman got out of her car and tried to usher the elk off the highway and back to a snow-covered field, to safety, but the elk stood her ground. The sheriff ordered us to drive around the elk, waved each car forward, and the woman stood and opened her coat to make a barrier between the elk and all those cars.

The next morning, Friday, I brought Coco to the bank for her visit with Evelyn and then came home to wait for Camilla. She hadn't confirmed what time she'd arrive, and given how often her schedule changed, we didn't know whether or when she would show. She arrived an hour after I'd dropped off Coco. I was due to pick up Coco in thirty minutes.

"We're going to start unsupervised visits next week," Camilla said. "This coming Monday."

"Aren't you supposed to move from supervised to monitored

first?" I asked. The last time we'd been in court, Camilla had assured both the judge and us that she'd move from supervised visits to monitored visits, which meant the Northstar team would still be present. They would drive Evelyn to see Coco and then wait in the car, going into the bank every thirty minutes or so to check on the baby. Evelyn was still deemed a flight risk.

"They've already been doing monitored visits," Camilla said.

Later, I asked both Northstar women if they had been doing monitored visits, and they said no, that they'd only ever left the baby alone with Evelyn if they'd had to use the restroom, and I called Camilla to tell her what they said, and she told me that one of the Northstar women told her the visits with Evelyn went so well, that Evelyn was so good with the baby, that sometimes the Northstar woman would fall asleep in the sun, and because she was asleep and therefore not exactly supervising the visit because her eyes were closed, Camilla had decided to call those visits "monitored."

"That's a stretch," I said.

"Yes," Camilla said. "It is."

The unsupervised visits on Mondays would be six hours long, Camilla explained. Evelyn would drive herself in her own car. She could take Coco wherever she wanted to take her, do whatever she wanted to do, spend time with whomever she wanted to spend time, but she had to submit plans in advance, had to let Camilla know where she planned to be, what she planned to do, who she planned to be with. "And if I pop in and she isn't where she said she'd be, if she isn't with who she said she'd be with, that's not good."

"Will you pop in?" I asked.

"I'll try," she said.

"Don't you think this is a pretty big jump?" I asked.

"Evelyn is making great progress," Camilla said and explained that Evelyn had just switched her work schedule from nights to days, that she'd rented her own apartment, that she'd graduated from her drug classes, passed her parenting classes with flying colors. "We expect her to relapse," Camilla said. "But that's part of recovery."

"You *expect* relapse?" Eric and I asked at the same time.

"That's part of recovery," she said again. "Now that all her classes are over, she'll let her guard down."

"You expect relapse, but you're letting her take a baby in a car for six hours?" I asked.

"Yes," she said.

"What about the second mental health evaluation you said you'd request months ago?" Eric asked.

"We've decided that would violate Evelyn's rights," she said.

"What about her son in foster care?" I asked. We'd been told Evelyn's son didn't want to live with Evelyn, that he wanted to stay with his foster family. "Doesn't it matter for Coco's case that Evelyn has another child refusing to live with her?"

"Not really," Camilla said. "She put him through the wringer."

We asked about CASA and when we should expect Alejandra to visit. "She's very hands off," Camilla said. "But courts expect CASA to be in monthly contact with the child."

"She's only visited Coco once in six months," I said.

"Once?" Camilla asked. "She's written in the reports she files with the court and with us that she has seen Coco every month."

"That's not true," I said.

"I should let you know that Alejandra and I are good friends," Camilla said. "But the fact that she's lying on her official reports is worrisome." She promised she'd follow up.

"Here's how it's going to go," Camilla said. "We'll do extended visits on Mondays for about a month, then we'll move to overnights for about a month, then two-night overnights, then three-night overnights, and then we'll say to Evelyn 'She's yours.' That could happen in June or it could happen in September."

Camilla had been at our house for about ten minutes. "I know this is a lot," she said, "But I need to get to the bank to see Evelyn with Coco."

hope

The next day my friend Erin sent me an email. *Was this your elk?* she wrote. *Fuckers.*

I clicked the link to an article in the local paper. When she wouldn't move, the sheriff called Idaho Fish and Game, and they arrived, guns drawn, and shot the elk, killed her, dragged her body off the road.

"We had a traffic hazard," their spokesperson said.

six months

I was afraid we would not get to see Coco turn one, so I decided to throw her a six-month birthday party. I invited our friends and their children. I ordered pink and white and gold balloons. I ordered crescent-moon- and heart-shaped rose-gold-glittered cupcake toppers. I bought party hats and sparklers. I baked chocolate cupcakes, whipped chocolate frosting. Claudia helped me plan games kids could play, crafts, snacks. I cut fruit and popped popcorn and opened bags of chips and dip and salsa. Eric made a blue cocktail to match Coco's eyes.

Though we'd said no gifts, people brought presents, filled our living room with new clothes and books and stuffed animals and blankets. At the party, kids played ping-pong in our basement and used black construction paper and white and gray paint and gold star stickers to paint moons in the night sky at the craft table Claudia and I set up in our kitchen.

We lit one candle and sang "Happy Birthday" and gave Coco her first bite of avocado. And though we all knew why we were there, in the photographs from that day everyone is smiling.

here, tend this

I wanted to keep Coco in a way I'd never wanted anything else. Before Coco, people used to tell me the love they felt for their child was unlike any love they'd ever felt, and I resented that idea, was insulted by it, felt it framed nonparents as deficient, limited. But with Coco, I could see they were, in some ways, right. My love for her was unlike any other love I'd ever felt.

My new love for Coco wasn't biological. It wasn't a result of having some part of me—my heart, my DNA—out in the world. And it wasn't because she was my child, however temporary or provisional our belonging. No. It was because Coco had been entrusted to me. My task was to care for her, to keep her safe, protected. *Here, tend this,* I heard the universe say to me about our vulnerable, fragile, beautiful, wiggly, curious, blue-eyed girl. And my heart expanded.

I want to believe it can expand for tree, for rock, for earth, for refugee, for hawk, for river, too.

Here, tend this.

When I shared my fear about losing Coco with other parents, they assured me my fear was exactly what it means to be a parent: You know your children will get hurt or get sick or die, and you can't protect them. With big love, the possibility of big loss. But our loss was not an abstract possibility, not a generalized risk you assume every time you love a mortal. Ours was inevitable, certain. And I'd first peered into its chasm at the meeting at Idaho Joe's, all that talk of Coco *going home,* of Coco *returning home,* of *Mama getting her back* echoing off the walls.

be the tree

My friend Jeanne's husband was dying. He was in terrible pain.
He was suffering. "When I see he's hurting," Jeanne told me,
"when I know there's nothing I can do but be present, I imagine
I'm a tree, rooted, my branches offering him shade."

why

"Why are we doing this?" I asked Juliana more than once.

"You tell me," she said.

"Because I want to live in a world where we take care of each other," I said.

"Yes," she said. "Remember that."

mama bear

Eric and I watched a video of a mama brown bear protecting her cub. A male black bear entered the mama bear's territory, and when she caught his scent, she chased him. The mama bear ran down a steep hillside covered with fallen trees and boulders and then followed the male bear up a tall pine tree, branches falling as she climbed.

For weeks, Eric had been trying to persuade me to put down some of my rage, at Camilla, at Alejandra, at CACA and DHW and the whole system. "There's no point to it. It does no good," he said. "Let go and let God."

I knew he didn't mean that. He hates that kind of theology. "What are you trying to say?" I asked.

"Let go," he said.

"I can't," I said. "I'm that mama bear."

"No," he said. "She had some control over her territory. You have no control here. You're not the bear. You're the tree."

XIV

OUR GIRL

hang out

Camilla sent me a copy of Evelyn's plans for her first six-hour unsupervised visit with Coco. Evelyn was required to outline a primary plan and a backup plan, in case her first idea didn't work.

Plan A: *Have Coco meet her family and play at home.*

Plan B: *Hang out at June's house.*

I called Camilla. "You're letting her drive Coco to Twin Falls for the first visit?" I asked.

"Yes," she said.

"That means three of the six hours will be spent in the car," I said.

"Maybe that's good," she said.

I forwarded a copy of Evelyn's plans to Eric. "Just sent you something," I shouted up the stairs to his closed office door. At the top of the document was Evelyn's new address. I opened Google Maps and entered the street name and house number. I moved the yellow human-shaped figure to the red teardrop marking the spot so I could see the street view. A housing complex. Small white structures arranged in neat groups. Freshly painted siding. A playground with a swing set and slide. Well-tended lawns. Lodgepole pines. Chokecherries. Maples.

Eric stood at my office door.

"There are trees," we said at the same time.

i can do this, mama

The day before the first six-hour unsupervised visit, I couldn't stop crying. I didn't think I'd be able to hand Coco to Evelyn, didn't think I could make my body do it. At the start of every other visit, I'd handed the car seat to Evelyn, Coco strapped safely inside. This time, I would have to take Coco out of her car seat, hold her in my arms, feel her little body against my heart, and then give her away. I kept picturing that moment, the hand-off. I kept having to lie down.

That night, I dreamt I held Coco. In the dream, she touched my face. "I can do this, Mama," she said.

The next morning, Eric and I drove to the bank. "Arrange to meet Evelyn at the parking lot," Camilla had told me. "It's still not safe to let her know where you live."

"But it's safe to let her drive Coco to a different town?" I'd asked.

We didn't see Evelyn at first. The only other car in the lot was a black sedan with a man at the wheel. Then Evelyn opened the passenger door.

"There's a man in the car," I said.

"Call Camilla," Eric said.

"Stall," I said.

Camilla answered. "There's a man in the car," I said.

"Who is it?"

"I don't know," I said. "She didn't list any other people on her plans."

"Oh, right," she said. "I forgot. She changed things at the last minute and said Jim might drive her."

"Who's Jim?"

"June's husband."

I got out of the car, opened the door to the backseat, leaned in to unstrap Coco. Evelyn stood so close I could feel her breath on my neck. I turned, handed Evelyn the blanket she'd knitted Coco with the gold thread running through it, the pink blanket she'd given Coco with the elephant on it, the unicorn rattle from Coco's brother. Then I gave her Coco.

"Hello, my beautiful girl," she said.

"Any questions?" I asked.

"Nope," she said.

"We just fed her," I said.

"Okay," she said, already turning away.

favorite toy

Eric and I passed the time while Coco was with Evelyn by getting massages. This was Juliana's advice. "Keep the energy moving," she said. "You don't want this trauma stuck in your body."

In the dressing room, a woman put her crying baby on a towel on the floor while she dressed herself.

"How old?" I asked.

"Five months," she said.

"I have a six-month-old baby at home," I said.

"Your first?" she asked.

"My foster daughter," I said.

"Cute," she said, and I wanted to punch her.

We drove to the bank and arrived fifteen minutes early. Evelyn was already parked in the lot. She technically had time left with Coco. I didn't know if we should wait in the car to respect their remaining time together or get out and say hello, but while I worried about this, Evelyn climbed out of the backseat of her car and carried Coco across the lot.

Coco didn't smile when she saw us.

"How'd it go?" I asked.

"Fine," she said.

"What was her favorite toy to play with?" I asked.

"Me," Evelyn said.

A black dog ran around the parking lot. "Is that your dog?" I asked.

"Yes," she said.

The dog came close, let me pet her. Evelyn handed Coco to me. She smelled like Evelyn's perfume and cigarette smoke. As soon as Coco was in my arms, Evelyn lit a cigarette.

At home, we gave Coco a bath. She played in the water with her bath toys, her two new teeth making a squeaking sound as she chewed on the dolphin, the octopus, the whale, the crab, the oyster shell. I watched her return to her body.

A few days later, Alejandra called. "I just wanted to let you know I saw part of Coco's visit with Mom, and it went well," she said.

"Thanks for letting me know," I said. "How long were you there?"

"Between ten and twenty minutes," she said.

"How did Coco seem?"

"The baby only got upset once that whole entire time," she said. "But Mom comforted her, showed her some toys, picked her up."

"What do you plan to recommend in court next week?" I asked.

"Mom's doing really well," she said. "We're moving toward overnights."

"Do you think that's safe?" I asked.

"I can't answer all your questions, Sarah."

bored

"I've heard there's really nothing to do where you live," Camilla said.

"I live in a resort town. People bring families to vacation here," I said. "There's a ton to do."

"Evelyn doesn't think there's anything to do there with the baby," she said.

"I'd be happy to share some ideas with Evelyn, but she doesn't really want to hear that kind of thing from me."

"You're the enemy right now, and it will only get worse," she said.

Camilla told me that she'd requested a new CASA worker for Coco but she'd met with some resistance from Tenner, Alejandra's boss.

"Did Alejandra really lie on the reports she submitted to court?" I asked.

"Yes," Camilla said. "I have her lies highlighted in a stack of documents right here on my desk."

"That's bold," I said.

"Pretty stupid to lie about something that can be so easily verified," she said.

"What about the mental health evaluation?" I asked.

"We're not going to do it," she said.

"What about her son who's refusing to live with her?"

"That doesn't matter," she said.

"It doesn't matter that another state has determined she's not safe enough to parent her son?"

"We consider one child at a time," she said.

"How likely is reunification at this point?" I asked. "Ninety-nine percent?"

"I wouldn't go that high," she said. "But I would say ninety percent. She's doing everything she's been asked to do. And remember, minimal parenting ability is all she needs to demonstrate."

"Being a social worker seems really hard," I said.

"I'd rather be doing what I'm doing than what you're doing," she said.

"Writing?" I asked.

"Being a foster parent," she said.

A few hours later, Evelyn texted me. *What should I do until four?*

When you're in Hailey with Coco next week? I texted back.

Yes.

I sent Evelyn some ideas—walks they could take, directions to the skate park where Coco loved to watch kids ride up and down the ramps, the best place to see the river, information about the children's library, maps of parks, the website for the local Y, which has a pool. She didn't respond.

Camilla sent me the plans Evelyn submitted for her next six-hour visit. Plan A: *Hang out at the library and if the weather is ok, take a walk. At 4 pm we will go to the Y.* Plan B: *Walk around the park and go to the Y at 4.*

I called Camilla. "It seems like Evelyn could use some support figuring out what to do with a six-month-old baby."

"I'll work with her on that," she said.

But she must not have, because Evelyn's next six-hour visit plan was this: *Visit the library.*

"All six hours at the library with a baby?" I asked Eric. "That's not going to go well."

Two hours into that visit, my phone rang.

"Can you come get her?" Evelyn asked. "We're bored."

she can see birds

Eric loved to hold Coco at the window in the middle of the stair-
way to look at the mountains across the road. She'd stand on the
windowsill, her body leaning against Eric's body, and he'd hold
her belly. She'd open her mouth and kiss the window, lick it.
She'd touch the glass with her hands, leaving fingerprints we
later refused to wash off. She'd giggle and turn back to look at
Eric and then out the window again.

"She can see birds," he said one morning, and I ran upstairs,
and it was true. Robins and cedar waxwings and magpies and
house finches and mourning doves—the outside world that had
been a blur of light and dark, of sun and shadow, now held birds
in flight for her.

bright spot

On Coco's seven-month birthday, Eric and I drove to Twin Falls for another court date. We arrived early enough to get a seat in the hallway. Evelyn and June said hello on their way to take a smoke break. When they returned, June walked by us, but Evelyn called her back.

"We can sit by Sarah," Evelyn said. She looked tired.

"Did you have to take the day off from work to be here for court?" I asked.

"No," she said. "I picked up an extra shift last night, worked from eleven P.M. to two A.M. But I'm taking tomorrow and Saturday off. I'm going back to see my son."

"That's great," I said.

"When this is all over, are you going to do it again?" Evelyn asked.

"Be a foster parent?"

"Yes," she said.

"No," I said.

"It's too hard, huh?" she asked.

"Yes," I said. "It's too hard."

"That's too bad," she said. "You two are great."

"Thank you," I said.

"I've heard there are some terrible foster parents," she said. "Everyone keeps telling me how lucky I am to have the two of you."

A friend of a friend in our town had just had her baby taken by Child Protective Services. The father was suspected of child abuse (though he was later cleared of all charges). The baby's foster mother lived in Twin Falls. She'd only let the biological mother see the baby if she came to church.

"I adopted a little girl a few years ago," June said.

"I didn't know that," I said.

"Through Catholic Charities," she said. "We found out we'd get to bring the baby home, but then we had to wait three weeks for her, and those weeks were so hard. It was foster-to-adopt, so the biological mom had six months to change her mind. I had to send the baby on an overnight with the bio mom, just once, and I was so scared we wouldn't get her back. I have some idea what you must be going through."

I looked at Eric, who was sitting next to me on the bench. I knew he was listening, but he didn't look up from *The New York Review of Books*. He was reading an article about Chernobyl.

"When I was at the library with Coco, I looked for your books, Sarah," Evelyn said. "But I couldn't find them."

I laughed.

"Is Alejandra here?" I asked. The one thing Evelyn and I bonded over was CACA. Alejandra had lied to and about both of us. She hadn't shown up at Evelyn's house, and she hadn't shown up at ours, though she told everyone she had. We agreed Coco didn't have the advocate she deserved.

"No," Evelyn said. "Something came up, I heard." We rolled our eyes.

"I know Alejandra lied about you in court," I said.

"She said she visited me four times, and I didn't answer the door," she said. "But that's not true."

"I told Camilla it wasn't true," I said. "Alejandra also lied in her official reports. She said she's visited Coco every month, but she hasn't."

The bailiff called Evelyn's name. Inside the courtroom, Camilla recommended that the judge grant "extended home visits with the mother." The prosecutor agreed with her recommendation, though he stressed to the judge that because of the mother's history, the move from six-hour visits to twelve-hour visits to overnights should be "measured and controlled and graduated."

The only concern the judge had was about Evelyn's finances. "I can see what you earn," he said to Evelyn. "It's not enough. You'll have to balance getting more hours of work with having to afford more hours of childcare to cover that time. But I agree with the department. Extended home visits at their discretion."

We left the courtroom, and Camilla pulled us into a room and closed the door. She told us her plan was to do a few more six-hour visits, then move to twelve-hour visits, then overnights. "I'm sorry," she said to Eric and me. "I know this is really hard for you."

Camilla was a mother, had several children, biological and adopted.

"Would you give Evelyn any of your children?" I asked.

"No," she said. "I wouldn't trust her to take care of my dog for an hour."

"You wouldn't trust her with your dog, but you're going to trust her with this baby," I said.

"That's not the rubric," she said. She suggested we wait at the courthouse for a while to see if we might be able to talk with the prosecutor. "Maybe he can request a new CASA representative," she said. "I'll tell him to find you when his meeting is finished."

Eric and I waited in the empty hallway. The judge walked by us, then an hour later he walked by us again. "I guess you just like it here?" he asked, his robe trailing behind.

The prosecutor found us in the hallway and took us back to the room where we'd talked with Camilla. We told him Coco had virtually no CASA representation, that Alejandra had lied in her reports, that Camilla told us she would not trust Evelyn with her dog.

"You've got to understand that eighty percent of the cases that come in front of this judge are meth cases," he said. "And in that courtroom, in comparison to what the judge usually sees, your bio mom is a bright spot. She's semi with it. She shows up to court. She attends meetings and her visits with her kid. She has a job, a place to live."

"Look at it this way," he added. "You're lucky that baby isn't on the floor of some trailer playing with bags of meth and needles with five strangers, one of whom is a sex offender whose name somehow nobody knows."

flooding

When I thought about Coco being taken away from us—which in the language of the foster care system sounds not like *taken away* but like *returned* or *reunified* or *sent home*—I couldn't stand. I had to lean on the kitchen counter. Lie on the bedroom floor. Put my hands on my knees. *Flooded,* my therapist called it. She taught me breathing exercises, taught me how to stay in the present. "Name five red objects in the room," she said, which sounded like the dumbest thing anyone had ever told me to do, but I tried it anyway, and it worked. Red block. Red paint. Red tongue. Red leaf. Red heart.

There was nothing I could do to change the outcome and there never was. All that was left to do was to love Coco, to be joyful and present, to teach her to trust and connect, to teach her how to sit and stand and chew and swallow and smile.

We fed her sweet potatoes, avocados, peas, bananas, rice cereal, oatmeal, broccoli, cauliflower, zucchini, lentils, coconut milk, peanut butter, scrambled egg yolks. We sat with her on the floor, put pillows all around in case she fell, helped her reach for blocks, for rings, for stuffed ducks and elephants and foxes. She made new sounds every day. *Eff, eff, eff,* she said. *Baa, baa, baa,* she said. She gurgled, yelped, giggled, cooed. She reached for the cats, petted their fur. Every morning when we came to get her in her crib, she wiggled and smiled and laughed. "Who's the happiest baby?" we asked. "Who is? Who is?"

I took Coco on a walk almost every day, and though there was still snow on the ground, I could hear the birds, who had returned. Vultures circled the blue, looking for what had not survived the winter. Groups of cedar waxwings flew from tree to tree. Red-winged blackbirds called to each other in the tall grasses. "Can you hear that?" I asked Coco.

When there was less human noise on the earth—less talking, less traffic, fewer machines, fewer airplanes—people could hear the other animals we share the planet with. They allowed themselves to be sung to.

"Wherever you are, there will be birdsong," I said. I pointed to the moon crossing the sky in the middle of the day. "Wherever you are, there will be moonlight."

dissolution

Again I handed Coco to Evelyn in the bank parking lot. "This is hard for me," I said. "I really love her."

"I know," Evelyn said.

I cried, turned my face away from Coco so she wouldn't see my tears.

"Do you have therapy today?" Evelyn asked.

"Yes, thank God," I said, and we both laughed. "How's your son?"

"We're in therapy too," she said. "He has a lot of walls up."

"Can I ask you a question?" I asked. "What motivated you to get sober this time?"

She pointed to Coco. "Getting my family back," she said. "And it turns out I don't do well as a drug addict."

Eight vultures circled above us, a kettle. That night, I will dream about those vultures. I am in our backyard, a vulture picks me up, puts me on his back. "Look," he says, and below I see the bones of the world's dead. We fly above the bank parking lot.

"This version of your relationship with Coco is dead," the vulture says.

"I don't want it to be," I say.

In the parking lot are three cocoons. I am inside one, Coco is inside one, Evelyn is inside one. "You are dissolving," the vulture says. "You will become something else."

"I don't want to," I say.

"It's okay," the vulture says.

"But it's not okay," I say.

"It's okay that it's not okay," he says.

gifts

Camilla texted me Evelyn's plan for her first twelve-hour visit with Coco: *Work on tummy time and find Coco's favorite toy.*

I called Camilla.

"Coco is way past tummy time," I said. "I know we won't get to keep her just because Evelyn's plans for these visits suck, but can we please use this as an opportunity to help her become a better parent? Can we please help support Evelyn to figure out what a baby needs, how to stimulate a baby's brain, how to keep her engaged? At the end of most visits, Evelyn tells me that Coco is fussy. But she isn't a fussy baby. She's bored."

"Why don't you go to her house on Monday, then?" Camilla said. "You can go there and help her learn about her child."

"You want me to go to Evelyn's house?" I asked.

"Yes," she said.

"If Evelyn agrees," I said, "I'd be happy to."

On Monday morning, I found myself driving Coco to Twin Falls for her first twelve-hour visit with Evelyn. The plan was that I'd stay for an hour.

"Bring a housewarming gift, like a plant," Juliana told me. "Bring a toy for her dog. Bring her some coffee. Treat this visit like you'd treat a visit with a good friend."

I brought Coco's favorite toys, her favorite books. I brought her frog chair, her favorite blanket, her favorite pacifier, her favorite stuffed duck. I brought Evelyn a planter filled with succulents. I brought a squeaky toy for her dog. I brought coffee.

Evelyn spread a blue blanket on the living room floor, and the three of us sat together and played. Framed photographs lined one wall of the living room and rested on the counter dividing the living room from the kitchen. I asked Evelyn to tell me about the people in the pictures—her sons, a niece, a nephew.

She brought a photograph from the bedroom to show me. "This is my mother," she said. She showed me a photograph of a little girl. "This is me," she said.

"You look like Coco in that picture," I said.

On the television stand was a photograph of Evelyn wearing an orange dress standing with a man, their arms around each other. When she saw me looking at it, she said, "That's Coco's dad, Cody."

"Do you keep in touch?" I asked.

"Yes," she said.

"Will he live with you when he gets out of prison?" I asked.

"I don't know yet."

"How are you feeling about being a single parent?" I asked.

"I'd rather do it alone than have some terrible person around," she said.

Through the living room window I saw a pine tree's green branches and a white-flowered tree.

"Do you like any of your neighbors? Have you made any friends here?"

"I've been told it's not a great neighborhood," she said. "There used to be a lot of drugs. I keep to myself."

We talked about childcare, about the fact that to reserve a place for Coco she needed to make a deposit, but she didn't have the money. She told me she'd been offered a promotion at work, but she wasn't sure she wanted to take it.

"Why not?" I asked.

"What if the machines don't work, and I can't figure out how to fix them?"

In Evelyn's bedroom was a changing table with a dinosaur-print changing pad. A blanket with a tiger on it covered Evelyn's bed. In an alcove of the bedroom was Coco's crib lined with beautiful blankets, stars pinned to the walls.

We played on the floor with Coco, and I took pictures of the two of them together.

"I can come back next Monday if you'd like," I said.

"Please," she said. "I enjoy spending time with you."

heartbeat

The next Monday I drove Coco to Twin Falls again. I brought coffee for Evelyn. I brought a pink blanket, stacking rings Coco loved to chew on, wooden boxes she loved to knock down, a plastic caterpillar with wheels, and some of her favorite books.

Evelyn and I sat on the floor across from each other with Coco between Evelyn's legs, and we sent the caterpillar back and forth, watching Coco laugh, watching her reach for the toy.

On the kitchen table was a sewing machine. "Do you sew?" I asked.

"Yes," she said. "Come look." She brought me to Coco's crib and showed me a quilt she'd just finished for her—purple on one side, a pink heart pattern on the other. In the crib was a stuffed monkey. Evelyn picked it up and pressed a button on its back. The noise was loud and staticky and I thought it would scare Coco, but it didn't.

"That's her heartbeat when she was still in my womb," she said, and we stood there, the three of us, and listened.

On the wall of the living room was a photograph of an older man and a toddler that I hadn't noticed during my first visit. Evelyn told me it was her father holding her second son. I'd thought he'd been adopted by someone at birth, but in the photograph with Evelyn's father he's not a baby.

"I couldn't get it together," she said. "I was in and out of his life, and I realized that wasn't fair to him, so I let him be adopted when he was two."

"Did you know the people who adopted him?" I asked.

"Yes," she said. "The woman was very nice. She was his foster mother at first, but then he started calling her *mama*, which broke my heart."

"I'm sorry I did that at the doctor's office," I said.

"I know," she said. "Losing a child leaves a hole that never gets filled. I don't want to do that again."

We talked about her third son, about her hope that he would come live with her, about her promotion at work, which she'd taken. "Everyone at work really likes me," she said.

"When you get her back, will you keep in touch with me?" I asked.

"Oh, Sarah," she said. "Yes. Of course. I want you to be part of her life."

"Thank you," I said.

"Can I ask you something?"

"Yes," I said.

"Did that first social worker tell you I was a poor prognosis?"

"Yes. She used exactly those words: *poor prognosis*. How did you know?"

"She said that to me, too," she said.

"That must have hurt," I said. "You proved her wrong."

"I know you thought you'd get to keep Coco," she said. "And if I was you, I'd be hoping that I'd fail. I'd want me to fail."

"I did at first," I said. "But I want Coco to be well and safe, and for her to be well and safe, I know you have to be well and safe. To root for her means to root for you. I understand now that I have to love you as much as I love Coco."

Evelyn cried.

"I know Coco wants me to love you," I said, "so I do."

We played with the baby, took turns reading books, stacking and restacking blocks. We watched her chew on rainbow-colored wooden rings.

"What do you like to eat?" Evelyn asked when I was packing up to leave. "Why don't you come back next Monday, and I'll make you breakfast."

different brains

People who donate kidneys to strangers have different brains than people who don't, scientists say. The region in their brain known to produce empathetic responses is larger than average, by 8 percent.

Scientists suggest it's having a different brain that makes people more empathetic and therefore more likely to donate an organ to someone they don't know. They are more sensitive to distress, scientists say. But because they study donors only after they've given away their kidneys, how do scientists know it's not the giving itself that transforms the brain? Maybe what renders you more sensitive to the suffering of others is having one of your organs in someone else's body. Maybe it's knowing there is no such thing as *mine*.

our girl

How's our girl? Evelyn texted.

we love

"I think you'll want to listen to this," Eric said and sent me a link to "The World's Smartest Animal," the final episode in "G," *Radiolab*'s series on intelligence. I put on my headphones and listened to Laurel Braitman, a writer and an anthropologist of science, arguing that sperm whales are the most intelligent animals.

Braitman based her argument on what she calls whales' "sixth sense." Sperm whales are very much like humans, Braitman said, but they have "stronger social and emotional bonds than we do." We tend to think of whale echolocation like boat sonar: a sound is sent out that bounces off something in the environment and then returns, giving a sense of the shape of the thing. But whale sonar doesn't communicate only shape, it also communicates feelings and emotions. In the mid-1980s, a neuropsychologist named Harry Jerison proposed that echolocated communications that are emotional in nature, like grief or joy, might be perceived by whales not only as shared information, but also as shared feelings. "Jerison thought that this might give rise to something called the communal self," Braitman said. "Whales . . . might not say 'I,' they might always be a 'we.'"

"We sad," she said.

As evidence of this communal self, Braitman pointed to whales beaching themselves. When a hundred whales strand themselves on the shore and die, and scientists then study the bodies of the dead whales, they learn that only one or two of the hundred were sick.

"We sick," Braitman said.

We happy. We lost. We hurt. We heal. We grieve.

I listened to the podcast and thought about Evelyn. She spent so much time driving between Hailey and Twin Falls, and

I often wondered how she passed the time. "Do you listen to podcasts when you drive?" I asked once in the bank parking lot.

"What's a podcast?" she asked.

Everything in our worlds—education and family and social class and addiction and diet and politics and housing and employment—is designed to keep Evelyn and me apart. We aren't supposed to like each other, much less love each other. But now we love the same girl.

We love.

"What looks like extreme empathy to us might just be them being themselves," Braitman says about the sperm whales. "Or maybe it's a new kind of intelligence," an intelligence that requires not just thinking about the feelings of others, but feeling the feelings of others. Communal feeling, communal self.

thank you berry much

The next Wednesday, Camilla texted Evelyn and me together: *After much consideration and staffing, it has been determined that we are going to move to overnights beginning this weekend. The visit will start at 7pm on Friday evening and end at 7pm Sunday evening. Plans do not need to be submitted and approved unless there is planned travel of more than one hour outside of the Twin Falls or Hailey area. Pickup and drop off will be in Hailey. This will be the plan that will last until court on June 20. As long as everything goes well, please plan on baby going with mom after court on June 20.*

Eric was out of town for work. My mother was on a plane to come spend the weekend with Coco. I called Camilla.

"A text?" I said.

"I know you're emotional about this," she said.

"You're moving from twelve-hour visits to two-night over-nights starting the day after tomorrow?"

"Yes," she said.

A few weeks before this text, out of the blue, we'd received a thank-you note in the mail from Camilla. On the front of the note were strawberries wearing sunglasses and the words *Thank you berry much.* Inside she'd thanked us for being Coco's foster parents. "I don't think this note is a good sign," Eric had said. "I think it means Camilla thinks this is over."

"What about the gradual timeline the judge approved?"

"Evelyn's ready," Camilla said.

"We have lives, schedules," I said. "We made arrangements according to the calendar of visits you sent us."

"Things change," she said.

"My mother is on a plane right now on her way to come visit Coco this weekend," I said. "And Eric is out of town."

"What does that have to do with anything?" Camilla said.

XV

ALL HER BELONGINGS

mother's day

Anything you need for the overnight? I texted Evelyn.

Just that baby, she texted back.

I brought Coco to the bank parking lot to hand her to Evelyn for their second overnight visit. Evelyn reached for Coco in my arms, and Coco leaned away from her, pushed her body into my body, but I had to give her away anyway. It was Mother's Day weekend. Evelyn gave me a yellow rose in a small white teacup with pink flowers on it. "Happy Mother's Day," she said.

I drove out of the bank parking lot. I was crying so hard I had to pull over. I screamed until my throat was raw. When I got home, the house was empty. Her slate-blue high chair, empty. Her chair attached to the kitchen island, the blanket I'd laid out in the living room with her toys all over it, her play mat, her crib, empty empty empty empty. Noises came out of my body that I didn't recognize.

Thinking of you, a friend texted.

all her belongings

Camilla changed the schedule again, moved the reunification date up. She sent the new schedule by email. In two weeks, Coco would begin spending more than half of her time with Evelyn, the email said. She would live with Evelyn Wednesday through Sunday. Reunification would occur on June 12, though the next court date wasn't until June 20. Camilla told us we were no longer welcome to attend court. *You will not be her foster parent at that time and hearings are closed,* she wrote. *Please have Coco's belongings ready to be given to Evelyn on June 12.*

In the PRIDE classes we took to become certified as foster parents, the facilitator had shared a story about a grandmother who was taking care of her grandchild because the child's biological mother could not. But then the grandmother could not, either, so the child was removed from the grandmother's home. The grandmother sent her grandchild to the new foster family with nothing but the clothes on her back.

"I bought that stuff for her," the grandmother said. "It's mine."

What will we send with Coco? Her play mat? Her frog chair? Stuffed duck and bear and elephant? Books? She learned to breathe by listening to our breath. Her heart learned to beat by listening to ours beat. Attachment, trust, joy—we will send these with her, too. I will send everything I have to give. My heart, my broken heart. All hers.

countdown

It was spring in the mountains when the final countdown began, and we marked her dwindling time with us by bloom. Will she see the lilac bloom in the corner of the yard? The yellow irises? The lilies?

I feel like crying about everything today, Evelyn texted.

Me too, I texted back.

separated

Parents in detention are lied to about the whereabouts of their children. Some are told their children are being taken for a bath or to play outside or to sleep. But then their children don't come back.

Newborn children are separated from their mothers right after they are born. The mothers are "distraught." One cried for seventy-two hours without stopping.

A three-year-old boy was crying when Border Patrol agents found him alone in a cornfield in Texas. Someone had written his name and a phone number on his shoes.

Once families are separated, I read in the news, it can become difficult for them to be reunited.

photobook

Eric and I spent hour after hour after hour creating a photobook to give to Evelyn. Pictures of Coco from the ten months she lived with us. At the back of the book, we wrote a letter to Coco. *May you always feel at home,* we wrote.

dust

I found a flying ant in my kitchen, and then another, and another. I trapped each one with a drinking glass. I studied their wings, the shape of their bodies, then took them outside and let them go. I wanted the flying ants to be termites. I wanted our house to be reduced to dust.

sick and hungry

Coco returned ravenous from her overnights with Evelyn. She returned tired, dark circles under her puffy eyes.

"Did she sleep well?" I asked in the parking lot.

"Kind of," she said.

"Did she nap?"

"Ten minutes here, ten minutes there."

"I think she needs more sleep than that," I said.

"You're making me feel bad," Evelyn said.

After a four-night visit, she came back with terrible diarrhea, with a diaper rash, red and raw.

"How long has she had diarrhea?" I asked.

"A few days," she said.

I called the doctor. "Bring her in," she said.

The new schedule—four days with Evelyn, three days with us—seemed to take a toll on Coco.

"Does she seem quieter to you?" Eric asked.

"Does she giggle less?" I asked.

She no longer experimented with new sounds. She seemed cautious.

"She doesn't trust us anymore," Eric said.

hide and seek

Eric put a burp cloth over Coco's head. "Where's baby?" he asked.

She pulled the cloth off her head.

"There she is," he said, and she laughed.

He covered her face again. "Where's baby?" he asked.

She pulled off the cloth.

"There she is," he said, and she laughed again.

He supported her so she could stand next to a miniature table with colorful buttons she could press, a mini keyboard that made noise, multicolored squares and circles and triangles that beeped. On the table was a box, and when its lid was lifted, music played. When Coco looked away, Eric hid toys in the box—a sheep, a pig, a cow, an orange triangle, a green square. When she turned back, she'd open the lid, find the object Eric had hidden for her, look at him with delight, put the toy in her mouth, hold the toy to Eric's mouth for him to kiss, and then throw it behind her.

Hide and seek and hide and seek and gone.

antelope

At night, in bed, we cried.

Eric talked about climate change, about scientists' predictions, about cities under water, rivers dried out, farmland turned to dust.

"One million people come to our borders every year trying to get in," he said. "But by 2050 there will be one hundred million people coming." He meant the information to be a kind of salve, a balm, the way for some people the idea that the universe is expanding, the idea that someday our planet won't exist, offers perspective, brings the relief of remembered smallness. Insignificance. Nothing matters.

"One billion people will be dislocated from their homes," he said. "Our girl is one of them."

The night before, he'd been watching a television show about extreme weather. People chasing a storm noticed something on the road. It was an antelope getting pummeled by hail.

"The world is indifferent to vulnerable things," Eric said. "The hail didn't care about the antelope. The ground didn't care about the antelope. Coco is that antelope now."

nest

There were magpie babies in a nest in a pine tree in our back yard. I couldn't see the nest, but I could hear the babies. I watched the adults disappear into the tree, heard the babies sing, watched the adults fly back out.

I spread a red blanket on the grass in the shade and brought Coco outside. I carried her from lilac tree to lilac tree. Showed her the maple leaves. Pointed out the tight iris buds, the peony bushes. Let her smell the chokecherry trees' white blossoms. On the blanket, we played with blocks. I put toys inside a box, and she reached inside to find them. I kissed the back of her neck. I kissed the top of her head. I kissed her cheek. We lay on our backs and watched the clouds.

"You can always come back," I said.

"Please come back," I said.

collapse

On a day when Coco was with Evelyn, Eric drove to Twin Falls to have our car serviced. I texted him the address of Coco's daycare.

Drive by, I texted Eric. *See what the facility is like from the outside.*

But Eric went inside. He talked to the daycare staff. He learned they were used to working with social workers, with mothers who'd had children taken away and then returned. They knew what to watch for. Two women gave Eric a tour, showed him the room where the toddlers were, showed him the baby room, the napping room. Through the open door Eric saw Coco. She was on her back on a play mat, a mobile above her head. She reached up.

The daycare worker asked Eric a question, and he answered, and when Coco heard his voice, she started to cry, and Eric was not allowed to comfort her.

He cried so hard his knees collapsed, and the woman tried to console him, to hold him up, and then he fled.

at least that long

At the end of Coco's nine-month checkup, her final doctor's visit while in our care, our favorite nurse pulled me aside. She told me what everyone tells me, that we had been there for Coco at a critical time in her development, that the foundation we laid for her would last her whole life, that there was nothing else we could do.

"I tell pregnant women that it took a year to put on that weight, so it will take at least a year for it to come off," she said. "You've had her for nine months. It will take at least that long for you to recover."

goodbye

People came to say goodbye. Our friends, their children. Erin asked people to give Coco their favorite children's books so we could send them with her when she returned to Evelyn. My friend Alli brought her two girls to visit, and they played with Coco in her room, on the floor, took out all her toys at once. The next day we had a picnic in the field behind Alli's house with Alli and her daughters, with Erin and her daughter, with Eric and Coco and me. Coco ate strawberries.

My friend Claudia, who had helped us take care of Coco, came over with her three children, and we walked to the park, wheeled Coco in her stroller. We pushed her in a swing. We went down a slide with her on our laps. Claudia invited us to dinner at her house. She prepared a feast, a long table set outside in her yard, her family there, her children, her husband, her mother, her brother. Her kids shared their toys with Coco, their Matchbox cars, their soccer balls. Coco played and laughed for hours in the late evening summer sun.

"I can't talk about it," Claudia said when I asked her how she wanted to say goodbye.

loved and safe and unafraid

On her last night in our home, Eric and I did rock-paper-scissors to see who would get to have the monitor on their side of the bed, and I won. We woke at 1:11 when she made noise, and we sat together on the couch and fed her a bottle. Coco rested her body against my body. Eric and I rested our heads on her head.

The next morning, we heard her cooing. "Who's the happiest girl?" we said, and she wiggled and smiled in her crib. I picked her up and held her.

We wanted to give her a beautiful, normal, happy, fun day. We played in the living room. We played in the backyard. We played in her bedroom. We went for a walk. Eric and I cried at different times, and one of us would have to leave the room, and when that person came back, the other would have to leave. We didn't want Coco to know we were crying. We didn't want her to be afraid. We wanted her to feel loved. We wanted her to feel safe.

While she napped, we packed the car with our gifts for Evelyn and Coco. A basket filled with the books our friends had collected for her. New clothes she could grow into. A basket of her favorite toys. The photobook. Canisters of formula. Teething biscuits. Her favorite stuffed animals. Her moose pacifier. A letter we'd written to Evelyn.

When she woke up, I took her downstairs. Eric was in the kitchen making oat cereal and peanut butter and banana for her, and I could hear him crying, though I knew he was trying to hide the sound, and it made me cry, too, so when I brought Coco into the kitchen, Eric and I were both crying and trying not to cry, and I put her in the chair attached to the island, and she told me with her sounds and with her body that she did not want to be in that chair, but I put her there anyway, strapped her in, because we only had a short time left to feed her. Then she did something I had never seen her do before. She crumpled. Hung her head. Slumped her shoulders. And cried.

I unbuckled her and picked her up right away. I comforted her. I held her in my lap while we fed her. She smiled and laughed. She touched my face.

But I cannot stop seeing her collapsed body.

She knew.

We changed her clothes. We brushed her hair. We played on the floor for a few more minutes, and then we had to carry her out of her room. We carried her down the stairs the way she loved to be carried down the stairs. I held her with Eric following behind. "Marching down the stairs," we said. "Marching down the stairs." Her mouth wide. Her body wiggling with delight.

We carried her through the living room. "Marching through the living room. Marching through the living room."

We carried her through the kitchen. "Marching through the kitchen. Marching through the kitchen."

She laughed and laughed.

Eric held her, and I anointed her body with rose balm, with cedar oil, and we put her in her car seat, and carried her to the car, and drove her to the classroom at the community college where we'd agreed to meet Evelyn.

I sat in the backseat and held her hand.

bring her body back

A grieving mother orca carried the body of her dead calf for two weeks, for more than a thousand miles. The baby had died a few hours after being born, and then her mother swam, balancing her daughter's body on her head. To keep her calf from sinking, the mother nudged her toward the surface of the Pacific. Her baby was heavy, four hundred pounds, and when she slipped off her head, her mother dived deep underwater to bring her body back.

Researchers knew about this mother whale before the calf was born; they had named her Tahlequah, which is the name of the oldest municipality in Oklahoma, the capital of both the Cherokee Nation and the United Keetoowah Band of Cherokee Indians. Tahlequah's pod, which roams between Vancouver and San Juan Island, numbers only seventy-five whales, and researchers are worried. They know their decline is caused by humans, who net the whales' salmon, who drive ships through their hunting lanes, who pollute their waters. Tahlequah's calf was the first in three years to be born into the pod.

You could watch Tahlequah mourn, watch videos that showed her surfacing with her daughter's body, and other mothers who had suffered miscarriages, stillborn births, the death of a child identified with her. She made their grief visible.

the end

I'm early, Evelyn texted.

She was already in the classroom when we carried Coco inside.

"Thank you for creating this amazing child," I said. "Thank you for trusting us with her."

"I never worried when she was with you," Evelyn said.

We showed her the photobook, the new clothes, the formula, the stuffed animals, the library of books. "We'll carry all of this to your car for you," Eric said. "You can stay here with Coco."

She handed me the keys.

"Which car did you drive today?" I asked. She always drove a different car, borrowed vehicles from friends. Her car was a gas guzzler, and it needed new tires, and she couldn't afford gas or tires.

"It's the car with no side mirror," she said.

"What color?" I asked.

"Maybe green?" she said.

"Where did you park?" Eric asked.

"I'm not sure," she said.

We wandered the parking lot until we found her car, which was parked right next to ours. We opened the trunk, and it was filled with someone's clothes and shoes. We put our gifts for Coco inside.

When we returned to the classroom, Eric took a picture of the three of us—Evelyn and Coco and me.

"I love you I love you I love you I love you I love you," we said.

And then we left.

empty

Eric drove us home, and we went inside, and we fell into each other, and we wailed and wailed and wailed. We put away the oat cereal and peanut butter and banana and avocado and the teething biscuits. We took everything else to the basement—the chair attached to the island, the bouncy gym, the high chair, the black-and-white artwork we'd taped to the walls, the bassinets, the multicolored eggs we'd just been playing with, the balls, the books, the blocks, the rings, the rattles. We went to her bedroom. We put the books on the shelf. We organized her toy bins. We put her clothes away. We lay on the twin bed and cried and cried and cried.

One minute she was there. And then, gone.

We cried until dark.

I went outside and looked at the moon. "You see the same moon I see," I said.

We went to bed and held hands.

"What are you thinking about?" Eric asked.

"Coco," I said.

"Give me something else to think about."

heartbreak

Day after day after day, my teeth ached. My jaw ached. I walked into a door and a bruise bloomed on my cheek. Somehow I bruised my forearm and both shinbones. My hips hurt. My eyelids swelled. My eyeballs were tender. My back knotted.

Eric refused to wash Coco's clothes. He put them in a bag in his closet. He carried them around.

My only plan for the summer-without-Coco was to hike and drink tequila, but drinking made everything worse, so I didn't drink.

I cried while hiking. I cried at my desk. I cried in the shower. I cried walking into the kitchen to get a glass of water. I screamed so loud alone in the car that I almost blacked out, my throat raw.

Record rainfall combined with snowmelt made the river rise and overflow its banks. Its raging matched mine, and I didn't trust myself to go near it.

a difference

How's that amazing, wiggly, curious baby girl? I texted Evelyn.

Terrific as always, she texted back. She sent me photographs. Coco trying to stand next to a couch. Coco watching fireworks. Coco sitting on Evelyn's lap while Evelyn holds a small chicken. Eric did not want to see them.

From someone who had been told not to talk to me anymore, I learned Coco had shown up vomiting at daycare, so they'd made Evelyn take Coco to the doctor's office, where Evelyn told the doctor Coco had fallen out of her crib.

Later Evelyn changed her story, said Coco had fallen out of her high chair.

Later she said she'd rolled off Evelyn's bed.

From someone who had been told not to talk to me anymore, I learned Coco had lost so much weight the doctor was worried about whether she was being fed properly. I learned Coco didn't like being near other children at daycare, that she pushed them away, kept to herself.

"Will any of this make a difference?" I asked and asked and asked.

"No," everyone said. "It will not make a difference."

i thought i heard her

I thought I heard her cry. I thought I heard her coo on the monitor. What if she is afraid? What if she is sad? What if she's hurt or tired or hungry? What if she wonders where we've gone? We keep her bedroom door closed, but sometimes I open the door, and the whole room smells like her. I bury my head in her sheets. We took care of her every second of every day for ten months, knew when she was asleep, when she was awake, when she was hungry, when she ate, when she played and laughed and smiled. Now we don't know anything.

evelyn does

"No one really understands what I'm feeling," I told Juliana.

"Evelyn does," she said.

"What do you mean?"

"She lost her child to you," Juliana said. "Then you lost your child to her."

you are not far from home

You Belong Here—that was the title of the first book I ever read to you, Coco. *The stars belong in the deep night sky and the moon belongs there too, and the winds belong in each place they blow by and I belong here with you,* I read, your little body nestled against mine. I turned page after page, showed you the pictures. Whales belong in the sea and waves belong to the shore and grasses belong to the dunes. Trees belong to the woods and deer belong to their shade. Birds belong to the sky and to nests and to trees. Fish belong to streams. Foxes belong to canyons. *And you belong right here, where you're home.*

You belong to sky. You belong to trees. You belong to music. You belong to laughter. You belong to gardens and prairies and mountains. You belong to rock. You belong to valleys. You belong to wildflowers. You belong to vistas. You belong to oceans and creeks and rivers. You belong to elk and buffalo and antelope and moose and hawk and hummingbird and vulture. You belong to bee and butterfly and spider. You belong to moon and sun and clouds and stars.

You were never ours, yet we belong to each other.

"When you kiss Coco, you kiss the earth," I hear in a dream. "And when you kiss the earth, you kiss Coco."

I kiss the grass in our front yard. I kiss the split tree at the top of the trail. I kiss the dirt. I kiss the maple leaf. I kiss the lupine. I kiss the sagebrush. I kiss the river. I open my mouth and kiss the rain. I kiss the wind. I kiss elk tracks. I kiss the sky. I kiss you. I kiss you. I kiss you.

Stardust, if that is what everything is, this house, this book, these bodies, then you are not far from home.

ready

My cellphone rang. *Grace*, my caller ID said, the name of the person who'd first called us ten months ago to tell us about three-day-old Coco, to tell us her biological mother was a poor prognosis, to ask us to come get her at the hospital. Eric and I were watching the World Cup, yelling at the television, rooting for our favorite soccer players.

"It's Grace," I said.

He muted the game.

I hoped Grace was calling to ask us to bring Coco home. I hoped she was calling to tell us she was ours to keep.

"Is this Sarah?" the woman asked when I answered the phone.

"Yes," I said.

"My name is Sarah, too," she said.

"Oh," I said.

"I'm calling because we have two children who need a home, starting tonight. A three-year-old and a six-month-old baby."

I didn't say a word.

"Are you there?" she asked.

"I'm here," I said.

"Are you ready?"

Maybe, someday, I will tell you this in person.

EPILOGUE

event horizon

Evelyn and I texted back and forth. She sent pictures and videos: Coco sitting in the wagon we gave her for her first birthday, Coco dressed as a ladybug for Halloween, Coco walking for the first time across Evelyn's living room.

And then, nothing.

Good morning, I texted. *How's that amazing walking girl?*

Nothing.

I hope you will be spending Thanksgiving with people you love and who love you. Please give Coco a hug from me.

Nothing.

I miss you.

Nothing.

We have Christmas presents for you and Coco.

Nothing.

Thinking of you.

Nothing.

Sending love.

Sending love.

Sending love.

I texted her friend June. I asked if she knew how Evelyn and Coco were doing.

Coco is okay, Evelyn is okay, she texted back. *Even if she isn't responding, she reads what you write. Keep reaching out. She doesn't have very many people in her corner.*

Then Evelyn cut June off too.

I'm worried about Coco, I texted her.

So am I, June texted back.

When Coco was reunified with Evelyn, all the supports DHW had given her while Coco was in our care were removed. No counseling, no rehab, no check-ins, no help with her finances, no supervision. The minute they returned her child and closed the case, Evelyn was on her own. The court had deemed Evelyn ready to parent, so the state had no legal basis for any kind of intervention. Evelyn only received help when her children were in foster care. A built-in incentive for relapse.

I started monitoring people connected to Evelyn on Facebook. Her son's foster parents. Her brother. Her friend June's sister-in-law. I checked their posts every few days, hoping to catch a glimpse of Coco and Evelyn, find some sliver of information that would let me know they were safe.

Then a post by Evelyn's brother: Months before, he'd moved to Twin Falls to live with Evelyn and help take care of Coco. Though he too struggled with addiction, Evelyn had taken Coco out of daycare and left her with him while she worked. In the post, her brother accused Evelyn of stealing his disability money. He accused her of inviting her drug dealer to live with them. He accused her of relapsing. He confessed to doing meth with her and her dealer. They got so high, he wrote, they didn't sleep for five days.

I called our social workers in Idaho. I was not the first person who had reported concerns, they told me, but no one knew where Evelyn and Coco were. They urged me to call the central intake line to report what I knew, so I did. There were already several open reports about Evelyn, but they would not stay open long. In Idaho, if DHW cannot locate the person in question within five business days, they close the case.

"But she's practiced at avoiding detection," I told every social worker I spoke to. "Five days isn't long enough."

"Everyone in this office knows exactly what she's up to," one of them said. "But there's nothing we can do. She's probably in the state where her son is living in foster care."

I tracked down her son's social worker, Dave. I left messages on his work phone. I left messages on his cellphone. I called again and again.

"We're looking for one woman and a baby in two different states," Dave told me when he finally returned my call. "It will be nearly impossible to find her."

I called Dave every week for months. I made a formal report about a drug-endangered child. Eric and I confirmed that our names were listed on the close relative registry. We talked with social workers in Idaho to make sure that if Coco came back into care she would be placed with us.

During one of our phone calls, Dave told me that his department had decided to terminate Evelyn's parental rights to her son. There had been a court date that morning and Evelyn had shown up, without Coco. When she learned they planned to terminate her rights, she ran.

"If you're terminating her rights to her son, what about her rights to Coco?"

"We haven't seen Coco. She might be fine."

"But you're saying Evelyn can't take care of her thirteen-year-old son, that it would not be safe for him to live with her."

"Yes, and I know that Coco is even more vulnerable," he said. "But we can't make an evaluation if she won't answer my calls and refuses to tell me where she's living."

"Could we issue an Amber Alert?" I asked.

"Coco hasn't been kidnapped," he said. "She's with her mother."

I learned from June that Coco's putative father—Cody—had been released from prison at the end of May. I knew in my bones that Evelyn had left Idaho to be with him.

"I know him," Dave told me when I called to tell him about Cody. "He's part of the reason her son was first put into care."

Dave sent a different social worker to visit Cody's home to determine if Evelyn and Coco were living with him. Cody told the social worker he'd seen Evelyn and Coco on Father's Day, but he hadn't seen them since.

The court could not legally set a date for terminating Evelyn's parental rights to her son without first giving her notice, but they couldn't give her notice because they couldn't find her. So they published notices in newspapers of all the towns where they thought she might be.

"You will be the first person I call when Coco comes back into care," Dave assured me every time we talked on the phone.

I kept calling Evelyn and leaving her messages. I texted her too.

Sending love.

Sending love.

Sending love.

One day I called and her phone was no longer in service.

In our backyard there is a window well for egress from the basement. Eric and I worry animals might fall in the well and not be able to get out, so we check it regularly. One afternoon, I looked inside and saw a fledgling, a baby robin. Two robins had built a nest in the eaves of our house, outside our kitchen window. The eggs hatched in early summer. The babies grew, then left the nest, and here was one of them, trapped. One of her parents hopped between branches of a nearby maple, agitated by my presence.

I went inside the house and called for Eric. He climbed the ladder into the well. I handed him the white bucket we use to collect food scraps for composting.

"I'm going to help your child," Eric said to the robin in the maple, singing at us with sharp cries.

Piled droppings along one wall of the well suggested the

fledgling had been there for quite some time and that the parents had been feeding her.

"It's okay," Eric whispered to the fledgling. "I'm not going to hurt you."

He managed to get her inside the bucket. He secured the lid and lifted the bucket and I reached for it. With the bird inside, it somehow felt lighter, as if her new wings were helping her rise, and I put the bucket on the grass, tipped it on its side, opened the lid, and the bird was free.

One morning in August, on the Facebook page belonging to Evelyn's son's foster mother, a new post: *It's a Girl.*

Wow, I didn't know you were pregnant, one of her friends posted in the comments below the pink-and-red-heart-filled image.

Wait until you see her, the son's foster mother replied.

Bravo, another friend wrote.

Finally, the son's foster mother replied.

I can't wait to see her, another friend posted. *It's about time she is where she needs to be.*

Whose baby? someone asked.

She's two, the son's foster father replied.

Coco.

I called Dave.

"I was about to call you," he said. "Coco came into care last night."

Eric had just left for a bike ride.

COME HOME, I texted.

COCO IS BACK IN CARE.

COME HOME.

NOW.

I called everyone I could think to call, and this is what I learned: Since Cody's release from prison, Evelyn had been living in a trailer in another state with Coco. Sometimes Cody stayed there too. The trailer had no water, no electricity. Evelyn was not employed. She had no money, no working car. A few nights before Coco was taken into care, Cody and Evelyn fought, and Cody broke Evelyn's arm with a hammer. He fired a gun across Evelyn's stomach, leaving powder burns on her skin. Evelyn had been pregnant at the time, but she had a miscarriage. He trashed her trailer. Broke every window. Poured paint all over the inside of her home.

Later Cody denied this. He told me Evelyn had pulled a gun on him. He told me Evelyn had fallen out of a window.

And Evelyn changed her story too. She said Cody did not break her arm with a hammer and he did not shoot a gun across her stomach. Wearing a purple cast on her arm, she told me she had fallen into a hole.

"Where was Coco when this was happening?" I kept asking.

The night social workers took Coco into care, they placed her with her half brother's foster parents—people she had never met. Coco's half brother is thirteen; she is two. On the foster father's Facebook page are Confederate flags, hateful messages about immigrants, sexist jokes. Evelyn and the foster father met when Evelyn was fifteen and he was twenty-three. He was the one who introduced her to drugs, her friends told me.

We knew enough to know we needed a lawyer. I called my dad, a retired attorney, and asked him to help us find someone familiar with foster care. I called my friend Erin too, and she sent a list. Eric called every lawyer they'd found. One of them was Ellie. She had decades of experience with the foster care system. She'd represented foster parents and biological parents and children in care. She'd won a major case against the department in favor of a gay couple, two foster dads.

"Ellie's the one," Eric told me after he talked to her.

Ellie told us to get in our car and drive to the town where

Coco had been taken into care. "Rent a house there," she said. "Email the social workers and tell them you're on your way. Tell them you can stay as long as needed." She explained that according to the department's own rules and regulations, Coco should have been placed with us. We were the kinship placement. We were listed on the close relative registry. "Kinship placement refers only to the caregiver," Ellie said. "Not to any sibling who might be living in the home." This new foster family was, for Coco, stranger care.

Ellie explained that where Coco was placed for the first two weeks would probably be where she was placed for the duration of the case. "Act confident," Ellie said. "Of course you're coming to get her. Of course she should be placed with you. She's lived with you longer than she's lived with anyone. She's lived in your home longer than she's lived anywhere. You are her family."

We did what Ellie told us to do. We collected paperwork to help with the transition between states. We made phone calls, sent emails. We packed our car with Coco's belongings. We went to parts of our house we'd been avoiding for a year—her bedroom, her closet, her toy bins, the basement. We packed her high chair. Her stuffed animals. Her stroller. Her car seat. Her toys. Her plastic dishes and spoons and sippy cups. Her blankets. I went to the grocery store and bought pouches of vegetables and fruit, cheese sticks, baby carrots, avocados, applesauce, peanut butter, apples. We knew what she loved to eat when she lived with us. We didn't know now.

We arrived on a Sunday. A social worker and her supervisor called us on Monday night.

"Why are you here?" the social worker asked.

"Who told you to come here?" the supervisor asked.

I explained that we'd been Coco's first home, that she'd lived with us for almost a year, that I'd been in touch with Evelyn's son's social worker, that I'd been worried about Evelyn and Coco for months.

"By your own rules, we are a kinship placement," I said.

"No, you're not," the social worker said.

"We are," I said. "We had a significant relationship with Coco before she came into care here, which makes us, by your definition, *fictive kin.*"

"But you didn't know her before she came into care in Idaho," she said.

"She hadn't been *born* before she came into care in Idaho," I said. "How could we have known her before she was born?"

Eric motioned with his hands for me to lower my voice.

"You're not kin," the social worker said.

"We are," I said.

"I don't understand why you drove here," the supervisor said.

"We brought Coco home from the hospital when she was three days old," I said. "She lived with us for almost a year. We've been trying to find her for months. And now she's back in foster care in a different state. If she was your child, wouldn't you come for her? Wouldn't you want to bring her home?"

"We will never move her from her current placement," the supervisor said.

"I don't understand," I said. "We are her family."

"You are not her family," she said. "She's with her brother."

"What could I share with you that might change your minds?" I asked.

"Nothing will change our minds," she said. "And it's been a year since you've seen her. Seeing you now would traumatize her."

"Go home," the social worker said.

June's sister-in-law gave my phone number to Evelyn, told her Eric and I were in town, ready to care for Coco as long as needed, told her we wanted to talk with her, make sure she was okay.

Eric was not in favor of talking with Evelyn. He thought we would get sucked into the madness that follows her around. But I wanted to hear her voice again. I loved her. And I believed she loved Coco, loved all of her kids, even if she could not take care of them.

"Love is not a feeling," Eric said. "Love is something you *do*."

My phone rang. I answered. I heard Evelyn's voice. And then I heard a man's voice.

"Well hello, Sarah," he said. "Tell me: What the fuck are you doing here?"

"We love your daughter," I said. "That's why we're here."

EVENT HORIZON, Eric wrote in all caps across the bottom of my notebook.

Later Eric explained to me what an event horizon is—the threshold around a black hole where the escape velocity surpasses the speed of light. What goes in never comes out, because nothing can travel faster than the speed of light. The event horizon is the point of no return. Gravity is so strong inside a black hole that not even light can leave it. The laws of physics that operate outside the event horizon don't operate inside the event horizon. The laws don't work, but their failure is hidden from view because all evidence of what is happening inside the black hole can't get out either. The only things we can see are massive streams of energy that black holes sometimes kick out. "The kind that gives you cancer," Eric said. "The kind that goes right through you, that destroys you."

We listened to Cody talk for nearly an hour. He told us about his guns, about being a marine, about earning back his right to carry a concealed weapon after prison, about meeting Coco for the first time. "She's cool as shit," he said. He told us about his felonies. About how to beat someone up without getting a felony assault charge. "Just don't kick them in the head or when they're on the ground," he explained. He told us about his construction business being a front. About being in four shoot-outs with the police. About being a suspect in two murders. About becoming a certified electrician in prison. About a bondsman who owed him tens of thousands of dollars. About the trucks and cars he owned and wanted to sell. About his son who had died. About how his son's death was the reason he started using drugs.

This was the first of many phone calls with Cody. Sometimes his voice was measured, calm. Sometimes he was charming. Sometimes he told us he wanted Eric and me to take care of Coco if anything were to happen to him or to Evelyn, told us all he really wanted was a fresh start. But most of the time, he was manic, pacing, swearing, threatening.

In the evenings, we sat on the front porch of our rental and watched the sky change. Every car that drove by was louder than the last, as if there were some contest in town for the noisiest vehicle. Once, a van drove by with ASSHOLE spray-painted in black along its side.

We'd made arrangements with the owner of the house we'd rented to extend our stay for at least a month, and when I told her why we were in town, she gave us a discount. The man who lived next door told Eric he was praying for us and for our foster daughter. He promised that things happen for a reason.

"I don't see it that way," Eric said, hands in his pockets.

"When one door closes, another opens," the neighbor said.

"No," Eric said. "That's not what's happening."

Cody had been calling to tell us he was sure that the social worker was friends with the foster family in whose care she had placed Coco. That was why she wouldn't change Coco's placement, he reasoned. She'd given her friends a child to keep, he told us. And she'd given her friends a stipend from the state. That was her plan all along, he said. That was why, on the day Coco first came into care, the foster mother posted *It's a Girl* on her Facebook page. Because she'd been promised a daughter.

Cody spent hours looking for proof of his hunch, and he found it on the social worker's Facebook page. Cody was right: She had a personal relationship with the foster family. They went to the racetrack together nearly every weekend; they were on the same racing team. And it turned out Cody knew the social worker's husband, he told us. When Cody was in jail a few years ago, the social worker and her husband had worked at the jail, and Cody had beaten up her husband. "I headbutted him," he said. "But for some reason I didn't get in trouble. There wasn't even an incident report."

What you did for her during her first year will be with her always, a friend texted.

I hope knowing you took amazing care of her brings you some comfort, texted another.

Your mother-love made a difference in her life, texted another.

Soon after we'd given Coco back to Evelyn, I'd bumped into a woman in the grocery store. I didn't know her well, but ours is a small town, and she knew what had happened.

"But she was your foster daughter, right?" she said. "You always knew she would leave?"

Having understood that her stay with us might be temporary did not bring any relief when we handed Coco to Evelyn. Just as knowing that everyone I love is mortal will not bring any relief if they die.

You gave her a great first year, a friend texted.

What does it matter now?

All life on earth was created in the furnace of now-long-dead stars. Knowing I am made of stardust used to make me feel closer to everything, related to everyone, kin of tree and whale and rock and child. But now it only makes me long for explosion, collapse.

Coco is so close. Coco is in care again. And somehow she is living in some stranger's house.

Weeks passed. We did not see Coco. She turned two, but we did not get to give her the birthday presents we'd bought her—a strider bike and helmet and butterfly stickers and handlebar streamers.

Cody kept calling us. He told us that the night Coco was taken into care, he'd been surrounded by cops, guns drawn.

He told us "some asshole" came to his house and got Evelyn high.

He told us he got mad and broke windows in Evelyn's trailer.

He told us Evelyn smashed the windshield of her truck.

"Where was Coco during all of that?" I asked, again and again, but no one would tell me.

Evelyn and Cody didn't want Coco to live with her son's foster family. They wanted Coco to live with us. To make their wishes clear, they granted us guardianship of Coco, signed consents a lawyer drew up.

We only had power as a united front—the birth parents and Coco's former foster parents and our attorneys all arguing for the same outcome—but that meant we had to keep Cody happy, keep him on our side, which was nearly impossible. He called most nights, and Eric and I spent hours listening to him talk, my phone between us, our eyes wide, exhausted. He'd read thousands of pages of department rules and regulations, he told us. They'd made mistakes, violated their own policies. They had nothing on him. He was going to get his daughter back. He was going to bring the whole department down.

The department was used to doing whatever they wanted, without question, without accountability, because most of the people they interact with are the most vulnerable among us— the poor and the addicted—who don't have the time or the resources to fight the department, even when social workers take their children. Eric and I were never supposed to see the inner workings of that system. We had peered over the event horizon, glimpsed that black hole's lawlessness, and the department would do everything in its power to send us away.

The department's best weapon was Cody. Like us, they needed him on their side. We kept hearing from Cody that the social worker was telling him that she would place Coco back in his care any day now, maybe next week, or the week after that. During our conversations, Cody would explain how the social worker warned him not to trust us, made him suspicious of our motives, told him if Coco was placed with us, he'd never see her again. But if Coco stayed with the other family, he'd get her right back. It sounded like the social worker was playing into Cody's fantasies, his belief that it was him against the world, every landscape a battlefield.

"I'm going to beat the department," Cody told us. "I don't need you."

In the early morning hours or late at night, Cody sent menacing texts. He threatened to report our lawyer, Ellie, to the state bar. He ranted about white collar crime. He made a PowerPoint, the last slide asking us for money. He said he'd recorded conversations during which we'd promised him thousands of dollars.

"They taught us to do one thing in the marines," he reminded us, and we knew he meant to kill.

We were scared. Eric and I tried to clean our home address

from the Internet. We talked about installing an alarm system. Meeting with the police chief of our small mountain town when we returned home. Buying a gun.

Astronauts who have been to the moon, who have had their boots and masks and gloves coated with those sharp and sticky particles, report that moondust smells like burnt gunpowder. For billions of years, meteoroids have been hitting the moon. Those impacts fuse the moon's topsoil into glass, then shatter it into tiny pieces. "Once their helmets and gloves were off," I read in an article by NASA, "the astronauts could feel, smell, and even taste the moon."

But moondust only smells like burnt gunpowder on the moon. When you bring that dust home to Earth, the smell is gone.

I watched the moon, its waxing and waning, watched it rise over one set of mountains and set behind another. I read about the moon's formation. I learned about Capture Theory, the idea that the moon was a "wandering body" formed in the solar system and captured by Earth's gravity as it came near. I learned about Accretion Theory, the idea that the moon was created along with the Earth at its formation. I learned about Fission Theory, the idea that the moon and the Earth were once one. The moon is a piece of the Earth that flew from our whirling planet and became her satellite. The Pacific Ocean, this theory proposed, occupies the space once filled by the moon.

But the most current origin story for the moon is not as gentle. At its heart are collision, calamity. It is called Giant Impact Theory—scientists now think the moon formed when an early version of Earth collided 4.5 billion years ago with another small planet, about the size of Mars, that scientists have named Theia, after the Greek goddess who gave birth to the moon. The impact produced enormous heat that created magma oceans and ejected debris into orbit around the Earth. That debris coalesced to form the moon.

But there is a problem with this story, details and facts and figures that have not been resolved. The Apollo missions that landed on the moon brought back rock and soil, a third of a ton of moon, and they learned its composition is very much like the Earth's. Where is Theia's material?

Scientists reason that the composition of Theia and the early version of Earth must have been similar too, so much alike that there is no discernible difference now. In all that vastness, they found each other, collided, and in that meeting, in that violence, made something new.

Which of us is the debris?

Cody told us that he was sure the social worker was going to give Coco to him. He insisted Evelyn was the problem, not him. He called himself "the non-offending parent," and his lawyer referred to him that way too. Cody said that the social worker promised him it would take just "a couple of weeks" for him to get Coco back.

Stay the fuck away from my daughter, Cody texted me.

Eric and I could not stop thinking about Coco being placed with Cody. We both thought it was possible that the department would place Coco with him to spite us. It would be the worst possible outcome. She might not survive it.

"They will never do that," Ellie assured us. "They will never place a two-year-old in his care."

But Eric and I were not so sure. We'd already watched our Idaho social workers put Coco in harm's way by reunifying her with Evelyn, despite so many red flags. If our fight against the department meant that the social worker would have to take back the baby it seemed she'd promised her friends, then we worried she would do anything to avoid having to place Coco with us—including giving her to Cody. It was possible that our fight for Coco was putting her in danger.

We drove home a second time, without Coco. A few days later, I went on a hike with my friend Erin.

"I don't want to quit," I said. "I don't want to give up. But I'm afraid our fight is putting Coco at risk. I'm afraid the department will place her with Cody to get back at us. And that could kill her."

Erin stopped walking and turned around on the trail to look at me. "You're framing it wrong," she said. "Your goal has always been to make sure Coco is safe. That is why you did all of this, why you hired lawyers, why you rented a house. Because you love her and you want to protect her. It isn't quitting to walk away now. It's love. It's the biggest possible act of love. To stop fighting is an act of love. You are not quitting. You are loving her. You are mothering her. You are keeping her safe."

Two days later, Cody and Evelyn withdrew their consents for guardianship. Eric and I were hiking on a trail near our house when Ellie called to tell us. We sat in the sagebrush. We sat in the dirt.

Stay the fuck out of MINE and my daughter's life as you cannot handle the fact that she is my daughter and not yours, Cody texted.

It was finished. On National Daughter's Day.

Evelyn later told me that Cody had punched her in the face, given her a black eye the night before they withdrew their consents. I heard from her friends that he cut the wires on her truck, cut the power lines to her trailer. She hid from him, skipped her scheduled visits with Coco because she was so afraid. She took out a restraining order against him. She called me and asked for her lawyer's phone number and told me Cody had taken her phone with all her contacts. I researched shelters for victims of domestic violence where she could stay. I mapped out legal steps to help her move to Idaho, to make sure she and Coco would be safe. I sent text after text showing her how it was still possible to protect her daughter. But, in a few days, she would lift the restraining order against Cody, and when her friend went to Evelyn's trailer to give her money to get the power turned back on, Cody would be there too.

She won't be happy until he kills her, one of her friends would text me.

She's going to keep choosing him, her lawyer would tell our lawyer.

Eric and I walked home, crying. We unloaded our car, which we'd kept packed and ready to return at any moment. We carried Coco's car seat, her stroller, and her high chair to the basement. We put her blankets in her crib. Put away her toys and stuffed animals. Unpacked her clothes.

The moon is far away. Yet her pull affects everything.

Will Coco ever know we fought for her, that we are fighting for her still? Will she ever know we came to get her, hired lawyers, rented a house, spent weeks and weeks and weeks driving back and forth and fighting the department? Does it matter?

She's safer now than she used to be.

That is no small thing.

But I want to bring her home.

And if we are not allowed to bring her home, then I hope, someday, I will see her again, walking down the street, in the aisle of the grocery store, at a restaurant, in the woods, by a river, on a playground.

She could be any stranger.

Any stranger could be our daughter.

Acknowledgments

I wrote most of this book in Idaho, on the original homelands of the Shoshone-Bannock people. The beauty of this land—rivers, mountains, valleys, trees—brought me comfort, peace. Yet I live three hours north of the Bear River Massacre Site, where the largest massacre of Native Americans in U.S. history occurred. The thefts, violence, and family separations that happen in the pages of this book—and that continue to happen in the United States and at our borders—are connected to the genocide and forced removal that took place here. I recognize the Shoshone-Bannock Tribe's continuing connection to and protection of land, waters, and culture. Thank you for teaching me what it means to love and tend a place. I pay my respects and offer my gratitude to Elders past, present, and emerging.

Thank you to my family for loving Coco while she was with us, and for loving us when she wasn't—my parents, Ann and Irwin, and my siblings and in-laws and nephews, Emily, Charley, Irwin, Rebecca, Della, Kristine, Dione, Barbara, Jerry, Sam, Elwood, Henry, Seth, and Mason.

Thank you to the team that brought this book to life. Thank you, Molly Friedrich, best reader, advocate, and agent a writer could hope for. Thank you for flying across the country to meet our girl—and for loving her. Thank you, Andy Ward, gift of an editor, gift of a human being. You made this book sing. Thank you, Marie Pantojan, careful, generous, brilliant editor. Thank you for understanding what I was trying to write and for helping me write it better. Thank you, Heather Carr, for your time and insights. Thank you, Adri Meyer, for your research. Thank you, Melissa Milsten, advocate. Your belief in this story and in me is everything. Thank you, London King, superb publicist and champion. I am grateful to work with you. And thank you to the extraordinary team at Random House: Jess Bonet, Evan

Camfield, Rachel Kind, Anna Kochman, Jo Anne Metsch, Allyson Pearl, Tom Perry, and Kaeli Subberwal. The books you help bring into being have been a balm for me; writers like those you publish have shown me the way.

Thank you, Juliana Jones-Munson. These pages are a love letter to you too—a testament to your transformative work in the world. Thank you, Lydia Missal, for the healing magic of EMDR. Thank you, Stephanie Hatzenbuehler, for helping us write Book Two. Thank you, Julie Lyons and your whole team, for taking such good care of Coco, and of Eric and me.

Thank you, Hedgebrook, for the gift of a residency and for the workshop with Carolyn Forché. I started writing this book in that beautiful place. Thank you, Willamette University, for supporting me to attend Forché's workshop. Thank you, Yaddo, for the gift of time and space, where this book took root. And thank you, Margaux Ogden and Dee Shapiro, for your friendship.

Thank you, Cheryl Strayed, for reading these pages and for taking Coco into your heart.

Thank you, Claudia Cayeros, Coco's favorite, and mine. Thank you for teaching us how to care for her and for your wide-open love. My heart, my heart, my heart.

Thank you, Erin O'Toole, for walking with me through every step of this heartbreak. My deepest gratitude for your friendship. You mother Maeve—and all of us—so generously. And thank you, Clancy.

Thank you, Alli Connolly, for loving our girl fiercely and with abandon—and for letting your girls love her too.

Thank you, Maylen Dominguez, for decades of unconditional love, and for decades more.

Thank you, Emily Rapp Black, for showing me what loving in the face of loss looks like.

Thank you, Katie Ford, for telling me in those early days

that Coco needed my "full-on in-loveness," for reminding me it's never wrong to choose love.

Thank you, Amy Walsh, for helping me become an artist.

Thank you, dear friends: Jenny Emery Davidson, Muffy Davis, Chantal Forfota, Courtney Gilbert, Sam Grant, Julie Green, Abby Greensfelder, Anne Guerry, Hether Holter, Lacy Johnson, Karen King, Erica Lauritsen, Amy Lief, Sara Levine, Becky Lopez, Elizabeth Malaska, Jeanne Meyers, Yuki Murata, Tovis Page, Vicki Politis, Kristin Poole, Kayleen Pritchard, Tara Rubinstein, Annie Staebler, and Laura Tuach. And for those of you not named here—who sent books and cards and texts and chocolate and soup and art and prayers and flowers—my deepest thanks. My friend the writer Wendy Hill said, "Grief is a new language, and you will recognize right away who knows how to speak it." You all know how to speak it.

Thank you to the participants in the WORD CAVE and RIGHT TO WRITE.

Thank you to the woman at Shutterfly who moved mountains to make sure the photobook arrived in time. I wish I knew your name.

Thank you to my cats, 2Lip and Googs, who sleep on my desk while I write, comfort.

Thank you, Ellie Boldman, champion and fighter for our girl. Thank you, Lisa Schoettger, Shannon Hathaway, and Tim McKeon. If anyone needs a lawyer as they navigate the foster care system, these big-hearted experts are your best bets.

Thank you, Kaitlyn Judy, for helping us find a new beginning.

Thank you, Gina and Angie. We tried.

Thank you, Evelyn, for making me a mother.

To the "child protection" teams in two states: None of this would have happened without you.

Thank you, Coco. We loved you as soon as we saw you, and

we will never stop. You brought us such joy. We are fighting for you. We will work to help build a world where you can have a beautiful life, no matter where you are. We miss you every minute.

And, finally, thank you, Eric Toshalis, partner, love of my life. Thank you for saying "Go write" every time my heart was breaking. There is no one else I would rather live this with. Someday, I know, we will bring our child home.

Notes

I. SHOW YOURSELF TO BE A MOTHER

7   **In the forest, underground, there is another world:** This section on tree communication and Suzanne Simard came from the following sources: Diane Toomey, "Exploring How and Why Trees 'Talk' to Each Other," *Yale Environment 360*, September 1, 2016; Suzanne Simard, "How Trees Talk to Each Other," TEDSummit June 2016, ted.com/talks/suzanne_simard_how_trees_talk_to _each_other?language=en; Derek Markham, "Trees Talk to Each Other and Recognize Their Offspring," *Treehugger*, May 9, 2020, treehugger.com/natural-sciences/trees-talk-each-other-and -recognize-their-offspring.html; Lacy Cooke, "Mother Trees Recognize Kin and Send Them Messages of Wisdom," *Inhabitat*, August 6, 2016, inhabitat.com/mother-trees-recognize-kin-and-send -them-messages-of-wisdom/; and Shannon Henry Kleiber, "Listening to the Mother Trees," *To the Best of Our Knowledge*, May 11, 2014, ttbook.org/interview/listening-mother-trees.

11   **The oldest known image of Jesus's mother:** "Milk from the Virgin's Breast," *WTF? Art History*, wtfarthistory.com/post/4653307 783/milk-from-the-virgins-breast, and "The Hidden Meaning of the Strangely Beautiful 'Lactation of St. Bernard,'" *ChurchPOP*, August 26, 2016, churchpop.com/2016/08/26/hidden-meaning -strangely-beautiful-lactation-st-bernard/.

11   **Through the Renaissance, breast milk was believed to be processed blood:** Jenny Bledsoe, "Feminine Images of Jesus: Later Medieval Christology and the Devaluation of the Feminine," *Intermountain West Journal of Religious Studies*, vol. 3, no. 1 (2011), 41, digitalcommons.usu.edu/cgi/viewcontent.cgi?article=1015& context=imwjournal.

11   **With the invention of the printing press:** David Gibson, "Christmas' Missing Icon: Mary Breastfeeding Jesus," *Religion News Service*, December 10, 2012, religionnews.com/2012/12/10/christmas -missing-icon-mary-breastfeeding-jesus/; David Gibson, "Jesus

Was Not a Bottle Baby: What Happened to Maria Lactans?" *Commonweal*, December 11, 2012, commonwealmagazine.org/blog/ jesus-was-not-bottle-baby-what-happened-maria-lactans; both articles engage a book by Margaret Miles, *A Complex Delight: The Secularization of the Breast, 1350–1750* (Berkeley: University of California Press, 2008).

13 **The video shows a four-story building in Syria:** "White Helmet Volunteer Sobs as He Rescues Baby Girl," CNN, September 30, 2016, edition.cnn.com/videos/world/2016/09/30/white-helmets -rescue-baby-girl.cnn.

16 **Most hornbills build their nests:** Thank you, Claudia Aulum, for telling me about hornbills. I researched hornbills and learned about them from these sources: Jeffrey Hays, "Hornbills, Their Nest-Building Behavior and Species in Asia," *Facts and Details*, November 2012, factsanddetails.com/asian/cat68/sub435/item2430 .html; "Why the Hornbill Shuts Its Nest," *Safari Ecology*, February 21, 2012, safari-ecology.blogspot.com/2012/02/why-hornbill -shuts-its-nest.html; and Michael Joseph Finney, "Conflict and Communication: Consequences of Female Nest Confinement in Yellow Billed Hornbills," September 2012, core.ac.uk/download/ pdf/146491463.pdf.

II. FAMILY PICTURE

21 **"Do you have kids?" strangers asked almost every day:** I first wrote about this idea for *O: The Oprah Magazine*, "The Other Mother: Sarah Sentilles on What to Expect When You're Expectant," *O: The Oprah Magazine*, July 2018 (vol. 18, no. 7), 30–32, oprah .com/inspiration/what-its-like-to-become-a-foster-parent.

26 **At that time in Oregon, there were more than eight thousand children:** These specific numbers are from 2012, but when I looked at other years, they were similar for the period of time in which we were working with DHW in Oregon: cwla.org/wp -content/uploads/2015/06/2015-State-Fact-Sheet-Oregon.pdf.

26 **In the United States about half of the children:** "What Is Foster

Care?," Annie E. Casey Foundation, February 5, 2014 (updated April 14, 2020), aecf.org/blog/what-is-foster-care/?gclid=EAaIQob ChMI4ZK4qvaA5AIVTj0MCh2xcwWrEAAYASAAEgIIa_D_BwE.

26 **A child in care is moved:** I found these statistics at this link, kinshiphouse.org/the-statistics, though it no longer works.

28 **In the photograph:** Kyle Almond, "The Life He Lived: Photos of the Last Male Northern White Rhino," with photos by Ami Vitale, CNN, March 2018, cnn.com/interactive/2018/03/world/last -rhino-cnnphotos/.

32 **Imagine that room:** Ariella Azoulay, *The Civil Contract of Photography* (New York: Zone Books, 2008), 184–85.

33 **The first time Lanier saw the image of Renty:** Joey Garrison, "Who was Renty? The Story of the Slave Whose Racist Photos Have Triggered a Lawsuit Against Harvard," *USA Today*, March 21, 2019, usatoday.com/story/news/nation/2019/03/21/harvard -slavery-lawsuit-who-renty-american-slave-photos/3232806002/.

33 **"Slavery was abolished 156 years ago":** Matthew S. Schwartz, "Harvard Profits from Photos of Slaves, Lawsuit Claims," NPR, March 21, 2019, npr.org/2019/03/21/705382289/harvard-profits -from-photos-of-slaves-lawsuit-claims.

34 **In a series that she titled** *Holding***:** Azoulay, *The Civil Contract of Photography*, 292–302.

III. ONE OF OUR OWN

44 *Stranger danger* **hangs on the belief:** Sara Ahmed, *Strange Encounters: Embodied Others in Post-Coloniality* (London and New York: Routledge, 2000), 3.

44 **Now the Department of Homeland Security tells us what to do:** dhs.gov/see-something-say-something.

44 **In** *Strange Encounters,* **Sara Ahmed argues:** Ahmed, *Strange Encounters,* 29.

44 **The stranger is "a mechanism** *for allowing us***":** Ibid., 3.

45 **Jackdaws, birds in the crow family:** Jakob von Uexküll, "A Stroll Through the Worlds of Animals and Men," in *Instinctive Behavior:*

The Development of a Modern Concept, translated and edited by Claire H. Schiller (New York: International Universities Press, 1957), 59–60.

45   **At the Amsterdam Zoo:** Uexküll, "Stroll Through the Worlds," 61.

55   **Later, I learned the FBI estimates:** nfyi.org/issues/sex-trafficking/.

57   **A woman in Germany:** I heard this story on NPR, but I cannot find it.

IV. MATERNAL IMPRESSION

61   **The average age of children in foster care is eight:** kinshiphouse .org/the-statistics.

63   **Sixty—that's how many years one woman carried a baby:** "Woman Delivers 'Stone Baby' after 60 Year Pregnancy," May 2, 2009, weirdasianews.com/2009/05/02/weirder-weird-chinese -stone-pregnancy/.

67   **On a September day in 1726, Mary Toft:** I learned about Mary Toft from Lucas Reilly, "The Woman Who Gave Birth to Rabbits," *Mental Floss,* January 28, 2014, mentalfloss.com/article/ 54643/woman-who-gave-birth-rabbits; "The Rabbit Babies of Mary Toft," museumofhoaxes.com/hoax/archive/permalink/ mary_toft_and_the_rabbit_babies/; and Niki Russell, "Mary Toft and Her Extraordinary Delivery of Rabbits," *The Public Domain Review,* March 20, 2013, publicdomainreview.org/2013/03/ 20/mary-toft-and-her-extraordinary-delivery-of-rabbits/#sthash .qdVlUUvE.dpuf.

V. FAMILY TREE

79   **But mapping family onto a plant:** Elizabeth Freeman, "Queer Belongings," in George E. Haggerty and Molly McGarry, eds., *A Companion to Lesbian, Gay, Bisexual, Transgender, and Queer Studies* (Malden, Mass., and Oxford: Blackwell, 2007), 308.

81   **Look up into the forest canopy:** Peter Wohlleben, *The Hidden Life of Trees: What They Feel, How They Communicate: Discoveries*

from a Secret World (Vancouver, B.C.: Greystone Books, 2016), 16, 4–5.

82 **We didn't know Idaho's reunification statistics are higher:** Idaho, Department of Health and Welfare, healthandwelfare .idaho.gov / Children / AdoptionFosterCareHome / tabid / 75 / Default .aspx#targetText=Currently%2C%20there%20are%20approximately %201300,very%20young%20children%20to%20teenagers.&target Text=The%20goal%20of%20foster%20care,about%2072%25%20o f%20the%20time.

90 **Mother trees raise their children:** Wohlleben, *Hidden Life of Trees,* 32–34.

93 **To guard against invaders like bacteria and fungi:** Alex L. Shigo and Harold G. Marx, "Compartmentalization of Decay in Trees," *Agriculture Information Bulletin* 45, July 1977, nrs.fs.fed.us / pubs / misc / ne_aib405.pdf.

96 **To graft is to join the root system:** I learned about grafting from "Grafting and Budding Nursery Crop Plants," North Carolina State University, content.ces.ncsu.edu / grafting-and-budding -nursery-crop-plants; "Graft," *Encyclopaedia Britannica*, January 4, 2019, britannica.com / topic / graft; and Marie Iannotti, *The Spruce,* October 21, 2019, thespruce.com / what-does-grafting-mean-412 5565.

97 **To create the illusion of bodies without kin:** Freeman, "Queer Belongings," 303.

VI. HOMESICK

101 **Homesick:** The title of this part is inspired by a manuscript in progress by Janine Mikosza.

108 **Black and Brown parents:** Stephanie Clifford and Jessica Silver-Greenberg, "Foster Care as Punishment: The New Reality of 'Jane Crow,'" *The New York Times,* July 21, 2017, nytimes.com / 2017 / 07 / 21 / nyregion / foster-care-nyc-jane-crow.html.

108 **More than 37 percent of children in the United States:** Trey

Rabun, "How We Found More Black Foster Parents and Confronted the Racial Disparity in Foster Care," *Youth Today*, February 28, 2018, youthtoday.org/2018/02/found-black-foster-parents-confronted-racial-disparity-foster-care/.

108 **"But for Black children, that number skyrockets":** Ibid.

108 **What's more, once these children of color are in foster care:** Tanya Asim Cooper, "Racial Bias in American Foster Care: The National Debate," abstracted from Tanya Asim Cooper, "Racial Bias in American Foster Care: The National Debate," *Marquette Law Review* 215 (Winter 2013), found online on *Race, Racism and the Law*, racism.org/articles/basic-needs/family/1784-racial-bias-in-american-foster-care-the-national-debate.

108 **Black parents don't abuse or neglect their children:** Ruth McRoy, "Foster Care for Minority Children," excerpted from Ruth McRoy, "Expedited Permanency: Implications for African-American Children and Families," *Virginia Journal of Social Policy and the Law* (2005), 475–89, found online on *Race, Racism and the Law*, racism.org/index.php?option=com_content&view=article&id=1078:adopto4-1&Itemid=118.

109 **Nevertheless, many professionals in the foster care system "routinely contend":** Cooper, "Racial Bias in American Foster Care."

109 **Based on this racist misperception:** Ibid.

109 **Racism means that if you're Black or Brown:** Amnoni L. Myers, "Black Children and Foster Care: On Surviving the Trauma of a System That Doesn't Care About Keeping Families Together," *The Root*, May 28, 2018, theroot.com/black-children-and-foster-care-on-surviving-the-trauma-1826121898#targetText=According%20to%20national%20data%2C%20there,23%20percent%20of%20those%20children. In 2015 in the United States, there were 428,000 children in the foster care system. Half of them were children of color, and 23 percent were Black. That same year, "more than 20,000 foster children of color aged out of the foster care system without reuniting with their families or finding permanent homes."

109 Landlords use the threat of foster care to bully their tenants: Clifford and Silver-Greenberg, "Foster Care as Punishment."

110 Next to an auction block hung a cotton sack: *The New York Times,* "I, Too, Sing America: The National Museum of African American History and Culture," multimedia, produced by Alicia Desantis and Josh Williams, photographs by Lexey Swall, written by Graham Bowley, interviews by Tamara Best, graphics by Anjali Singhvi, video by Johan M. Kessel, September 15, 2016, nytimes .com/interactive/2016/09/15/arts/design/national-museum-of -african-american-history-and-culture.html.

110 Mark Auslander, an associate professor of anthropology: Amina Al-Sadi and Jeannie Yandel, "A Slave Mother's Love in 56 Carefully Stitched Words," KUOW, December 23, 2016, kuow.org/post/ slave-mothers-love-56-carefully-stitched-words.

117 The first elephant arrived in North America: George G. Goodwin, "The Crowninshield Elephant," *Natural History,* natural historymag.com/editors_pick/1928_05-06_pick.html; "Scientists Unravel the Secret World of Elephant Communication," *PhysOrg,* May 23, 2005, physorg.com/news4211.html; "Seismic Communication," *Elephant Voices,* elephantvoices.org/elephant -communication/seismic-communication.html; and "Gigantic," *The Memory Palace,* episode 32, July 3, 2010, thememorypalace.us/ 2010/07/episode-32-gigantic/.

119 In the exhibit *The Hampton Project:* Greg Cook, "Exhibit Revisits Old Uncomfortable Questions," *The Boston Globe,* March 21, 2007, archive.boston.com/ae/theater_arts/articles/2007/03/21/ exhibit_revisits_old_uncomfortable_questions/.

119 Though most of the boarding schools closed: Becky Little, "Government Boarding Schools Once Separated Native American Children from Families," A&E Television Networks, *History,* History Stories, November 1, 2018, history.com/news/government -boarding-schools-separated-native-american-children-families #:~:text=Government%20Boarding%20Schools%20Once%20 Separated%20Native%20American%20Children%20From%20

Families,-Once%20they%20returned&text=Rather%2C%20the
%20Carlisle%20Indian%20Industrial,%2C%20and%20save%20the%
20man.%E2%80%9D.

119 **By the 1960s, between 25 and 35 percent of all American Indian children:** Christie Renick, "The Nation's First Family Separation Policy," *The Chronicle of Social Change*, October 9, 2019. In the late 1960s, Bertram Hirsch—a New York–based attorney employed by the Association on American Indian Affairs (AAIA)—was sent to North Dakota to help with a kinship dispute case on behalf of the Spirit Lake Tribe. Child welfare workers were removing children from their families by force and putting them in the homes of White people, sometimes out of state. One grandmother had been jailed after she refused to give up her grandchildren. As Hirsch worked on the case, he began to help with a nationwide data collection project, which showed that a third of all Native American children had been taken from their families and put in foster care with White families. Hirsch helped write the Indian Child Welfare Act (ICWA), which he describes as "a huge grassroots effort spanning eleven years and involving thousands of people across the country." It was passed in 1978. With the act, tribes won the ability to determine the residency of children in that tribe.

120 **In *The Undercommons*, Fred Moten writes:** Jack Halberstam, "The Wild Beyond: With and for the Undercommons," in Stefano Harney and Fred Moten, *The Undercommons: Fugitive Planning and Black Study* (New York: Minor Compositions, 2013), 10.

VII. FAMILIES BELONG TOGETHER

135 **The Associated Press reported:** Elliot Spagat, "US Sees Limitations on Reuniting Migrant Families," *AP News*, February 2, 2019, apnews.com/48210bbf243e423ea151ff04e4878ce6?utm_medium=AP WestRegion&utm_campaign=SocialFlow&utm_source=Twitter. In this passage—"Removing children from sponsor homes to rejoin their parents 'would present grave child welfare concerns,'

officials insisted. It would be 'traumatic to the children'"—the quotes belong to Jonathan White, who led the Health and Human Services Department's effort to reunite migrant children with their parents.

135 **A woman from Guatemala who lived in Missouri:** Rachel Nolan, "Destined for Export: The Troubled Legacy of Guatemalan Adoptions," *Harper's,* April 2019, 54.

136 **wet nurse:** I learned about this practice from Emily West and R. J. Knight, "Mothers' Milk: Slavery, Wet-Nursing, and Black and White Women in the Antebellum South," *The Journal of Southern History* 83, no. 1 (2017): 53, 51, 59, 55, 66. West refers to John Davis, *Travels of Four Years and a Half in the United States of America During 1798, 1799, 1800, 1801 and 1802* (New York, 1909), 93–94.

137 **"The Convention on the Prevention and Punishment":** Nolan, "Destined for Export," 49.

143 **A committee of more than three hundred vultures:** Kingsville Station, U.S. Customs and Border Patrol, cbp.gov/border-security/along-us-borders/border-patrol-sectors/rio-grande-valley-sector-texas/kingsville-station.

143 **Agents know that vultures avoid areas where other vultures have died:** Katherine J. Wu, *Smithsonian,* January 13, 2020, "Vulture Poop Has Compromised a Customs and Border Protection Radio Tower in Texas," smithsonianmag.com/smart-news/vulture-poop-has-compromised-customs-and-border-protection-radio-tower-texas-180973948/.

143 **The roosting vultures drop flesh and bones and fur:** Leah Asmelash and Hollie Silverman, "Hundreds of Unwelcome Vultures Are Perched on US Border Patrol's Texas Radio Towers," CNN, January 10, 2020, cnn.com/2020/01/10/us/vulture-customs-border-protection-trnd/index.html.

VIII. FLESH AND BLOOD

155 **The vulnerability of infants:** Judith Butler, *Precarious Life: The Powers of Mourning and Violence* (New York: Verso, 2004), 26.

158 **In some communities, it is not birth that creates:** Marshall Sahlins, "What Kinship Is (Part One)," *Journal of the Royal Anthropological Institute,* vol. 17, 2011, 3.

158 **In other communities, family is formed by food:** Ibid., 4.

162 **Kinship is not something you *are*:** Elizabeth Freeman, "Queer Belongings," in George E. Haggerty and Molly McGarry, eds., *A Companion to Lesbian, Gay, Bisexual, Transgender, and Queer Studies* (Malden, Mass., and Oxford: Blackwell, 2007), 298.

167 **For the Ilongot of the Philippines:** Sahlins, "What Kinship Is," 5, referring to R. Roaldo, *Ilongot Headhunting, 1883–1974: A Study in Society and History* (Palo Alto: Stanford University Press, 1980), 9.

167 **For the Malays:** Sahlins, "What Kinship Is," 5, referring to J. Carsten, *After Kinship* (Cambridge: Cambridge University Press, 2004), 40.

167 **In some Inuit groups:** Sahlins, "What Kinship Is," 5.

167 **For the Amazonia it is not blood but "affinity":** Ibid., 6.

167 **Plants are the children of the Amazonian women:** Ibid., 15.

167 **The Trukese use the category:** Ibid., 14.

167 **Feasting at the same table:** Ibid., 5, 14.

167 **If everything descends from the same creators:** Ibid., 15.

168 **In the local paper I saw a picture:** Joshua Murdock, "Hailey Woman Allegedly Neglected Baby, Lied," *Idaho Mountain Express,* November 15, 2017, mtexpress.com/news/cops_courts/hailey -woman-allegedly-neglected-baby-lied/article_41590a6a-c97f-11e7 -b108-b74d464889e6.html.

170 **When a woman is pregnant, cells from the fetus cross the placenta:** Viviane Callier, "Baby's Cells Can Manipulate Mom's Body for Decades," *Smithsonian,* September 2, 2015, smithsonianmag .com/science-nature/babys-cells-can-manipulate-moms-body -decades-180956493/, and Nancy Shute, "Beyond Birth: A Child's Cells May Help or Harm the Mother Long After Delivery," *Scientific American,* April 30, 2010, scientificamerican.com/article/fetal -cells-microchimerism/.

IX. BIG LOST

181 **In the second and third centuries, people argued about what happened to Mary's body:** Jennifer A. Glancy, *Corporal Knowledge: Early Christian Bodies* (New York: Oxford University Press, 2010), 81.

181 **Some feminists try to reclaim Mary's birthing body as holy:** Ibid., 88.

181 **The Mary story I like best, because it reads to me now like an adoption story:** Ibid., 100.

193 **When the mine stopped yielding copper:** "The World's Deepest, Biggest and Deadliest Open Pit Mines," *Mining People International*, February 15, 2016, miningpeople.com.au/news/the-worlds -deepest-biggest-and-deadliest-open-pit-mines.

193 **When birds are migrating, people stay close to the pit:** "Snow Geese Update," *Pit Watch*, December 9, 2016, pitwatch.org/snow -geese-update/.

X. FLIGHT RISK

212 **Robbed of both flight and flock:** All of what follows was learned from Charles Siebert, "What Does a Parrot Know About PTSD?," *The New York Times*, January 28, 2016. For more about Serenity Park, visit lockwoodarc.org/serenity-park.

XI. NO OTHER WAY

234 **The wild inhabitants of damaged lands:** Sarah Gilman, "Corvid Conservation Corps," *Audubon* (Winter 2019), 22.

234 **The jays gardened:** Scott Sillett, a scientist at the Smithsonian Migratory Bird Center, asked the question this way: "Could the jays have been their own accidental gardeners, and recovered their own habitat?" Gilman, "Corvid Conservation Corps," 20–25.

243 **Months before, I'd heard an art historian say that failed perspective:** When I heard this story on the radio, I wrote down the historian's name—Eliza Griswald—and the date—July 23, 2018—but now I can't find the story or any writing about failed perspective

as a form of prayer. I did find this: Sandra Willard, "The Illusion of the Renaissance," Yale–New Haven Teachers Institute, March 1986, teachersinstitute.yale.edu/curriculum/units/1986/3/86.03 .08.x.html.

244 I remembered a story I'd read: Maryam Sachs, *The Moon* (New York: Abbeville Press, 1998), 58.

XII. A TALE OF TWO MOTHERS

250 In the early twentieth century, government pamphlets used to warn parents: Deborah Blum, the biographer of Harry Harlow, talks about Harlow's experiments and about the psychologist John Watson on Episode 317 of NPR's *This American Life*, "Unconditional Love," September 15, 2006, thisamericanlife.org/317/ unconditional-love.

251 I watched a video of Harlow's experiments: "Harlow's Monkey Experiment: The Bond Between Babies and Mothers," *The Psychology Notes HQ*, February 14, 2020, psychologynoteshq.com/ psychological-studies-harlows-monkey/.

259 To prove that a mother's love is essential: "Harry F. Harlow, Monkey Love Experiments," *The Adoption History Project*, University of Oregon, pages.uoregon.edu/adoption/studies/Harlow MLE.htm.

259 To further make his point, Harlow turned the cloth mothers into abusive mothers: Harlow wrote the words quoted in this paragraph, but another scientist is reading his words during Episode 317 of NPR's *This American Life*, cited above.

272 I took a copy of the magazine: Uriah Smith, "Discover the Diamonds," *The Standard Bearer*, vol. 32, no. 3, 7.

XIII. BE THE TREE

297 Ho'oponopono, a practice of reconciliation and forgiveness: "Ho'oponopono," *Wikipedia*, en.wikipedia.org/wiki/Ho%CA %BBoponopono, and Jonathan Davis, "The Ancient Hawaiian

Practice of Forgiveness," *Uplift*, September 5, 2018, upliftconnect
.com/hawaiian-practice-of-forgiveness/.

XIV. OUR GIRL

323 **When there was less human noise on the earth:** Jamie Sams and
David Carson, *Medicine Cards: The Discovery of Power Through the
Ways of Animals* (New York: St. Martin's Press, 1999), 200-203.

331 **People who donate kidneys to strangers:** Stephanie Stahl, "People Who Donate Organs to Strangers Have This Special Brain
Feature, Researchers Say," 3CBSPhilly, July 8, 2019, philadelphia
.cbslocal.com/2019/07/08/people-who-donate-organs-to-strangers
-have-a-special-brain-feature-researchers-say/.

331 **Scientists suggest it's having a different brain:** "Brain Structure
of Kidney Donors May Make Them More Altruistic," September
15, 2014, *Georgetown University,* georgetown.edu/news/abigail
-marsh-brain-altruism-study.html.

333 **"The World's Smartest Animal":** "G: The World's Smartest Animal," *Radiolab,* July 29, 2019, wnycstudios.org/podcasts/radiolab/
articles/worlds-smartest-animal.

XV. ALL HER BELONGINGS

354 **Researchers knew about this mother whale before the calf was
born:** Avi Selk, "Update: Orca Abandons Body of Her Dead Calf
After a Heartbreaking, Weeks-Long Journey," *The Washington
Post,* August 12, 2018, washingtonpost.com/news/animalia/wp/
2018/08/10/the-stunning-devastating-weeks-long-journey-of-an
-orca-and-her-dead-calf/.

EPILOGUE

377 **Later Eric explained to me what an event horizon is:** Charles
Q. Choi, "What Exactly Is a Black Hole Event Horizon (and What
Happens There)," space.com, space.com/black-holes-event-horizon
-explained.html, April 9, 2019.

382 **Astronauts who have been to the moon:** "The Mysterious Smell of Moondust," *NASA*, January 30, 2006, science.nasa.gov/science -news/science-at-nasa/2006/30jan_smellofmoondust#:~:text= Although%20it%20happens%20too%20slowly,Apollo%20astronauts %20were%20specific.

382 **I read about the moon's formation:** Kerry Lotzof, "How Did the Moon Form?," Natural History Museum, nhm.ac.uk/discover/ how-did-the-moon-form.html#:~:text=What%20is%20most%20 widely%20accepted,Earth%20to%20form%20the%20Moon; and Rebecca Boyle, "What Made the Moon?," *Quanta Magazine,* August 2, 2017, quantamagazine.org/what-made-the-moon-new-ideas -try-to-rescue-a-troubled-theory-20170802/.

382 **Giant Impact Theory:** Lotzof, "How Did the Moon Form?"; Christian Schroeder, "How the Moon Formed: New Research Sheds Light on What Happened," *Phys.org,* March 10, 2020, phys .org/news/2020-03-moon.html; and "Where Does the Moon Come From?," August 22, 2018, history.com/news/where-does-the -moon-come-from#:~:text=Charles%20Darwin's%20son%20 George%2C%20an,and%20became%20our%20planet's%20satellite.

ABOUT THE AUTHOR

Sarah Sentilles is the author of *Draw Your Weapons,
Breaking Up with God,* *A Church of Her Own,* and
Taught by America. A graduate of Yale University and
Harvard Divinity School, she lives in Idaho's Wood
River Valley.

sarahsentilles.com

ABOUT THE TYPE

This book was set in Dante, a typeface designed by Giovanni Mardersteig (1892–1977). Conceived as a private type for the Officina Bodoni in Verona, Italy, Dante was originally cut only for hand composition by Charles Malin, the famous Parisian punch cutter, between 1946 and 1952. Its first use was in an edition of Boccaccio's *Trattatello in laude di Dante* that appeared in 1954. The Monotype Corporation's version of Dante followed in 1957. Though modeled on the Aldine type used for Pietro Cardinal Bembo's treatise *De Aetna* in 1495, Dante is a thoroughly modern interpretation of that venerable face.